Pierre Teilhard de Chardin
on
People and Planet

edited by
Celia Deane-Drummond

D1713747

Equinox Publishing Ltd

London   Oakville

Published by

UK: Equinox Publishing Ltd., Unit 6, The Village, 101 Amies St., London SW11 2JW
USA: DBBC, 28 Main Street, Oakville, CT 06779

www.equinoxpub.com

First published 2006

Library of Congress Cataloguing-in-Publication Data
A catalogue record for this book is available from the Library of Congress

ISBN   1845531604   (paperback)
        9781845531607   (paperback)

Typeset by Forthcoming Publications Ltd.
www.forthcomingpublications.com

Printed and bound in Great Britain by Lightning Source UK Ltd., Milton Keynes and
Lightning Source Inc., La Vergne, TN

Dedicated to Teilhard de Chardin and Siôn Cowell

CONTENTS

ACKNOWLEDGMENTS

This book is a revised version of a collection of essays first published in 2005 in the journal *Ecotheology: Journal of Religion, Nature and Environment*, issue 10(1) April and 10(2) August, also published by Equinox.

Two of the chapters in this book have been published in revised versions previously. John Grim and Mary Evelyn Tucker's chapter, 'An Overview of Teilhard's Commitment to "Seeing" As Expressed in His Phenomenology, Metaphysics, and Mysticism', is based on their 'Introduction' to *Teilhard in the 21st Century: The Emerging Spirit of Earth* (ed. Arthur Fabel and Donald St John; Maryknoll New York: Orbis Books, 2003), pp. 1-12, ISBN 1-57075-507-8, copyright 2003, The American Teilhard Association. Sion Cowell's chapter, 'Newman and Teilhard: The Challenge of the East', is a revised English version based on the original French given at the International Teilhard de Chardin Colloquium, Centre Spirituel, Hautmont, Lille, on 27 October 1991, and subsequently published in *Colloques Internationaux Teilhard de Chardin, 2001 Lille-Hastings; 2002 Paris-Le Caire* (Paris: Aubin Éditeur, 2003).

I would like to acknowledge the special work that Sion Cowell put into the early stages of this project, showing characteristic dedication, enthusiasm and support for all work related to Teilhardian witness and scholarship. His dedication was exemplified not just in the way he wrote and spoke, but also in his lifestyle and in his manner of dying. Shortly before he died, he had the occasion to celebrate a house mass with Billy Hewett (SJ) who visited Sion and his wife Caroline in August 2004. Sion later told me that 'We concluded with words from Teilhard's Journal from 1941: '...il y a cependant quelque chose de si exaltant dans la Mort Chrétienne : *Le* Trouver... Quel « thrill » ! ' (Pierre Teilhard de Chardin SJ, *Notes de Retraites*, 7th day, 1942, Éditions du Seuil, 2003, p. 223)'. Such words speak for themselves.

All of Sion Cowell's books on Teilhard now form a special collection at St Deiniol's residential library in Hawarden, Flintshire, Wales.

If any reader of this book wishes to either benefit from or contribute to a special memorial bursary fund dedicated to Teilhardian scholarship, please name the Sion Cowell Bursary Fund and write to Peter Francis, The Warden, St Deiniol's Library, Hawarden, Flintshire, CH5 3DF, email, deiniol.warden@btconnect.com. Special thanks are also due to the staff at St Deiniol's library, who have consistently provided a warm welcome for those seeking serious scholarship. I owe the library a special debt of gratitude for their ongoing support and encouragement, as well as providing the venue for meetings with other scholars and students.

The Christendom Trust (now M.B. Reckitt Trust) has also supported this project indirectly by providing ongoing funds between 2002 and 2005 for the Centre for Religion and the Biosciences at the University of Chester. This project forms an aspect of the research work of the centre. The work towards this book would not have been feasible without their support, and this is gratefully acknowledged. I would also like to thank my colleagues at the University of Chester for supporting my sabbatical leave for the period September 2004 to September 2005 during which time both the special issues for *Ecotheology* and this book were prepared for publication in 2005 and 2006 respectively.

LIST OF CONTRIBUTORS

Siôn Cowell served as Chairman of the British Teilhard Association from 1991–2002 before becoming its President. He was formerly President of the European Teilhard de Chardin Centre. He was studying for a doctorate in theology at the University of Chester before his death in September 2004. He is author of over a hundred papers and articles on Teilhard over the past twenty five years, and he is also author of the *Teilhard Lexicon: Understanding the Language, Terminology and Vision of the Writings of Pierre Teilhard de Chardin* (Sussex Academic Press, 2001) and translator of a new edition of Teilhard's work (*The Divine Milieu*, Sussex Academic Press, 2004). This chapter is published posthumously.

André Daleux lives in Lille, France, and is a retired medical practitioner. He has been a member of the Centre Teilhard de Chardin de Lille for almost 45 years, and has authored four books on Teilhard de Chardin: *Teilhard de Chardin, Science et Foi réconciliées* (Gabriandre, 1994), *Pierre, la force de l'amour* (Gabriandre, 2004 [an illustrated book for children]) *Teilhard de Chardin: une vision cohérente du monde compatible avec la Science* (Aubin, 2005), and *Teilhard de Chardin: permis de croire en l'au delà* (Aubin, 2006).

Celia Deane-Drummond is Professor and Director of the Centre for Religion and the Biosciences at University College Chester and editor of *Ecotheology: Journal of Religion, Nature and Environment*. She was chairperson of the *Science and Religion Forum*, based in the United Kingdom from 2003–2006. She is the author of a number of books including, most recently, *Creation Through Wisdom: Theology and the New Biology* (T. & T. Clark, 2000), *Biology and Theology Today; Exploring the Boundaries* (SCM Press, 2001), *The Ethics of Nature* (Blackwells, 2004), *Genetics and Christian Ethics* (Cambridge University Press, 2006), *Wonder and Wisdom: Conversations in Science, Spirituality and Theology* (DLT, 2006). She is also co-editor (with B. Szerszynski) of *Reordering Nature: Theology, Society and the New Genetics* (Continuum/T. & T.

Clark, 2003) and editor of *Brave New World: Theology, Ethics and the Human Genome* (Continuum/T. & T. Clark, 2003) and joint editor with Peter Scott of *Future Perfect: God, Medicine and Human Identity* (Continuum/T. & T. Clark, 2006).

Robert Faricy is a Jesuit priest and theologian who lives at Marquette University in Milwaukee, Wisconsin, USA, and is an emeritus professor of spiritual theology at the Pontifical Gregorian University in Rome. He has written over thirty books, most translated into several languages, and several hundred articles. His most recent publications are *Praying with Mary: Contemplating Scripture at Her Side* (co-authored with Lucy Rooney, Pauline Books, 2002) and *Knowing Jesus in the World: Praying with Teilhard de Chardin* (co-authored with Lucy Rooney, St Pauls Publishing, 1999).

Ludovico Galleni is Professor of General Zoology and Environmental Ethics, Pisa University. He is on the Editorial Board of the journals *Biology Forum, Studies in Science and Theology, Issues in Science and Theology,* and *European Journal of Science and Theology.* He is a member of the Council of the European Society for the Study of Science and Theology (ESSSAT) and he was nominated among the founder members of the International Society for Science and Religion (ISSR). His published books are *Scienza e Teologia, proposte per una sintesi feconda* (Queriniana, Brescia, 1992), *Da Darwin a Teilhard de Chardin, Interventi sull' Evoluzione (1983–1995)* (SEU, Pisa, 1996), and *Biologia* (La Scuola, Brescia, 2000).

Mary Grey is D.J. James emeritus Professor of the University of Wales, Lampeter, and currently Professorial Research Fellow, St Mary's University College, Strawberry Hill, Twickenham. She was formerly the Editor of *Ecotheology* and is Founder Trustee of the NGO *Wells for India.* Recent publications include: *Sacred Longings: Ecofeminist Theology and Globalisation* (SCM Press, 2003), and *Pursuing the Dream: a Jewish -Christian conversation* (Darton, Longman & Todd, 2005).

John A. Grim is Coordinator of the Forum on Religion and Ecology with Mary Evelyn Tucker and series editors of 'World Religions and Ecology', from Harvard Divinity School's Center for the Study of World Religions. In that series he edited *Indigenous Traditions and Ecology: the Interbeing of Cosmology and Community* (Harvard, 2001). He has been a Professor of Religion at Bucknell University and Sarah Lawrence College where he taught courses in Native American and

Indigenous religions, World Religions, and Religion and Ecology. His published works include: *The Shaman: Patterns of Religious Healing Among the Ojibway Indians* (University of Oklahoma Press, 1983) and edited volumes with Mary Evelyn Tucker entitled, *Worldviews and Ecology* (Orbis Books, 1994 [5th printing 2000]), and a *Daedalus* volume entitled, *Religion and Ecology: Can the Climate Change?* (American Academy of Arts and Sciences, 2001). John is currently President of the American Teilhard Association.

Thomas M. King is a Jesuit priest and professor of Theology at George-town University in Washington, DC. After graduation from the University of Pittsburgh he entered the Jesuits and obtained his doctorate at the University of Strasbourg. He has published nine academic books, most recently, *Jung's Four and Some Philosophers* (Notre Dame, 1999) and *Teilhard's Mass* (Paulist Press, 2005).

Ursula King is Professor Emerita in Theology and Religious Studies, University of Bristol, and Professorial Research Associate at the Centre for Gender and Religions Research, School of Oriental and African Studies, University of London. She has published many books and articles on religion, gender, spirituality, and on Pierre Teilhard de Chardin, especially the biography *Spirit of Fire* (Orbis Books, 1996) and an edited selection of his spiritual writings in the 'Modern Spiritual Masters Series' (Orbis Books, 1999).

Richard W. Kropf holds doctorates in theology from the University of Ottawa and Université St-Paul in Canada. His published books include *Teilhard, Scripture, and Revelation* (Fairleigh Dickinson University Press, 1980), *Evil and Evolution: A Theodicy* (Fairleigh Dickinson University Press, 1984 [2nd edn 2004]) and *Faith: Security and Risk: The Dynamics of Spiritual Growth* (Paulist Press, 1990 [2nd edn 2003]) and he is the author of the forthcoming *The Faith of Jesus: The Jesus of History and the Stages of Faith*. A former parish priest, college chaplain, and instructor in philosophy, psychology, religious studies, and the-ology, he now resides in northern Michigan.

Diarmuid O'Murchù, a priest and social psychologist, belongs to the Sacred Heart Missionary Congregation. Currently he works in London as a counsellor in a project for homeless people, while spending time each year facilitating international workshops on spiritual trends of our time; in this capacity he has worked in the USA, Canada,

Australia, India, the Philippines, and in several African countries. His written works include *Quantum Theology* (Crossroad Publishing, 1997), *Reclaiming Spirituality* (Crossroad Publishing, 1998), *Religion in Exile* (Gateway, 2000), and *Evolutionary Faith* (Orbis Books, 2002).

Francesco Scalfari teaches at Polo Universitario Asti Studi Superiori, Italy. He is a member of the European Society for the Study of Science and Theology (ESSSAT), and co-authored an article (with Ludovico Galleni) titled 'Theology of Nature as a Contextual Theology: Ethical Implications', which appeared in *Studies in Science and Theology* 9 (2003), pp. 43-58.

James W. Skehan, SJ, is Professor and Director Emeritus in the Department of Geology and Geophysics at Weston Observatory, and has a PhD degree in geology from Harvard University and an MDiv degree from Weston College. His geological research has been concerned mainly with the geology of New England, the Appalachian Mountains and the geology of Europe and Africa in the context of the Assembly and Breakup of Supercontinents through time. His writings on Teilhard de Chardin have focused on an evaluation of the quality of Teilhard's voluminous geological and paleontological research in light of probable motivation derived from his 'new' mysticism of action.

Mary Evelyn Tucker is a Research Associate at the Harvard-Yenching Institute and the Reischauer Institute at Harvard. She is co-founder and co-director of the Forum on Religion and Ecology. With John Grim, she organized a series of ten conferences on World Religions and Ecology at the Center for the Study of World Religions at Harvard Divinity School. They are series editors for the ten volumes from the conferences distributed by Harvard University Press. She is the author of *Worldly Wonder: Religions Enter Their Ecological Phase* (Open Court Press, 2003) and *Moral and Spiritual Cultivation in Japanese Neo-Confucianism* (SUNY, 1989). She co-edited *Worldviews and Ecology* (Orbis Books, 1994), *Buddhism and Ecology* (Harvard, 1997), *Confucianism and Ecology* (Harvard, 1998), and *Hinduism and Ecology* (Harvard, 2000) and *When Worlds Converge* (Open Court Press, 2002). With Tu Weiming she edited two volumes on *Confucian Spirituality* (Crossroad Publishing, 2003, 2004). She also co-edited a *Daedalus* volume titled *Religion and Ecology: Can the Climate Change?* (American Academy of Arts and Sciences, 2001).

INTRODUCTION

Celia Deane-Drummond

This volume offers a contribution to Teilhardian scholarship with a particular focus in mind, namely his significance for current debates about the human relationship with the natural world. His cosmic mysticism and intense interest in both cosmological and evolutionary sciences are highly relevant to current debates about how best to construct a meaningful spirituality for the twenty first century. There are, nonetheless, aspects of his thought that need to come under careful scrutiny in the light of both an increased sophistication of biological understanding, but also more awareness of how and to what extent humanity is culturally and historically situated in given, limited contexts. The book is divided into five sections that deal with different aspects of Teilhard's thought relevant to the theme, namely *Teilhard and the Cosmos, Teilhard and Mysticism, Teilhard and Ecotheology, Teilhard and Environmental Responsibility* and *Teilhard Between East and West*. The topics in each section necessarily overlap with the others, but the sections serve to highlight those features of his thinking that deserve special attention.

The first section, *Teilhard and the Cosmos*, brings together chapters by James Skehan and André Daleux, both of which deal with cosmological aspects of Teilhard's thinking that sets the scene for the development of more mystical aspects of his thought. James Skehan demonstrates, moreover, that Teilhard's mystical thinking cannot be detached from his reflection on the cosmos. He argues that while Teilhard was very much a child of his time, speaking out of particular contexts in which he found himself, such as his experience of the second World War, his writing has more enduring significance. It is also increasingly being accepted within Roman Catholic circles, in spite of initial condemnation, as reflected Vatican II statements that show a clear dependency on his insights. He argues that not only was Teilhard a pioneer in relating science and theology, but more specifically, he built up a way of thinking about the earth and God in mystical terms that can still serve to influence and inform today's culture.

André Daleux's chapter in French is a fitting tribute to the language in which Teilhard expressed his ideas. He explores more fully the relationship between science and theology that are integral to Teilhard's thought, hinted at in Skehan's chapter. He shows how while Teilhard was strongly committed to science; he opposed the philosophical presumption that often accompanies scientific activity, namely materialism. Teilhard believed that if science is dominated by materialist goals, it loses its spirit and its freedom and becomes deterministic. Daleux argues that the way Teilhard viewed the future for science was prophetic of the new physics of the twentieth century, since it resists rigid notions of determinism, and is more inclined to speak in terms of probabilities. It is possible to add to Daleux's discussion by suggesting that even more recently evolutionary biology has tended to use the language of probabilities, rather than determinism, and the balance between what evolutionary theorists generally call chance and necessity veers more on the side of chance, rather than deterministic law. Teilhard also comes very close to 'vitalism', long resisted by biologists, through his notion of the existence of the cosmic spirit in the natural world, though his clear sense of the transcendence of God effectively steers him away from any such conclusion.

The second section, *Teilhard and Mysticism*, takes the analysis of Teilhard's mysticism further in three chapters that each in their own way highlight significant features of his mystical thinking. John Grim and Mary Tucker's chapter provides an informative and instructive overview of Teilhard's phenomenology, metaphysics and mysticism. Teilhard challenges mechanistic models of physical matter by pointing to the possibility that it too has psychic properties that eventually flower into complexity and consciousness. The emergence of complexity is one of the great challenges of evolutionary theory. For Teilhard, a particular way of 'seeing' how this complexity emerges and in particular, its appearance in humans, flows out of the dialectical relationship between matter and spirit. Grim and Tucker remind us of Teilhard's concept of involution, that is an inward turning towards greater complexity/consciousness by a synthesis of matter and spirit. In this sense matter is neither denigrated or reformulated through a Platonic idealism, but contributes itself to the evolutionary process. In addition, the participation of humanity in the evolutionary process becomes what Teilhard calls the centration of persons, a discovery of the human place on earth by means of active participation in the evolutionary process. The authors are also aware of some aspects of Teilhard's work that were time bound, such has his ideal of progress, his tendency to emphasise the importance of the human, and his failure to pay due attention to bioregions. In spite of these limitations they argue strongly that Teilhard's vision provides an important corrective to much of the way we think about the earth, for it is a uniting vision that serves to challenge humanity towards greater responsibility and action.

Ursula King's chapter takes on board the more specifically ecological imperative of spirituality that arises out of our own present context, and asks how far and to what extent Teilhard can contribute to such an ecologically balanced spirituality. Like Skehan, she suggests that he puts forth a cosmic vision, but she takes this further in putting more emphasis on the evolutionary web of life that is integral to ecological reflection. She argues that Teilhard's ecological spirituality has relevance for four key areas that are important in order to develop ways of thinking ecologically about the earth. In the first place Teilhard's vision makes us conscious that we are living on one planet. In the second place, his vision enables us to see connections between ecology, spirituality and the world as a whole. In the third place spirituality becomes more deeply embedded in the biological world, through the way Teilhard envisioned the mutual interaction between the biosphere, common to all creatures, and the noosphere, characteristic of humanity. Finally, she suggests that his vision provides us with a spiritual heritage that is global in outlook and one that can be ecologically balanced. Above all, she believes that the kind of holistic vision that is essential for bringing together different religious traditions is exemplified in the work of Teilhard, whose ideas resonate with more recent statements such as that found in *The Earth Charter* at the turn of the twenty first century.

The chapter by Diarmuid Ó Murchú is practical in orientation and seeks to highlight Teilhard's contribution to a form of spirituality that is centred on creation. He argues, like other writers in this book, that Teilhard's contribution to the dialogue between science and religion is just one strand of his thinking that is significant. He believes that Teilhard is responsible for a new wave of mysticism that integrates the earth and creation with spirituality in a way that is highly relevant to more contemporary forms of spirituality that seek to do the same, but are writing outside the Christian tradition. In this respect we can be grateful to Teilhard for his enduring legacy, for by implication, there are resources embedded in his work that can meet the need of contemporary spiritualities that seek to identify more fully with the earth. Perhaps it is fair to say that Teilhard would not necessarily have recognised this extension of his work in terms of its practical outcome. But in this respect we might have to concede that Teilhard was blind to the full implications of his own mystical vision, which reached beyond himself and his culture and speaks to the needs of today.

The third section on *Teilhard and Ecotheology* has two chapters that are concerned more specifically with ecotheological themes, while taking up threads apparent in the previous sections on mysticism and cosmic communion. Mary Grey's chapter takes up the liturgical, eucharistic elements in Teilhard's thought through a focused study on his *Mass on the World*. Like Skehan, she begins by tracing some of the reasons behind Teilhard's condemnation by the Vatican, and finds it wanting. However, she also asks important questions about the value of his Eucharistic texts, which pointed to a world that was charged with psychic energy. She recognises the way Thomas Berry and others have been indebted to Teilhard's vision, in particular the way humanity is situated in a universal, cosmic context. His emphasis on the cosmic Christ as an anchor for spirituality also finds echoes in contemporary ecotheology. Yet Grey sees the Eucharist as the heart of Teilhard's spirituality, but it is an offering that is infused with both the presence of cosmic matter and spirit, based on his deep appreciation of the importance of the incarnation of Christ. Like many other authors in this book, she is particularly appreciative of his cosmic vision, which she argues overcomes tendencies towards anthropocentrism, and his concept of the God of the future luring the cosmic world into full participation. She also draws on the work of David Toolan, who develops Teilhard's eucharistic vision, but manages to ground it more successfully in the historical context of the reality of Jesus as Jew approaching his own suffering and death. She also believes that Toolan gives more place to the role of the Holy Spirit in the transformation of creation compared with Teilhard, and in this provides an important corrective to his work. She also argues that it spite of his lack of attention to practical issues of justice, his mystic vision remains important as a means of nourishment for those who are activists and who regularly identify with the suffering of both people and planet.

Robert Faricy's chapter argues that Teilhard's writing helps to overcome any dichotomy that may exist between nature and humanity, and as such is an important prelude to the development of ecotheology. He believes that one of the legacies of the Reformation is an undue emphasis on the separation of the orders of creation and redemption. He suggests, in particular, that while this gap between nature and humanity and between nature and grace remains, exploitative attitudes to the natural world stay unchallenged. Yet once the gap is closed, as in, for example, the works of Teilhard and Rahner, then it becomes impossible to exploit the natural world and treat it simply as a resource for humanity's benefit. He is also critical of two sharp a separation between immanence and transcendence and a failure to recognise the importance of immanence that he suggests is characteristic of Reformed theology. In addition, counter trends in Reformation thought that make the earth sacred also fail, rather the earth should be thought of as holy as it exists in relationship to God. In particular, it is Teilhard's attention to the energy of love uniting the whole cosmos that informs his spirituality and mystical vision. Like Mary Grey, he points to the harsh experiences of Teilhard as a stretcher-bearer in World War 1 as the context in which his vision for love energising the world developed. He also argues strongly against those interpretations of Teilhard that believe he succumbed to pantheism, drawing on both Teilhard's visionary experiences and his subsequent reflections. The love that Teilhard pointed to is a love that differentiates and personalises, rather than one that confuses or merges individuals. In this sense the love becomes connected with all of creation, and hence forms a basis for thinking in a more holistic way about the earth.

The fourth section on *Teilhard and Environmental Responsibility* has three chapters that deal with Teilhard's thought in the light of pressing issues in environmental ethics, taking up threads that were also apparent in the section on *Teilhard and Ecotheology*. Richard Kropf's paper argues that Teilhard's understanding of the evolutionary process and his belief in the emergence of an 'ultra-humanity' that is both a summation of the evolutionary trajectory, but transcends its limits, is significant for environmental ethics. He is conscious of the advances in cosmological and planetary science and its relationship with Teilhard's views on the future of human evolution. He believes, in particular, that research, which indicates that life once existed on other planets, will be significant, as it shows that life has come into being and then been destroyed, and further, the possibility that life is sustainable on other galaxies becomes more likely. He believes that Teilhard was aware of the way cosmology could provide challenges to classical notions about human uniqueness, the doctrine of the Fall of humanity and the need for redemption. He was also aware of the pessimism about the future that pervaded the cosmology of the period, the ultimate futility of the earth according to its predicted destruction in a heat death. Teilhard's optimism needs to be situated in such a scientific context in order to be understood as a counter trend to this pessimistic secular eschatology. He was also aware not just of the need to counter pessimism, but also of the need for engagement, rather than withdrawal, and solidarity, rather than isolation. Kropf believes that these three strands have inescapable implications for the way we treat the planet. Teilhard seemed to be more concerned that humanity would run out of psychic energy before material resources were exhausted. While he may have been naïve about the environmental dangers, the difficulties that are faced by environmentalists today concern the lack of will to change, apathy in spite of knowing what the dangers might be. In this sense, Teilhard is correct in his estimation that psychic energy is a prerequisite to action and knowledge. Kropf also believes that we need to learn to be co-creative with the earth in engaging with it, rather than withdrawing from it by turning away from its demands. Kropf also argues that the question of whether the evolution of the cosmos has a goal remains the ultimate question to be tackled. He argues, in particular, that Teilhard's vision can help to sustain hope even in the midst of more pessimistic accounts about the future of the universe and planet earth.

Ludovico Galleni and Francesco Scalfari's chapter looks more deeply into the evolutionary context in which Teilhard developed his ideas. They explore, for example, the way Teilhard draws on the evidence for increased complexity in the animal evolution of canalisation and parallelisms, the most important of which was the development of a central nervous system, or cerebralisation. Teilhard was also deeply appreciative of both biological research that helped to uncover the processes behind the complexity of life and geo-biology that formed the science of the evolving biosphere. The authors, who write as biologists, are deeply appreciative of the way Teilhard manages to develop a synthesis between his biological understanding of evolution and his theology. They also trace the importance of Teilhard's work as a paleontologist and assess its significance in the light of contemporary discussions about the evolution of complexity. They acknowledge the way Teilhard is a pioneer in more holistic ways of thinking about the relationships on the earth, alongside pioneering work of the geologist priest Stoppani, whose writing finds its contemporary expression in the Gaia hypothesis of James Lovelock. They believe that Leonardo Boff drew out the social implications of Teilhard's work in his early writing on liberation theology. They argue that Boff also recognised the importance of Teilhard's thinking for environmental ethics, for it avoided the difficulties associated with either anthropocentrism or biocentrism. Hence, implicit in Teilhard's vision is a call for ecological responsibility, for his eschatology and the coming of Christ presuppose the preservation of the biosphere. In addition, they argue that the biological concept of symbiosis, where each creature is dependent on the other for its existence, is also implicit in the close dependency between the biosphere and the noosphere, or region of consciousness as expressed in humankind.

Thomas King's chapter also engages with the environmental implications of Teilhard's thought. He recognises how Teilhard's spirituality has been useful in building up an ecologically aware manifesto. However, he is also conscious that many of those who are working towards environmental consciousness have a certain ambivalence towards Teilhard, not least because in order to achieve the kind of unification with the earth Teilhard also called for the development of modern industry, commerce, economic development and so on. In other words, the way he envisioned his theory in practical terms was through globalisation and development, which swims against the tide of an active ecological manifesto as it is normally understood. Thomas King argues that Teilhard would, had he been alive when Rachel Carson published her work, almost certainly have had sympathy with her position, but at the same time he would have supported the use of science and technology in order to achieve such aims. The earth could be, he believed, served by such technology, as long as it was done responsibly. Thomas King also, significantly it seems to me, traces an ambiguity even within Teilhard's thought, one that both drew him to matter, but also one that saw Christ in the globalisation of human activities.

The final section entitled *Teilhard Between East and West* raises some of the ecumenical implications of Teilhard's vision for theology, science and ecology. Siôn Cowell's chapter, published posthumously, is important as it places due emphasis on this transcendent aspect of Teilhard's thinking, and seeks to analyse from a historical perspective how far both Teilhard was influenced by John Henry Newman, in particular the latter's attraction to the Eastern Fathers of the early church. It also seems that Teilhard was influenced more directly by writers of the early church, including Irenaeus of Lyons, Origen of

Alexandria, Gregory of Nyssa and Gregory of Nazianzus. Cowell argues that the influence of the Eastern Fathers on the writings of Teilhard has been insufficiently recognised, so that aspects of their thinking including the divinisation of the cosmos and the stress on apophatic theology has become embedded in his thought. He also hints at an intriguing possibility for Teilhard scholarship, namely that he can become the means through which Churches from the East and West begin to find the resources for reconciliation.

In my own chapter I turn the spotlight onto Teilhard's understanding of the Virgin Mary, and I argue that his devotion to her finds expression in the prose poem *Hymn to the Eternal Feminine*. I am particularly interested in the way Teilhard links his understanding of the Eternal Feminine with Sophia, comparing his understanding of Mary with that found in the work of the Russian Orthodox writer, Sergei Bulgakov. Both authors offer accounts that bridge the divide between the Eastern and Western traditions of Christianity. Both authors are conscious of the cosmic significance of Mary. However, I argue that by confining Sophia to Mary, and by putting due emphasis on her subsidiary place in relation to Christ, Teilhard does not go as far as Bulgakov in developing an adequate Sophiology. On the other hand, Teilhard is more aware than Bulgakov seems to be of the importance of evolution in understanding the way the world has emerged. I am, none the less, critical of Teilhard's ideal of progress which seems to blind him to the ethical dangers in modern technology and science. He was less aware, of course, of the implicit dangers in the ever-increasing demand for progress by humanity in a way that lacked attention to environmental concerns. There are other strands in his thinking that counteract this trend somewhat, such as have been pointed out by Galleni and Scalfari in the preceding section. I also argue that implicit in both Teilhard and Bulgakov are ways of perceiving Mary that allow her to have significance for environmental responsibility. She becomes, through embodiment of Sophia in its creaturely expression, representative of idealised humanity, who speaks of what the world as redeemed may become. As creaturely Sophia incarnate and divinised, Mary represents both the connectivity and care for the earth that is possible for humanity to achieve.

Teilhard died before concerns about ecology and environmental issues were fully recognised on the cultural landscape. However, this does not mean that his work is irrelevant to such issues, for, as this book has aimed to show, his vision and his insights still have enduring relevance, not only in relation to how humanity is related to the world, but also in terms of his cosmic vision of how to understand God's engagement with the world in the light of what we know about evolutionary biology and its cosmic rootedness in evolutionary history. Not only does this book aim to probe more deeply into his mystical insights in a way that challenges the reader's understanding of spirituality, it also offers a critical revision of aspects of his thought in the light of current debates in evolutionary science, ecotheology and the challenges posed by environmental ethics. By focusing on the human person, *people,* and the *planetary* context in which people are situated, Teilhard takes us beyond the current debates between anthropocentrism and biocentrism that have characterised contemporary discussion about environmental ethics.

This book is dedicated to the memory of Pierre Teilhard de Chardin on the occasion of the fiftieth anniversary of his death on Easter Sunday, 10 April 1955. It is also dedicated to my colleague and friend Siôn Cowell, lately President of the Teilhard de Chardin Association of Great Britain, who was involved in the early stages of this project, but regretfully passed away on 12 September 2004.

Part I

TEILHARD AND THE COSMOS

1

EXPLORING TEILHARD'S 'NEW MYSTICISM': 'BUILDING THE COSMOS'*

James W. Skehan, SJ

Teilhard's Life Goal

Pierre Teilhard de Chardin (1881–1955), was a distinguished French geologist-paleontologist, Jesuit priest and mystic. As a fully educated and trained paleontologist his chief scientific interest was in human paleontology. He was uniquely shaped both intellectually and spiritually by nature and education from early youth. I will note how some persons contributed importantly to his intellectual and spiritual growth.

A few major questions preoccupied Teilhard throughout his life and he was in part formed by them. Some of these were philosophical, some theological, but many grew out of the interaction of science with both. Teilhard had a life-long preoccupation with human evolution from a scientific perspective mainly in the same way in which other scientists studied the phenomenon. However, Teilhard brought to his paleontological research a perspective that was unique by

* Acknowledgements: I am grateful to Siôn Cowell for discussions which have helped improve the accuracy of my prior statements surrounding the request made of Teilhard to prepare a summary of his views on original sin, and the still-mysterious way in which that paper came into possession of the Vatican's Holy Office; in addition, written and oral discussions with Cowell, Celia Deane-Drummond, Robert V. Paskey, SJ and Mark A.S. McMenamin were stimulating and fruitful. To Ursula King (1976, 1977, 1980) I am indebted for her in-depth and lucid explanations of aspects of Teilhard's 'new mysticism' that provide important insights helpful to Teilhard's readers to develop a practice of 'communion with God through earth', the central focus of this paper. I am grateful to Maureen Burke, Tracy Downing and Christine Bronchuk for assistance in manuscript preparation.

reason of his sound theological and philosophical education in addition to his doctoral studies and subsequent research in the geo-
sciences. By reason of this breadth of background and interest
Teilhard's principal goal seems to have been to probe and gain some
understanding of the mystery of Christ, the God-man, especially as
this might shed light on the role of mankind in the universe. He
plowed new ground at the time by stretching the traditional boundaries of evolutionary science 'to include a study of the human person
in relationship to the material world'. Teilhard set out

> to rethink within his own distinctive evolutionary system the data of
> Christian revelation concerning the Person of Christ. This he tried to do
> primarily because he believed that Christ, as God Incarnate, revealed in
> himself not only the mystery of God but also the meaning of man, and
> therefore the ultimate meaning of that evolutionary process of which God
> is the cause and man the culmination. (Mooney 1964: 5)

A growing number of authors have examined various aspects of
Teilhard's voluminous writings and his fascinating life. One of my
goals is to note the commonly neglected significance of Teilhard's
contributions to his scientific fields of paleontology and geology as
well as his recognition of aspects of mysticism involved in the process
of scientific research that allowed him to gain fuller insight into his
'new mysticism'. Teilhard was a recognized scholar in the fields of
paleontology and more specifically human paleontology for which he
was best known. Additionally, Teilhard had a keen pastoral sense of
the urgent need for Christianity to become more in tune with the
culture and spirit of the times. He felt that the harmony that he
recognized between biblical texts of St Paul and St John and evolution
could help Christians and non-Christians to develop a similar harmonious understanding of how they might go about 'building the earth'.

Recognition of Need for a New Mysticism

Teilhard recognized for years the unfulfilled spiritual hunger of many
of his fellow Christians who felt separated simultaneously from a
total dedication to both 'building their world' and a heartfelt 'communion with God'. As a result he wrote:

> We need a new theology and a new approach to perfection…to meet the
> new needs and aspirations… But what we need perhaps even more…is for
> a new and higher form of worship to be gradually disclosed by Christian
> thought and prayer, adapted to the needs of tomorrow's believers without
> exception. (Teilhard de Chardin 1968: 220; cited by U. King 1997: 2)

What factors shaped Teilhard's influential life and scientific career, led him to recognize the need for a new mysticism, and caused some of his biographers to regard him as a religious mystic? Thomas King (1988), a Jesuit theologian and Teilhardian scholar, distinguishes several kinds of mysticism and indicates a fundamental difference between Teilhard and many earlier scholars. These spiritual writers, in general, required that one leave behind lower stages of creation as one ascended to God. Teilhard, on the other hand, claimed that 'one is able to ascend only by uniting oneself with the material world. For Teilhard, the material world contains the power we need for the ascent to God. So for Teilhard the basis for any form of mysticism required that one begin with the Cosmic Sense' (T. King 1988: 64). This, in a word, is what Teilhard regarded as a 'new mysticism'.

Family, Jesuit and Early Scientific Influences

A brilliant and devout person such as Teilhard, combining extraordinary talents and accomplishments in science and spirituality, does not just appear fully-developed on life's stage. I will note some persons and influences that, in my view, may have been among the most important in shaping Teilhard's life.

Teilhard was not only endowed to an extraordinary degree by nature and grace but he was influenced by caring and insightful parents and other mentors. Teilhard tells us of the indelible and distinctive religious influences exerted on him as a child by his mother, Berthe-Adele de Dompierre d'Hornoy, a great-grandniece of Voltaire. On learning of her death, Teilhard said: 'To her I owe the best part of my soul'. Many years later, in 1936, in reflecting on the interplay of the emotional and the scientific sides of his life, he observed: 'I find a continual source of strength in recognizing that the evolutionary effort may be reduced to the justification of a love (God's love, in fact) and its development. This is just what my mother used to tell me. But it will have taken me a lifetime to integrate this truth into an organic vision of things' (Cuénot 1965: 2).

Emmanuel, Teilhard's father, a graduate of the École des Chartes, specialized in the history of his own province of Auvergne. He was widely read, was interested in everything about the land and its history, and the well-being and education of his family. He inculcated in his family an interest in the neighboring mountainous landscape and stimulated in them a desire to make natural history collections of insects, birds and rocks. He might best be described as a 'gentleman farmer-naturalist'. The emotional impact of the beautiful,

mountainous volcanic terrain of Auvergne, and the desire to understand the geologically young craters that stretched out before his
gaze and which permeated his psyche, can hardly be overemphasized (Cuénot 1965).

> Auvergne molded me... Auvergne served me both as a museum of natural
> history and as a wild-life preserve. Sarcenat in Auvergne gave me the first
> taste of the joys of discovery...my delight in nature...my most precious
> possessions: a collection of pebbles and rocks still to be found there, where
> I lived... I was interested specially in mineralogy and biological observa-
> tion. I used to love to follow the course of the clouds, and I knew the stars
> by their names... To my father I owe a certain balance, on which all the
> rest is built, along with a taste for the exact sciences. (Cuénot 1965: 3)

Teilhard began his formal education in 1892 when he was enrolled in
the Jesuit secondary school at Notre-Dame de Mongré, Villefranche-
sur Saône (Rhone). 'Although no prodigy, Pierre achieved a high
standard in a wide range of subjects, including Latin, Greek, German
and Science...and passed without trouble the two-part matriculation
examination of the University of Clermont-Ferrand' (Cuénot 1965: 4).
Teilhard was active in religious activities throughout these years and,
as elected prefect of the Sodality of Mary, left a record in the minutes
of the concern that the Jesuits had for the interior life of their pupils.
During a year's 'sabbatical' following his graduation due to being
run down in health, Teilhard improved his mathematical skills under
watchful tutors and enjoyed weekend field trips searching for mineralogical specimens (Cuénot 1965).

Early Years as a Jesuit

On 20 March 1899 Teilhard was admitted to the Jesuit Novitiate at
Aix-en-Provence. Here for two years he was immersed in a personal
development program at the heart of which was the *Spiritual Exercises*
of Ignatius of Loyola the Founder of the Jesuits, absorbing the spirit
and history of the Jesuit order. For two years Teilhard studied literature at the University of Caen after which he pursued a program of
studies in philosophy, theology and the sciences. This four year
period of study on the Isle of Jersey came about when Jesuits, including himself, were expelled from France. Here Teilhard spent his spare
time and holidays studying the geology of the bedrock along its
shores, and constructing a map of its geological structure. Teilhard
obviously took satisfaction and delight in this field of research that
resulted in a preliminary geological and mineralogical note published
in the Annual Bulletin of the Jersey Geological Society. This was a
time that:

His inner attraction to the great forces of nature, so deeply rooted in earlier childhood experiences, became so immensely strong that it awakened in him a vibrant cosmic consciousness… [B]ut when surrendering himself 'to the embrace of the visible and tangible universe', he learned to feel the hand of God. And then he saw, 'as though in ecstasy, that *through all of nature I was immersed in God'*. (U. King 1996: 19)

Molded by Science and Spirituality

From the time that he was a young Jesuit in studies, Teilhard had a consuming interest in geology. Even before specializing in paleontology, he was concerned with evolution as a significant biological as well as a religious concept and process. Teilhard's lifelong goal in terms of the Christological problem was 'to rethink the total mystery of Christ in terms of *'genesis'* or 'becoming'. Additionally Teilhard's scientific studies of evolution in paleontology enhanced his understanding that he was living in a dynamic universe (Mooney 1964: 62).

Teilhard's perspective throughout life was that evolution was 'the main melody of the cosmic symphony', as I refer to it, and it shed light on a theological problem that St Paul addressed briefly and in general terms. Two of Teilhard's burning questions were: in light of the Incarnation, 'what is the relationship between Jesus of Nazareth and evolution? And what is the relationship of the cosmos to the same Jesus', the second Person of the divine Trinity? Teilhard's writings and thought are generally regarded as of great significance in light of his theology of the Incarnation and of Creation. Teilhard appreciated the theological richness of humans participating in the process of what may be referred to as 'ongoing Creation' or of humans participating in 'building the Earth'.

It was during the formative years of Teilhard's life of scholarship and spirituality that he began to formulate some of his important concepts, one of which links the cosmic significance of Christ's life, death and resurrection to the cosmic evolution of life itself, for which Jesus as Creator of the universe is responsible. In Teilhard's view, the *Parousia* represents the final culmination of God's salvific plan for the human race and as such corresponds, first of all, to Teilhard's initial understanding of Omega as the totality of earth's collective reflection at the end time. More fundamentally, Teilhard accepted the term 'Omega' in Scripture as referring to 'the supreme personal Being here and now responsible for the time process itself, the real Omega, the Prime Mover ahead, who not only is, but has always been'. Teilhard assumed that if the Christ of revelation is identical with the Omega of

evolution, then by whatever means the final culmination of God's
salvific plan for the human race is accomplished, it must somehow
already be present in the life, death and resurrection of Jesus of
Nazareth. This must be so because:

> in the Person of Jesus the real Omega took flesh and became part of that
> evolutionary current for which he himself as Creator is responsible…all
> the great Christological events must somehow be obedient to evolution's
> most fundamental law. Somehow we must be able to speak of a genesis
> which is Christic as well as a genesis which is cosmic, and in some sense
> we must be able to speak of them both as ultimately one and the same. It is
> precisely to speak in such a way, while yet remaining faithful to the testi-
> mony of revelation, which is the aim of Teilhard de Chardin's Christology.
> (Mooney 1964: 63)

Theological Studies and Ordination

In 1905 Teilhard began regency, a three year experience as a teacher
of chemistry and physics as well as curator of the museum in the
Jesuit College de la Sainte Famille in Cairo, Egypt. Although he was
at this stage an amateur scientist, Teilhard undertook geological field
excursions into the desert to collect fossils. These brought him into
contact with leading researchers in Egypt and France. Three species
of fossils, a *lepidopteron*, a *hymenopteron* and a variety of *Gisopygus*,
were named after Teilhard. Impressions derived from these field
studies 'contributed to an increasing awareness of the immensity of
matter and the grandeur of Christ' (Cuénot 1965: 10).

At the end of three years in 1908, Teilhard was called back to Hastings, England where he began a four year theology program. Toward
the end of the third year of theological studies in 1911, he was
ordained to the priesthood. After a final year of theological studies
Teilhard returned to Paris where he was interviewed by the famous
geologist and specialist in vertebrate paleontology, Professor Marcellin Boule. Teilhard recalled this meeting joyfully on a celebratory
occasion for Professor Boule in 1937, possibly the latter's retirement,
as an interview that launched him 'into what has been my whole life
ever since: research and adventure in the field of paleontology' (U.
King 1996: 41).

Stretcher Bearer in World War I

Teilhard's final year of formal Jesuit training in ascetical theology
began in Canterbury in 1914 but was interrupted by his being

inducted into the French army as a medical orderly. At his own request Teilhard served as a stretcher bearer in a regiment of Zouaves and Moroccan Tirailleurs who participated in the main battles of the war. His choice of service was dangerous to the point that death and the prospect of death were his constant companions while serving his troops. Complete dedication gave rise to his great popularity because these mainly Muslim soldiers came to rely on him as a source of courage and strength.

What in other circumstances would have been Teilhard's final year of Jesuit training, was spent instead in military service at the Front. Normally, the young Jesuit priest would be engaged in a one year program devoted to ascetical and pastoral theology, including once again a 30-day secluded retreat engaged in the *Spiritual Exercises* of Ignatius. Teilhard's preparation for final vows consisted instead, of the asceticism of rescuing the wounded and retrieving his dead companions from the field of battle where they fell. Teilhard served four years as a stretcher-bearer soldier, mainly at the battle front.

During World War I Teilhard had arranged to send the essays that he composed while not actually engaged in his stretcher bearer duties, to his cousin, Marguerite de Teillard de Chambon, for safe keeping. Teilhard must have been constantly writing as he authored eighteen essays amid the confusion and horrors of life at the front. His constant lyrical and heartfelt prayer in the trenches called 'The Priest' was written during this time. Another deeply moving prayer that he composed later and which he recited during long geological treks in the deserts of eastern Asia bore the title 'The Mass on the World' under date of 1923. Marguerite had assembled these essays together with 'The Priest' and 'The Mass on the World' as a volume entitled *Writings in Time of War* (1965). Speaking of Teilhard's essays, François Mauriac enshrined them as follows: 'The most optimistic view a Christian thinker has ever held of this criminal world was conceived at Verdun' (U. King 1996: 66). Teilhard was mustered out of the army on 10 March 1919.

A New Mysticism: Communion with God through Earth

Towards the end of World War I Teilhard expressed in an essay a deeply felt, urgent pastoral need for 'evangelization of a new age'. He saw that in the modern world of twentieth century science, technology and globalization, it is important to find a 'new understanding of the meaning of holiness, a new way of embodying the ideal of

Christian perfection'. This was a recurring life-theme that reappeared in his final paper written on 10 April 1955 just before his death (U. King 1996: 2).

'Christians', he wrote, 'must learn to perceive and revere the sacredness of matter and the cosmos; the experience of the cosmos is a necessary dimension of human experience that must be integrated into the Christian faith'. What Teilhard refers to is a form of mysticism that he designates a *'communion with God through earth'*, *'a new synthesis between the forward and the upward'*. Teilhard describes this 'new mysticism' as a 'communion with God through earth' (U. King 1997: 87) in which 'the human being is united with the Absolute, with God' by means of the unification of the universe (Teilhard 1970: 56). This new mysticism is regarded by Teilhard as a dynamic transformational process in which the individual participates actively. He speaks of it as a 'mysticism of evolution' and a 'mysticism of action'.

Ursula King, a distinguished scholar of Teilhard's thought and spirituality, insightfully points out that the time of post-modernity for which Teilhard was writing and lecturing was one of great opportunity:

> In an earlier age when Christian religious ideals still informed the entire culture, the human being was primarily understood in relation to the Divine, to God. The dominant scientific approach of today tends to relate the human being primarily to the animal and life worlds of our natural environment and that [in turn], to God — [these] need to be combined and linked with each other in a way that is new and culturally transformative and creative... Perhaps it is the very questions and problems raised by modernity, and the possibilities opening up with new postmodern perspectives, that will provide us with the opportunities for developing a truly holistic and transformative spirituality. (U. King 1997: 4)

Teilhard's impassioned cry for a modern theologically-based perspective was muted drastically in his lifetime because he was forbidden by his religious superiors from publishing on theological topics. Nevertheless, from World War I onward he wrote unceasingly until his death in 1955, although it was only after his death that his writings were published widely in English. Almost simultaneously with his death, his eagerly sought-after writings, that had been entrusted to one of his special friends, were published. Fundamental starting points for Teilhard's thought and spirituality were a number of passages in the writings of St Paul and St John, the Nicene Creed and scientific topics that he considered relevant and adaptable to his project of 'finding God in all things'.

A fundamental Christian theological position on divine creation of the Earth and Universe was established by the Council of Nicæa in 325 AD and was given primacy in the beginning of the Church's profession of Faith as a basic tenet of Christian theology. In the Nicene Creed Christians from the early days of the Church have affirmed that 'we believe in one God, the Father, the almighty, maker of heaven and earth, of all that is seen and unseen' and, therefore, believers from the earliest part of the Christian Era and Jews as well, as we know from Hebrew Scriptures, have held that God is ultimately responsible for the existence of the entire material universe. Today, as was never possible before space travel and satellite photography, the Earth and Universe are objects of wonder and beauty as well as the object of scientific study. The Eastern Churches have preserved a long tradition of creation-theology.

More than a few Western Churches also have come to recognize that the sacramentality of all of creation is harmonious with Teilhard's mystical concept of 'communion with God through earth'. Expressed in a slightly different way Teilhard's phrase, '*the above with the ahead*' (Cowell 2001: 3, 5-6) expresses the fundamental core of his action-mysticism. By this he meant that it is impossible to rise '*above*' without moving '*ahead*'—or '*to progress ahead without rising toward the above*' (Cowell 2001; Cuénot 1965: 369), in reality an '*on-going-creation theology*'. The phrase 'above' and 'from above' so meaningful to Teilhard's 'new mysticism' is actually a time-honored phrase that was familiar to Teilhard from Ignatius Loyola's Fourth Week of the *Spiritual Exercises* (Skehan 1991: 155-56; 1994: 77).

From Chair of Geology to Exile in China

On 22 March 1922 Teilhard defended his doctoral thesis on mammals of the Lower Eocene period in France by which time he was well-known and highly regarded in scientific circles. Teilhard was appointed to the chair of geology in the Institut Catholique, amid expectations that he would rise quickly to the upper reaches of his profession. After World War I, he recognized among other signs a yearning on the part of young people, a widespread and growing attraction to Buddhism and other forms of spirituality and pointed out the urgent need on the part of the Catholic Church to discover new ways of expressing worship and adoration' (Skehan 2001: 27).

'Since the war [World War I] he realized that humankind formed a single whole, a large, cosmic reality that far transcended individuals and groups. This human reality…was like a dynamic, living organism…, a network whose threads stretched over the face of the whole earth' (U. King 1996: 87). Teilhard had previously called the thinking Earth the 'anthroposphere' but in 1925 settled on a new name, the 'noosphere', the notion of which has been attributed to Vladimir I. Vernadsky (Levit 2000, 2001) in discussion with Teilhard de Chardin and Édouard Le Roy, SJ. The term noosphere is widely used and accepted today. In fact in various quarters some of Teilhard's fans have considered that this concept of 'noosphere' predicted in principle the modern 'worldwide computer internet'.

> This [the noosphere] was to become one of his [Teilhard's] key ideas, an absolutely central element in his vision. Just as the zone of life — the total mass of living organisms — was the biosphere, a living layer above the non-living world of the geosphere, so there was yet another, thinking layer, a sphere of mind and spirit surrounding the globe. It is like a thinking envelope of the earth of which all humans are a part. All contribute to it through their thinking, feeling, connecting, and interacting with each other, and above all through their powers of love. The emergence of the noosphere is an important step forward in becoming human, in the process of transformation he called 'hominization'. (U. King 1996: 88)

About the same time that Teilhard was getting established as Chair of the Department of Geology at the *Institut Catholique*, he was also returning to a long-standing concern for the implications of anthropology for the question of original sin: 'Teilhard was already acutely aware of, and concerned with, a religious crisis that brought traditional understanding of God into conflict with new perspectives of the natural world' (Skehan 2001: 27). Siôn Cowell (written communication, 2004) corrected my earlier statement on the circumstances surrounding Teilhard's distressing discovery that the 'destination of the written summary of his [Teilhard's] views on original sin…was the Vatican's Holy Office' (Skehan, 2001: 29). Cowell clarifies the historical facts: 'He was in fact a Belgian confrère and friend, Louis Riedenger, professor of dogmatic theology at Enghien, who asked Teilhard before Easter 1922 to prepare a private discussion paper (that we now know as *Note sur quelques représentations historiques possibles du péché originel*). Riedinger was in no way responsible for what happened concerning Teilhard's Summary subsequently. In late 1924 (while Teilhard was still in China) he received a letter from Costa de Beauregard ordering him to Lyon (13 November)'. Teilhard's reaction: 'One of my papers (the one in which I develop three possible ways of representing original sin) has been sent, I do not know how, to Rome… I expect I shall be labeled a heretic or a hurly-burly'.

Cowell's comment: 'The paper had been removed from his [Teilhard's] desk during his absence in China by a person or persons whose identity remains unknown to this day. It was, of course, as you say, this paper which led to Teilhard's exile' (Cowell, written communication to J.W.S., SJ, 2004).

By 1925 Teilhard's influence had so disturbed a bloc of conservative French bishops that they complained to the Holy Office in Rome which in turn put pressure on the Jesuits (Lukas and Lukas 1977). This incident only exacerbated the turmoil that surrounded Teilhard at the time. Accordingly 'Teilhard was ordered to leave his position at the *Institut Catholique* and to go into exile', which he did, joining other Jesuits in China who as a team were engaged in paleontological and geological research (Skehan 2001; Lukas and Lukas 1977).

By 26 April 1926 Teilhard was on board the ship, *Angkor*, and on 10 June he arrived once again in Tientsin (Peking), this time indefinitely as it turned out. 'Teilhard had left for China before it had been finally decided that the severance of his connection with the *Institut Catholique* should be permanent'. Teilhard's masterpiece of spirituality, now known in English as *The Divine Milieu*, was completed in China in 1926–27.

It is of interest to know Teilhard's frame of mind as he went into exile. 'Teilhard's adaptability enabled him…to make a new home in China, as he did later in America. Paris, however, was still the centre of his world' (Cuénot 1965: 63). On 16 January 1927 Teilhard wrote to a friend who had sent him news that his appointment to the *Institut Catholique* had been terminated. Teilhard's reaction: 'I am little affected by this news. When I left Paris in April it was with the impression that my future was wholly uncertain; and I have since lived in China with the growing feeling that in this country I have found a new home' (Cuénot 1965: 63).

By February 1927 the Carnegie Foundation invited Teilhard to supervise research on vertebrate and human fossils throughout China, an offer that increased enormously both his responsibilities and available resources, while he remained a representative of the Paris Museum. With several colleagues he was in charge of geological work in all of China. What an unparalleled opportunity to work collaboratively with teams of well-qualified fellow scientists! 'In my own special field my concern is now to clear up some geological formations over an area as large as half Europe… My most active moments are still when I am saying my "Mass upon the altar of the world" to divinize the new day' (Teilhard 1962: 137-40).

Teilhard's New Mysticism

Ursula King believes that Teilhard's new synthesis became possible only through 'the emergence of the modern world wherein the religious and the mystical are closely interdependent with our knowledge of the natural world and with the construction of our social world. This unification appears to be what Teilhard means by 'Building the earth'. King (1997: 87-88) points out that Teilhard is the only writer known to her 'who wrestles with the similar seriousness and integrity demanded by contemporary needs without reducing them to primarily an inward quest. For Teilhard it is the integration of the inner and outer as experienced in the modern world that provides the road to a new synthesis and the possibility of a new mysticism' (U. King 1997: 88).

Teilhard refers to three types of mysticism. The first he calls 'communion with earth'; the second, 'communion with God' and the third which is a new synthesis which he advocates, between the forward and the upward directions, 'a communion with God through earth', a new mysticism that focuses on 'building the earth' (U. King 1996: 87). The phrase and concept 'forward and upward' (Cowell 2001: 84, 209) refers to 'two complementary currents' of which Teilhard was very conscious, namely an attraction to a supernatural union with Christ but also a strong attraction to matter. Early on, these seemingly divergent attractions gave rise to a psychological conflict within him, which when resolved in a positive way gave rise to his synthesis, a 'new mysticism'. Mooney (1964: 27-28) illustrates this point: 'It will be remembered that the cult of the Heart of Christ enabled Teilhard to 'materialize' what was divine, to bring into a single concrete focus both his attraction for matter and his adoration of the Person of Christ'.

Teilhard in a letter written on 15 March 1916 from the trenches during World War I to a Jesuit friend and theologian, explains more fully the nature of the problem of 'the forward' and 'the upward' in his life: He explains as follows the problem vexing him as he was arriving at a statement of his 'new mysticism':

> It is all very well to study science…to please God, and to fulfill an assigned task. But this is not enough; unless I recognize…the possibility of loving my work; unless I see that I must give myself to it completely, that I consolidate my progress towards an absolute by reason of the conquests themselves.
>
> …I have been trying to discover what there could be that is divine and predestined within the matter itself of our cosmos, our humanity, and our

progress...cannot the object, the matter itself, of our human love be transfigured, transferred into the absolute and, in short, into the divine? ... I want to love Christ with all my strength in the very act of loving the universe...Besides communion with God and communion with the earth, is there not also communion with God in and through the earth? (Mooney's translation 1964: 28-29 of Teilhard's 15 March 1916 letter in de Lubac 1967: Appendix 1, 241-45)

Teilhard perceived that the heart of spirituality is to be found in mysticism, of which for him, the supreme expression is a mysticism of action activated by 'the fire of love'. It is not at all surprising to me to find in Teilhard's discussion of mysticism, echoes of two action-oriented examples by Ignatius Loyola in the final meditations that form the *grand finale* of the 30 days of the *Spiritual Exercises*: 'love ought to show itself in deeds over and above words' and 'love consists in a mutual sharing of goods (Fleming 1980: 139; Skehan 1991: 158-61; 1994: 75-77).

Teilhard's Preoccupation: The Mystery of God and the Mystery of Evolution

Teilhard de Chardin's multi-faceted life and writings are of great importance to modern civilization because he has given us a foundation for thinking about the meaning of Christ, as God Incarnate. Jesus revealed in himself both the mystery of God and the mystery of all of creation, including mankind. During Teilhard's lifetime the theory of biological evolution was a most pressing and exciting, although controversial scientific concept, impacting theological discussions. Teilhard undertook the project 'To rethink within his own distinctive evolutionary system the data of Christian revelation concerning the person of Christ'. Teilhard 'believed that Christ as God Incarnate, revealed in himself not only the mystery of God but also the meaning of man, and therefore the ultimate meaning of that evolutionary process of which God is the cause and man the culmination' (Mooney 1964: 7).

Evolution & Theology: The Relationship of the Cosmos to Christ

Teilhard believed that the scientific discovery of evolution was of great theological importance, because it shed a totally new light upon a theological problem that St Paul addressed in his letters, the relationship of the cosmos to Christ. Teilhard thought that it made a world of difference. 'A satisfactory answer to this problem in terms of evolution, Teilhard felt, could do much to bridge the chasm which exists today between Christians and non-Christians on the question of building the earth' (Mooney 1964: 6).

The Christian who feels secure in the knowledge that a certain avenue of escape to the next world is at hand, frequently sees no ultimate value to human progress in the present world. The results of human effort precisely as human, tend to hold little interest. The unbeliever is quick to sense this ambivalence because the planning and shaping of the modern world are seen as of supreme importance: and so the Christian is faulted...for an apparent lack of interest in grappling with the grimy machinery of society that is linked to social progress (Mooney 1964: 6). Conversely, the Christian may regard the diligent unbeliever as a godless materialist. Teilhard's goal is to show that the city of mankind is also the city of God and that human achievement must also be regarded as sacred accomplishment.

Years of Magnificent Achievement

The twenty-one years after his exile from France and his return to China were for Teilhard a time of great productivity in geology and paleontology on three continents. His work at first was mainly involved with projects in China, and then with those that included neighboring countries over a vast area of eastern and central Asia. These brought him into close contact with the leading scientists of this vast area including those from the wider international community. In 1929 Teilhard was appointed Scientific Adviser to the Chinese Geological Survey.

Also in 1929 the skull of 'Peking Man' was found in the now-famous Chou-Kou-Tien deposit. Although Teilhard did not discover the skull, he was closely involved with aspects of its identification and the problematic geologic setting of the discovery and consequently its age determination. He continued to take on more responsibility for geologic information in the service of paleontology in general and of human paleontology more specifically. George Barbour, Teilhard's collaborator and friend, noted that the 'isolated position of Chou-Kou-Tien — thousands of miles from the nearest localities where other Late Cenozoic strata were known'...required meticulous regional geologic correlations to determine the deposit's age. This situation ruled out straightforward correlations by which the exact age of the Peking Man 'horizon' could be established. Davidson Black, Teilhard's Canadian colleague and close friend as well as Director of the

Cenozoic Laboratory, determined that reconnaissance studies had to be extended across China and into Central Asia. Teilhard's participation in this project requiring both paleontological and geological skills would be essential.

> Black had already made contact with authorities in India and the Middle East, as a first step in his plan to lead a Cenozoic Expedition into the mid-continent. He came to New York with Teilhard and [Dr. Amadeus W.] Grabau in the summer of 1933, just before the Washington meeting of the XVIII International Geological Congress, with a view to securing from the Rockefeller Foundation approval for this project (Barbour 1965: 60).

Much has been written about the well-deserved significance of Teilhard's publications on spirituality. However, as a professional geologist, I think it is important for me to emphasize the high quality of Teilhard's geological as well as his paleontological research. Teilhard was a highly respected, meticulous researcher in the field of biological paleontology as well as in regional geologic correlations while carrying out research for the China Geological Survey. George Barbour, a distinguished geologist in his own right, for many years a professor at the University of Cincinnati, worked closely with Teilhard on several projects for a quarter of a century and regarded him as a world-class geologist and paleontologist.

Barbour writes about his association with Teilhard in his delightful book, *In the Field with Teilhard de Chardin*, in which he describes discussions around the campfire during fieldwork. Barbour's words represent a significant commentary by a highly respected American geologist on the scientific skills and accomplishments of Teilhard, which have been under-reported elsewhere because of the overwhelming interest and significance of his writings on spirituality. Teilhard inscribed one of his important papers, 'How I believe', 'to my other self, George B. Barbour' (Barbour 1965).

In 1929, after the discovery of teeth of the Peking man, Davidson Black organized the Cenozoic Laboratory as a joint research center in the Geological Survey of China, supported by the Rockefeller Foundation. Teilhard worked in Peking and at the Chou-Kou-Tien site, where he was in charge of identifying the fossils. Black died suddenly in 1934, and Teilhard was appointed acting director of the Cenozoic Laboratory. Teilhard spent a part of 1935–36 first in India in the Siwalik Hills with the Yale-Cambridge research team under Helmut de Terra, explorer and geographer, and later in Burma with the Harvard-Carnegie expedition led by Professor Hallam Movius of Harvard University with whom I became acquainted while I was a graduate student in Harvard's Department of Geological Sciences in the late 1940s and early 1950s (Skehan 2001).

Teilhard, one of forty scientists and engineers, was chosen as the official Citroen Expedition Geologist for its trans-Asian expedition that left Peking in May 1931 to cross the Gobi Desert. This ten month project traversing incredibly difficult terrain, under adverse climatic and other challenging conditions, was Teilhard's most rewarding expedition because it consisted essentially of ten months of uninterrupted research through mountainous terrain that would have been impenetrable except for the experimental Citroen vehicles.

When the Japanese army invaded North China in 1940, Teilhard's ability to continue fieldwork was tightly constrained by the invading army. As a result he and Pierre Leroy, SJ, not to be confused with an older colleague, Édouard Le Roy, organized the Geobiological Institute in the Legation Quarter of Peking, rescuing, as possible, collections from the Cenozoic Laboratory and the Tientsin Museum. A volume of essays written at this time entitled 'The Future of Man' was assembled after Teilhard's death.

Groundwork for Teilhard's best known book, *The Human Phenomenon* had begun in 1928 and 1930 with two brief essays; however, he spent two years from June 1938 to June 1940 completing the manuscript. Teilhard had written his first essay on the topic '"Le Phénomène humain" in 1928 in Paris'. 'He told his friend Father Valensin that beyond geology the true passion of his life was now the human phenomenon' (U. King 1996: 171). His hope at this time that 'his quite long work' on 'Man' would be published', came to fruition with the publication in French of *Le Phénomène humain*, translated into English in 1959 by Bernard Wall. A recently available major reference is Teilhard's *The Human Phenomenon*, the definitive revision translated and edited by Sarah Appleton-Weber (1999).

Teilhard's Final Years

By Christmas 1945 Teilhard received official permission to return to Paris where Father d'Ouince, one of his strongest supporters who had collected all Teilhard's writings in spite of official censure, was the Superior of the Jesuit house at Études. Teilhard was preparing to join George Barbour in 1947 on the University of California's expedition to South Africa when he experienced a heart attack. This turn of events forced him to postpone until July 1951, when he had sufficiently recovered his health, his long cherished desire to carry out research in South Africa with financial support of the Viking Fund in New York, later called the Wenner Gren Foundation of Anthropological Research. After eight weeks of research in South Africa, Teilhard returned to St Ignatius Parish, 980 Park Avenue, New York, a fifteen minute walk from the conveniently located Viking Foundation. I had the privilege of meeting Teilhard on two occasions in the 1950s, one of which was during the Annual Meeting of the Geological Society of America in Atlantic City, New Jersey.

> On New Year's Day, 1955 Teilhard completed a short essay, The 'Death-Barrier and Co-Reflection'. He proposed that 'science needed the stimulation of religion, and the understanding of revelation could develop more fully only if it took into account the new contributions that scientific research is gradually making to human consciousness...' (U. King 1996: 225)

'Teilhard's science, religion, and mystical spirituality came together in his understanding of Christ in whom all things are made one'. Ideas that were most important to Teilhard in the few months that remained in his final year of life are those contained in this beautifully described Christic vision, his spiritual autobiography, *The Heart of Matter*. Teilhard tells us that 'The Christic' is a distillation of *The Divine Milieu*, 'The Mass on the World', and *The Heart of Matter* (Mortier and Auboux 1966: 162; U. King 1996: 225).

Teilhard wants us to know what was in his heart as he wrote this last essay:

> It is a long time now since, in 'The Mass on the World' and *The Divine Milieu*, I tried to put into words the admiration and wonder that I felt as I confronted perspectives as yet hardly formulated within me.
>   Today, after forty years of constant reflection, it is still exactly the same fundamental vision, in its mature form, for the last time. With less exuberance and freshness of expression perhaps, than at my first encounter with it, but still with the same wonder and the same passion. ('The Christic' in *Heart of Matter*, 1978: 83; U. King 1996: 226)

Toward the end of his life Teilhard summarizes his vision of the creation of 'a new spiritual atmosphere...through the coming together of the love of God and the new faith in the world'. Teilhard had the confidence that 'Everywhere in the world...the fusion of these two faiths would sooner or later occur and provide a new energy that would spread like fire. His vision was that 'the development of something 'Ultra-human' would eventually lead to Christ-Omega, the center and summit of the universe, of all creation (U. King 1996: 228).

Teilhard's Biblically-Rooted Thought and Spirituality

The basic premise for Teilhard's synthesis is that evolution is a fundamental process in nature and as such characterizes the behavior of the entire universe at all times. Teilhard developed insights based on several Pauline texts that place creation and incarnation in an evolutionary context: The three so-called cosmic Pauline texts, translated by Mooney (1964: 95, 97, 98), considered by Teilhard as most relevant to determining Christ's relationship to the material world, are presented below.

In the passage that follows, Paul expresses reasons for the Christians of Rome to hope in the face of suffering and death saying that if we suffer with Christ we will share his glory and that this glory will more than compensate for the sorrows of this life. Teilhard interprets Paul as saying that it is '*the whole of creation*, ...through the bodies of men', now better translated as the human body, 'that redemption extends to the rest of creation. The use of the Greek word *ktisis* to designate all things is quite common both in the Septuagint and the New Testament, and is so used by Paul himself in Rom. 1.25' (Mooney 1964: 95).

> For creation is waiting with eager longing for the revelation of the [children] of God: if it has been condemned to frustration — not through its own fault but because of him who so condemned it, — it also has hope of being set free in its turn from the bondage of decay and of entering into the freedom of the glory of the children of God. We know indeed that the whole of creation has been groaning until now in an agony of birth. More than that, we ourselves, who already possess in the Spirit a foretaste of the future, groan also in our hearts, waiting for the redemption of our bodies. (Rom. 8.19-23)

'The restoration of the entire universe in Christ...became...a dominant theme of Colossians and Ephesians, both written while Paul was captive in Rome... In the famous two-strophed hymn of Colossians 1.15-20... Paul asserts the supremacy of Christ as *Kyrios*, Lord and Master, over the whole universe'. Paul recurs to 'the pre-existence of Christ with the Father, in whose image he is the source as well as the instrument and final end' [goal] 'of creation. The Incarnation, crowned by the triumph of the Resurrection, is seen as placing the human nature of Christ at the head not only of the whole human race but also of the entire created universe' (Mooney 1964: 96).

> He is the image of the unseen God, born before every creation.
> In him all things were created.
> Heavenly and earthly, seen and unseen,

Thrones, dominions, princedoms and powers—
All things were created through him and for him.
He takes precedence over all and in him all things subsist.

He is also Head of his Body the Church;
For he is the beginning, first-born from among the dead,
That he might come to stand first in everything.
It was God's good pleasure to make reside in him all the
Plenitude.
And to win back all things through him and for him, on earth and in
heaven.
Making peace with them through his blood shed on the cross.
(Col. 1.15-20) (Mooney, 1964: 97)

Mooney (1964: 98) notes that this passage in Eph. 1.9-10, 2-23 appears to be a remarkable development in Paul's thought. It begins with 'a description of God's plan of salvation as a "re-establishment", a "summing up" of all things in Christ' whose root meaning of the Greek word is 'to head up'. From the context it seems that 'Paul's intention is to situate within a cosmic framework his Body-of-Christ theme, and at the same time to present the relationship between Christ and the cosmos as an extension of the physical and sacramental relationship between Christ and the members of his Church. Not only is Christ Lord of the universe, he is also its "Head"'. Mooney suggests further that 'the Church, as the risen Body of Christ', is 'equated with the dimensions of the Pleroma'... The 'fullness of time' in which this Plenitude is to be realized refers most probably to *both* comings of Christ, his Incarnation and work of Redemption in time and his Parousia at the end of time.

> It was [God's] loving design, centered in Christ, to re-establish all things in him when the fullness of time should come, all that is in heaven, all that is on earth, summed up in him... [God] has put all things under his feet and made him the indisputable Head of the Church which is his Body, the Plenitude of him who is everywhere and in all things complete. (Eph. 1.9-10, 22-23)

These texts mystically view anthropogenesis and cosmogenesis as a Christogenesis based mainly on the cosmic vision of St Paul in Colossians and Ephesians. One line of Teilhard's theological thought based mainly on the cosmic vision of St Paul in letters to the Colossians and Ephesians concerns the physical relationship between the Body of Christ, mankind and the material world. He viewed humankind as the spearhead of evolution, in whom evolution has become self-conscious. Building on the analogy of the spheres of the earth, Teilhard postulated a spiritual, world-encircling sphere of thought, that he called the 'noosphere', that has been in process of forming since humankind developed reflective consciousness. Teilhard was thinking of Christ as intimately involved in the processes of evolution in the widest sense when he said:

> Because everything in the universe is in fact ultimately moving towards Christ–Omega: because cosmogenesis, moving in its totality through anthropogenesis, ultimately shows itself to be a Christogenesis;...if the whole movement of the world is in the service of a Christogenesis (which is another way of saying that Christ is attainable in his fullness only at the end and summit of cosmic evolution)... We have seen that Christ, by reason of his position as Omega of the world, represents a focus toward whom and in whom everything converges... What can this mean except that every action, as soon as it is oriented toward him, takes on, without any change in itself, ...the psychic quality of an act of love... Now he (the Christian) can unite himself directly to the divine Centre through action itself, no matter what form that action takes. (Mooney 1964: 161-62, citing Teilhard's 'Super-humanité, super-Christ, super-charité', 1943, Oeuvres, ix: 213-17)

Evaluations of Orthodoxy of Teilhard's Writings

Because criticism of Teilhard's prolific writings have at times been acrimonious during the twentieth century, I believe it is important to say a word about the orthodoxy of Teilhard's writings. Teilhard's religious superiors requested that Cardinal Henri de Lubac, a highly esteemed scholar and Jesuit theologian, provide them with an evaluation of Teilhard's written work. Cardinal du Lubac, a Jesuit and a younger contemporary of Teilhard, provided the requested evaluation. In the resulting volume published in French in 1962, *The Religion of Teilhard de Chardin*, de Lubac (1967) wrote a detailed and generally laudatory review of Teilhard's spirituality and thought. It is significant that de Lubac at the time was already a Cardinal with enormous prestige in scholarly theological circles as well as in the secretariats of the Vatican. The laudatory implications written by de Lubac in the dedication to his review volume, *The Religion of Teilhard de Chardin* (1967) unmistakably refers to Teilhard by indirection: 'To the memory of a great contemplative Father Charles Nicolet (1896–1961) who was a devoted friend of Father Teilhard, and was consumed by the same fire'.

Cardinal de Lubac's implied message regarding Teilhard's writings taken as a whole is very positive. During Teilhard's early career he circulated written copies of many of his papers and ideas to sympathetic fellow Jesuits for their review and feedback, so de

Lubac, several years younger than Teilhard, was generally familiar with the content of Teilhard' writings many years before he was asked to prepare the above review. The esteem in which Cardinal de Lubac was held by officials at the Vatican may be measured by the fact that he and Yves Congar, a distinguished Dominican theologian, were commissioned to prepare the agenda for the Second Vatican Council.

In his lifetime, and since his death in 1955, the cloud of misunderstanding of Teilhard's ideas and spirituality within the Catholic Church, still continues to confuse some of the general public in spite of clear evidence to the contrary. On the occasion of the twenty-fifth anniversary of Teilhard's death, Cardinal Agostino Casaroli on behalf of Pope John Paul II sent a congratulatory message to the International Assembly of Teilhard Societies and encouraged them to celebrate Teilhard's contributions to spirituality and culture. This welcome message was published in *Origins*, 16 July 1981 (Skehan 2001: 64).

Building the Earth and the Cosmos

One of Pierre Teilhard de Chardin's important perspectives that is relevant to our relationship to the Earth and the Universe as responsible human beings, is summed up in his multifaceted concept of 'Building the Earth'. That concept refers not only to progress 'ahead' resulting from human effort but 'upward movement of human beings toward the above'. His was what we might call an ecotheology spirituality in the sense of regarding all of Creation as Sacred, an all encompassing spirituality of finding God in every aspect of human endeavor. One who regards all of Creation as sacred, must necessarily think of the Earth with the kind of reverence that we would accord a lower case 'sacrament' because by sacrament is meant a 'sign' pointing to God's action in our lives.

The Earth and Universe, as we are reminded by Scripture, are God's handiwork and they reveal to us the 'workman' who fashioned them (Rom. 1.22). Are not our personal activities a kind of 'stewardship' or even a kind of 'priestly duty', as Fred Lawrence of Boston College (written communication, 1990) refers to the privileged intimacy and corresponding responsibility that we scientists bear as caretakers of 'on-going creation' of the material world around us? In the title of this paper I have used the term 'building the cosmos' as well as the more familiar phrase that Teilhard used, 'building the earth'. I chose to do that because Teilhard, who thought in cosmic terms, dedicated *The Divine Milieu* 'to [for] those who love the world', giving as his reason 'Sic Deus dilexit mundum', meaning that "God so loved the world' (all of creation, the cosmos) that He gave us His only Son'. I think it would be harmonious with Teilhard's cosmic thought to use the phrase 'Building the cosmos' in connection with this 'new mysticism'.

Teilhard's attitude was that all Creation is sacred; that the entire lives of human beings are significant because we participate in creation so-to-speak not only by 'building the earth but the entire cosmos'. Based on his understanding of key passages of St Paul, Teilhard envisioned that each of us with Christ serves as 'co-creator' and 'co-redeemer' of the Earth and Universe during our time and place on planet Earth (Skehan 2001: 45-52). These understandings impart a new appreciation of the link between the created world and our own 'action-oriented' spirituality of 'building the Earth and the Cosmos'.

References

Barbour, George B.
    1965   *In the Field with Teilhard de Chardin* (New York: Herder & Herder).
Bouma-Prediger, Steven
    1995   *The Greening of Theology: The Ecological Models of Rosemary Radford Reuther, Joseph Sittler, and Jürgen Moltman* (ed. B.A. Holdrege; American Academy of Religion, 91; Atlanta: Scholars Press).
Cowell, Siôn
    2001   *The Teilhard Lexicon: Understanding the Language, Terminology and Vision of the Writings of Pierre Teilhard de Chardin* (Brighton, UK/ Portland, OR: Sussex Academic Press).
Cuénot, C.
    1965   *Teilhard de Chardin: A Biographical Study* (Baltimore, MD: Helicon Press).
de Lubac, H.
    1965   *Teilhard de Chardin: The Man and His Meaning* (New York: Hawthorn Books).
    1967   *The Religion of Teilhard de Chardin* (New York: Desclee Company).
Egan, SJ, H.D.
    1982   *What Are They Saying About Mysticism?* (Ramsey, NJ: Paulist Press).
    1987   *Ignatius Loyola the Mystic*, in O'Donoghue (ed.): 1987.
Fisher, George W.
    2000   'Sustainable Living: Common Ground for Geology and Theology', in Jill S. Schneiderman (ed.), *The Earth Around Us: Maintaining a Livable Planet* (New York: W.H. Freeman & Co., 2000).
Fleming, SJ, D.L.
    1980   *The Spiritual Exercises of St Ignatius: A Literal Translation and A Contemporary Reading* (St Louis: The Institute of Jesuit Sources).

Haight, Elizabeth
    2002   Review of George S. Levit's *Biogeochemistry-Biosphere-Noosphere: The Growth of the Theoretical System of Vladimir Ivanovich Vernadsky* (Chicago: University of Chicago Press), *Isis*, v. 93, p. 150. [significant review]

Hallman, D.G. (ed.)
    1994   *Ecotheology: Voices from South and North* (Maryknoll, NY: World Council of Churches/Orbis Books).

King, SJ, Thomas
    1981   *Teilhard's Mysticism of Knowing* (New York: Seabury).
    1988   *Teilhard de Chardin*, in O'Donoghue (ed.): 1988.

King, Ursula
    1980   *Towards a New Mysticism: Teilhard de Chardin and Eastern Religions* (New York: Seabury).
    1996   *Spirit of Fire: The Life and Vision of Teilhard de Chardin* (Maryknoll, NY: Orbis Books).
    1997   *Christ in All Things: Exploring Spirituality with Teilhard de Chardin* (Maryknoll, NY: Orbis Books).
    2002   *Mysticism and Contemporary Society: Some Teilhardian Reflections* (Teilhard Studies, 44; New York: American Teilhard Association for the Future of Man).

Lachance, A.J., and J. Carroll (eds.)
    1994   *Embracing Earth: Catholic Approaches to Ecology* (Maryknoll, NY: Orbis Books).

Levit, G.
    2000   *The Biosphere and the Noosphere Theories of V.I. Vernadsky and P. Teilhard de Chardin: A Methodological Analysis* (Archives Internationales D'Histoire des Sciences, December).
    2001   *Biochemistry – Biosphere – Noosphere: The Growth of the Theoretical System of Vladimir Ivanovich Vernadsky* (Verlag fur Wissenschaft und Bildung: Berlin).

Lukas, M., and E. Lukas
    1977   *Teilhard: A Biography* (New York: Doubleday)

Mc Menamin, Mark A.S.
    2001   *Evolution of the Noosphere* (Teilhard Studies, 42; New York: American Teilhard Association for the Future of Man).

McMenamin, Mark A.S., and Dianna L.S. Mc Menamin
    1990   *The Emergence of Animals: The Cambrian Breakthrough* (New York: Columbia University Press).

Mooney, C.F., SJ
    1964   *Teilhard de Chardin and the Mystery of Christ* (Harper & Row: New York, 1964).

Mortier, Jeanne, and Marie-Louise Auboux (eds.)
    1966   *Teilhard de Chardin: Album* (New York/Evanston: Harper & Row).

O'Donoghue, Noel Dermot, ODC (ed.)
    1988   *The Way of the Christian Mystics* (Wilmington, DE: Michael Glazier).

Schmitz-Moorman, K., and N. Schmitz-Moorman (eds.)
    1971   *L'oeuvre scientifique de Teilhard de Chardin* (12 vols.; Freiburg: Walter Verlag).

Skehan, J.W., SJ

1991   *Place Me with Your Son: Ignatian Spirituality in Everyday Life* (Washington, DC: Georgetown University Press, 3rd edn).

1994   *Place Me with Your Son: Ignatian Spirituality in Everyday Life, Director's Guide to Third Edition* (Washington, DC: Georgetown University Press).

2001   *Praying with Teilhard de Chardin* (Winona, MN: Saint Mary's Press).

Teilhard de Chardin, SJ, Pierre

1959   *The Phenomenon of Man* (ed. and trans. Bernard Wall; London: Collins).

1960   *The Divine Milieu* (New York: Harcourt Brace).

1962   *Letters from a Traveler* (London: Collins).

1965   *Writings in Time of War* (New York: Harper & Row).

1968   *Science and Christ* (London: Collins).

1970   *Activation of Energy* (London: Collins).

1978   *The Heart of Matter* (London: Collins).

1999   *The Human Phenomenon* (ed. and trans. Sarah Appleton-Weber; Brighton, UK: Sussex Academic Press).

2003   *Notes de retraites, 1918–1955* (Introduction et notes de Gérard Henry Baudry; Préface de Gustave Martelet, SJ; Paris: Éditions du Seuil).

Vernadsky, Vladimir I. (Foreword Lynn Margulis...[*et al.*]; Introduction by Jacques Grinevald)

1998   *The Biosphere* (trans. David B. Langmuir; rev. and annotated Mark A.S. McMenamin; New York: Copernicus/Springer Verlag, complete annotated edition).

2

LA LIBERTE SELON TEILHARD ET LA SCIENCE

André Daleux

1. Qu'est-ce que la liberté pour la science?

1.1. Position des scientistes du siècle dernier
Pour bon nombre de scientifiques du siècle dernier, la liberté, tout comme l'esprit, était un phénomène illusoire, un épiphénomène, sans aucun lien réel avec le monde physique qu'elle ne pouvait en rien influencer.

Comment en était-on parvenu à cette conviction?

1.1.1. *Déterminisme newtonien*. Ce sont les lois de Newton et leur succès dans la prédiction du mouvement des astres, qui convainqui-rent les chercheurs des 18e et 19e siècles que '*Le monde fut mis en mouvement et a continué depuis toujours à tourner, semblable à une machine gouvernée par des lois immuables*' (Capra 1979: 1). '*Une fois définies les conditions initiales d'un système, la loi le détermine complètement, permet de déduire son évolution, de calculer son état pour n'importe quel instant antérieur ou ultérieur*' (Prigogine et Stengers 1979: 1, 5, 6).

1.1.2. *Hypothèse de Laplace*. L'apogée de cette vision d'un monde réglé comme un mécanisme d'horlogerie fut l'hypothèse de Laplace, mathématicien français de l'époque napoléonienne, qu'il énonça comme suit:

> '*Un intellect qui à un moment donné connaîtrait toutes les forces en action dans la nature, et la position de chaque chose dont le monde est fait (…) comprendrait dans la même formule les mouvements des plus grands corps de l'univers et ceux des atomes les plus infimes; rien ne serait incertain pour lui, et l'avenir comme le passé, serait présent à ses yeux*'. (Capra 1979: 1)

La conséquence d'une telle vision du monde allait de soi: il n'y avait plus la moindre place pour le libre arbitre, pour l'acte libre, dans un univers où aucun acte libre ne pouvait s'opposer à l'implacable engrenage des causes et de leurs effets. Cette position persiste encore de nos jours chez de nombreux scientifiques pour qui nous sommes aussi prisonniers du déterminisme, qu'un caillou obéissant à la pesanteur.

De ces restrictions des prérogatives de l'âme à la suppression pure et simple de l'âme, il n'y avait qu'un pas qui fut vite franchi par les scientifiques classiques du 19e siècle qui adoptèrent une vision déterministe et mécaniciste jusqu'à une époque relativement récente. Ainsi, pour les mécanicistes, l'organisme des animaux, parmi lesquels figurent les humains, n'était qu'un mécanisme de précision, merveilleux sans doute, et d'une complexité invraisemblable, mais rien de plus. L'esprit, l'âme, n'avaient pas d'existence vraie. Tel biologiste célèbre résumait bien cette position en disant: 'Je n'ai jamais trouvé l'âme à la pointe de mon scalpel'.

Dans le cadre d'une telle conviction scientifique, les hypothèses de Teilhard de Chardin sur la liberté humaine et son émergence en l'homme, que je vais maintenant exposer, ne pouvaient être que des balivernes pour les scientifiques du XIXe siècle, enfermés dans des convictions déterministes. Mais nous verrons que:

> *En fait, cette évidence s'effondre avec l'apparition de la physique quantique. Les relations d'incertitude découvertes par le physicien Werner Heisenberg mettent un terme au rêve laplacien d'un 'univers engrenage' dont une intelligence supérieure pourrait déduire, en s'appuyant sur la causalité, tout le passé et l'avenir. Heinsenberg établit qu'au niveau quantique il est impossible de connaître avec précision à la fois la vitesse et la position d'une particule. Tout progrès dans la connaissance de la position augmente l'incertitude sur la vitesse, et réciproquement. De ce fait, l'horloge de précision que représentait le déroulement des événements matériels, pour les scientifiques, depuis le XVIIIe siècle, bat la breloque. Ses rouages prennent du jeu.* (Daleux 2001: 1-3)

2. La liberté humaine selon Teilhard de Chardin

2.1. Les limites de notre liberté

Teilhard était très conscient des limites imposées à l'exercice de notre volonté libre, par le milieu extérieur. Qu'il s'agisse des contraintes physiques ou des traits de caractère indélébiles qu'imprime en nous l'hérédité inscrite dans nos chromosomes.

C'est ainsi que pour Teilhard:

> *Quand nous agissons, semble-t-il avec le plus de spontanéité et de vigueur, nous sommes en partie menés par les choses que nous croyons dominer'. 'Si nous y prenons garde, en effet, nous nous apercevons avec une sorte d'effroi, que nous n'émergeons dans la réflexion et la liberté que par la fine pointe de nous-mêmes.* (Teilhard de Chardin 1965: 2)

Cet ocean dont nous émergeons à peine est '... la nuit de tout ce qui est en nous et autour de nous, sans nous et malgré nous' (Teilhard de Chardin 1965: 2).

Nous sommes plongés dans le milieu extérieur où aucun effet ne peut apparaître sans être déterminé par une cause. C'est la base même du déterminisme scientifique. Ce monde extérieur, dit Teilhard, '*par les innombrables tentacules de ses déterminismes, et de ses hérédités, s'insinue au coeur même de ce que chacun d'entre nous avait pris l'habitude d'appeler familièrement son âme*' (Teilhard de Chardin 1963: 2, 3, 5, 8).

2.2. Critique du mécanicisme

2.2.1. *Réponse de Teilhard au scientisme mécaniciste*. Selon lui, l'erreur des mécanicistes provient de leur méthode d'étude du réel, qui fait appel essentiellement à l'analyse.

Sous la corrosion de l'analyse, tout système complexe se dissocie en ses éléments constituants. C'est alors que les organismes vivants sont réductibles en organes, en cellules et, à la limite, en substances chimiques. (Un organisme humain, c'est 80% d'eau et 20% de matière minérale.) L'acte libre, scruté par l'analyse, révèle son infrastructure de circuits cérébraux, de sécrétions hormonales ou autres, le tout étroitement enchaîné en une série de causes et d'effets.

Mais, selon Teilhard, chaque analyse laisse échapper l'essentiel du système analysé, c'est-à-dire la puissance, la force qui maintenait la cohésion de cette structure, lui assurant ainsi son identité propre et sa capacité de fonctionner. Cette force de cohésion, c'est ce que Teilhard appelle l'âme de cette structure, de cet ensemble, par analogie avec l'âme humaine.

> '*L'analyse, admirable et puissant instrument de dissection du réel, abandonne entre nos mains des termes toujours moins compréhensibles et toujours plus appauvris.(...) Chaque degré nouveau de réduction au multiple (de matérialisation) laisse échapper une âme*'. (Teilhard de Chardin 1965: 2)

Dans ces conditions, il est évident que le scalpel n'est pas l'instrument adéquat pour détecter l'âme.

Au point de vue matérialiste qui réduit le monde à de la matière et fait de l'Esprit une illusion, Teilhard oppose la notion d'*Esprit-Matière* selon laquelle l'étoffe cosmique n'est pas double, formée d'une part de matière, d'autre part d'esprit, mais unique. Cette entité unique présente deux aspects. Sa face interne, spirituelle, avec laquelle nous entrons en contact par notre propre intériorité, lors de la méditation, la prière ou simplement la réflexion profonde. Par contre, la face externe, matérielle de cette entité unique est sa traduction par nos organes sensoriels, sous forme d'objets et d'êtres situés dans l'espace-temps physique. Selon Teilhard nos organes sensoriels nous trompent, la face solide de l'Esprit-Matière n'est pas son apparence matérielle, mais sa face spirituelle. C'est-à-dire que *pour Teilhard, le monde est Esprit*, nos sens nous induisent en erreur quand ils le traduisent en matière statique. C'est ainsi qu'il écrit à son amie philosophe Léontine Zanta en 1929: « *Maintenant, 'l'Esprit' est assez bizarrement devenu pour moi une chose toute réelle, la seule réelle…*» (Teilhard de Chardin 1965: 2).

2.3. *Origine de notre liberté*
2.3.1. *Evidence intuitive de la liberté.* Selon Teilhard le seul instrument capable de déceler notre liberté est d'ordre psychologique. Seule l'introspection, le regard intérieur, peut nous mettre en contact direct avec notre propre psychisme, doté d'une volonté libre qui devient, dès lors, l'objet d'une certitude intuitive. Souvenons-nous aussi que, pour Teilhard, le seul fait de déceler avec certitude l'existence de l'Esprit en un seul point de l'univers (nous mêmes), implique la présence plus ou moins diffuse de ce même Esprit jusqu'aux niveaux les plus élémentaires de la trame de l'univers. « *A cette certitude de base, Teilhard applique le principe scientifique selon lequel un phénomène observé soigneusement en un point de l'univers doit avoir des prolongements plus ou moins diffus dans la totalité cosmique* » (Daleux 2001: 1-3).

2.3.2. *La liberté humaine.* Pour Teilhard, les éléments infimes qui constituent l'étoffe de l'univers, sont dotés d'une 'spontanéité embryonnaire', qui peu à peu s'enrichit dans *'le lent mais progressif rassemblement d'une conscience diffuse'* et finit par se manifester au grand jour, dans la liberté humaine. *'De ce point de vue, l'Homme n'est autre-chose dans la Nature, qu'une zone d'émersion, où culmine et se trahit précisément cette évolution cosmique profonde'* (Teilhard de Chardin 1962: 2). Voici qu'apparaît le maître mot par lequel Teilhard rend compte de l'apparition de la liberté chez l'homme. La *liberté est une émergence*, c'est-à-dire la manifestation devenue apparente d'un phénomène qui était resté caché jusque là et qui apparaît dès lors au grand jour. La liberté émerge par le franchissement du seuil de la pensée réfléchie humaine.

> La notion de franchissement de seuil est à l'œuvre de Teilhard ce qu'est la catalyse à la chimie. Le seuil rend compte de l'émergence du 'tout autre' au cours de l'évolution. Il s'agit d'un changement de nature des éléments impliqués dans la cosmogénèse. (…) La banalité des phénomènes physico-chimiques qui ont amené son apparition ne doit pas nous masquer le fait essentiel. Grâce à une transformation,

anatomiquement minime, l'être humain, parce que réfléchi, représente du 'tout autre' dans le monde. Un fossé désormais infranchissable le sépare des autres vivants ». (Daleux 2001: 1-3)

Nous verrons tout à l'heure que certains scientifiques contemporains dont nous étudierons les hypothèses, considèrent également la liberté comme une émergence.

Selon l'hypothèse de Teilhard, l'organisme humain fonctionne comme un système collecteur et amplificateur de la spontanéité élémentaire qu'il puise jusqu'au niveau quantique de l'étoffe cosmique, pour en extraire la possibilité d'actes libérés du déterminisme.

2.3.3. *Pourquoi l'absence apparente de liberté de la matière?* Un esprit rationnel ne manquera pas d'opposer à Teilhard l'objection suivante: 'Si chaque corpuscule élémentaire et doté d'un embryon de liberté, comment expliquer l'inertie, l'absence totale de spontanéité constatée dans l'étude de la matière non-vivante? 'La réponse de Teilhard est que les libertés élémentaires des corpuscules infimes de l'étoffe cosmique se contrecarrent, s'annulent mutuellement, par un effet de grands nombres. Ce qui explique l'apparente inertie de la matière et son assujettissement au déterminisme, c'est-à-dire aux lois physiques précises qui régissent les rapports entre les causes et leurs effets.

> '*En vertu du jeu des Grands Nombres, la multitude désordonnée des consciences élémentaires, prise en masse, se comporte exactement comme si elle était privée de tout 'dedans' (de toute intériorité), c'est-à-dire elle développe exactement les mêmes déterminismes d'ensemble que ceux engendrés par l'énergie granulaire primordiale des physiciens'.* (Teilhard de Chardin 1963: 2, 3, 5, 8)

De façon imagée, on pourrait dire que des humains enserrés dans une foule, se trouvent privés de toute liberté d'action. L'écoulement de cette foule à travers un passage dépend aussi étroitement de la largeur de ce passage que l'écoulement d'un fluide dans une canalisation. Il en va de même pour les éléments infimes de l'étoffe cosmique élémentaire dont la spontanéité reste masquée par cet 'effet de foule'. Ce qui aboutit à l'apparente inertie de la matière.

Cette explication, qui pourrait à première vue passer pour une subtilité gratuite, est en fait la base de l'un des arguments les plus solides de Teilhard à l'encontre des théories matérialistes pour lesquelles le monde n'est que matière, l'Esprit n'étant qu'un épiphénomène illusoire, sans existence vraie. Aux matérialistes, Teilhard pourrait objecter: 'Vos théories dont l'esprit est exclu, expliqueront peut-être parfaitement le fonctionnement cosmique, mais ne peuvent rendre compte de l'existence de la conscience et de la liberté humaines. Au contraire, ma théorie selon laquelle un embryon d'Esprit imprègne dès l'origine chaque corpuscule cosmique, non seulement rend compte de l'Esprit et de la liberté de l'Homme, mais encore explique l'inertie de la matière et son obéissance aveugle aux lois physiques, par un effet statistique de grands nombres qui occulte ces libertés élémentaires'.

> *Une Evolution à base de matière ne sauve pas l'Homme: car tous les déterminismes accumulés ne sauraient donner une ombre de liberté. En revanche une Evolution à base d'Esprit conserve toutes les lois constatées par la Physique, tout en menant directement à la Pensée: car une masse de libertés élémentaires en désordre équivaut à du déterminé'.* (Teilhard de Chardin 1969: 3)

Il est intéressant de noter que, en raison de cette accession de l'Homme à la liberté, sa coopération est désormais nécessaire à l'évoution spiritualisante cosmique, puisqu'il est devenu libre de lui prêter on non son concours.

Mais reconnaissons honnêtement, avec Teilhard que le processus exact du passage, en l'Homme, d'un organisme totalement dépendant du déterminisme cause-effet, à un psychisme qui semble en être, au moins partiellement, devenu indépendant, reste assez mystérieux. Teilhard lui-même concluait en 1948: *'Celà nous le comprendrons peut-être mieux un jour'* (Teilhard de Chardin 1955: 3).

3. *Evolution de la science depuis le début du 20e siècle:*
critique du déterminisme absolu

Nous l'avons vu les choses ont bien évolué depuis le début du XXe siècle, avec la critique de plus en plus aigue de la notion de déterminisme absolu.

Le physicien Léon Brillouin en donne une excellente expression dans son livre: Vie, matière et observation:

> *'Affirmer le déterminisme, c'est faire acte de foi. Pour le prouver, il faudrait partir de mesures infiniment précises, infiniment nombreuses, irréalisables; il faudrait ensuite effectuer des calculs infaisables et observer pendant un temps infini. Poésie pure, sans aucune réalité concrète.*
>
> *Le déterminisme est impossible à prouver, dans le domaine de la physique classique, mais lorsque l'on passe à la physique atomique et à la mécanique des quanta, le déterminisme sombre complètement'.* (Brillouin 1959: 4)

3.1. *Indéterminisme quantique*
C'est en effet la physique quantique qui s'avère le grand fossoyeur de la notion de déterminisme absolu. Niels Bohr, l'un des fondateurs de cette physique quantique l'exprime clairement dans son livre

'Physique atomique et connaissance humaine', recueil de conférences tenues entre les années 30 à 50. Tant que l'on en reste à un point de vue déterministe, nous dit-il, l'idée de la liberté d'agir est évidemment exclue. Mais la physique atomique nous a appris la portée limitée d'une description mécaniste des phénomènes biologiques (Bohr 1961: 4). Trois éléments interviennent dans cette limitation quantique du déterminisme: l'interaction entre l'observateur et l'objet observé; les relations d'incertitude de Heisenberg, et la prévision seulement statistique des événements futurs.

3.1.1. *Limites de l'observation.* A l'échelle microscopique, tout événement observé est modifié par l'instrument de mesure, d'une façon qui nous est inconnaissable, ne serait-ce que par la lumière dont le flux de photons bombarde littéralement la particule quantique observée. De plus, le choix de l'instrument de mesure, qui incombe à l'expérimentateur, modifie radicalement la nature du phénomène observé. Selon l'instrument utilisé, la particule atomique observée se présente soit comme une onde (de localisation imprécise et d'extension spatiale indéfinie); soit comme un corpuscule (bien localisé et d'extension spatiale limitée). A la limite, nous dit Niels Bohr, la notion de localisation de la particule sur tel ou tel point de sa trajectoire, perd tout sens précis. Ce qui, avouons le, se prête mal à une description mécaniste des phénomènes, en un sens analogue à des mécanismes d'horlogerie parfaitement engrenés (Bohr 1961: 4).

3.1.2. *Relations d'incertitude de Werner Heisenberg.* Ces particularités des phénomènes quantiques ont été traduites par le physicien Werner Heisenberg en une *relation d'incertitude* selon laquelle: '*La connaissance que l'on peut avoir de l'état d'un système atomique doit toujours comporter une 'indétermination' particulière*' (Bohr 1961). De façon schématique, on ne peut connaître de façon précise, à la fois la position et la vitesse d'un objet atomique (Bohr 1961: 4). Notons bien que cette imprécision n'est pas due à un défaut de nos moyens d'observation, mais fait partie intégrante de la structure même du monde microphysique.

3.1.3. *Prévisibilité seulement statistique.* La troisième notion qui limite le déterminisme est le caractère imprévisible d'un événement quantique individuel. Par exemple, dans un bloc de radium (substance qui se désintègre spontanément), nous ne pouvons prédire le moment où aura lieu la désintégration de tel atome particulier de radium. La prévision ne peut être que statistique; c'est-à-dire qu'au bout d'un laps de temps bien déterminé, la moitié des atomes de radium se sera désintégrée. Un physicien classique aurait tendance à dire: l'impossibilité de prédire la désintégration de tel atome particulier vient de l'insuffisance de nos moyens d'observation. Mais le physicien quantique affirme que c'est dans son principe même que la prévision d'un événement individuel ne peut être effectuée. Il y a donc là un événement sans cause immédiate, qui échappe par principe au déterminisme absolu, à l'enchaînement étroit de cause à effet (Heisenberg 1967: 4).

Teilhard de Chardin a d'ailleurs tenu compte de ces notions quantiques, au moins en une occasion. L'un des problèmes que pose l'acte libre, phénomène sans cause directe, est la source d'énergie que nécessite cet acte. Si celui-ci n'a pas de cause immédiate, comment admettre qu'apparaisse spontanément, faudrait-il dire 'miraculeusement', l'impulsion énergétique nécessaire à sa réalisation? Il y aurait là une violation de la loi de conservation de l'énergie que l'on peut schématiser par l'aphorisme: « Dans la nature, rien ne se crée, rien ne se perd »; Teilhard appuie sa réponse sur les relations d'incertitude de Heisenberg qui introduisent dans le comportement de la particule quantique une marge d'imprécision où le calcul de l'énergie dépensée n'est plus possible.

> *Le rayon de choix accordé à chaque corpuscule élémentaire peut être pris assez petit pour rester à l'intérieur de la sphère d'indétermination reconnue par la Science la plus déterministe comme un attribut particulier de l'Infime. Autrement-dit, la 'création' d'énergie impliquée par le choix (…) peut être imaginé(e) comme de grandeur si faible qu'il n'affecte pas appréciablement la somme de l'Energie universelle.* (Teilhard de Chardin 1963: 2, 3, 5, 8)

L'ensemble de ces notions quantiques entraîne donc à la fois une dématérialisation progressive de l'objet physique, et un estompage croissant de la notion de déterminisme absolu. Le rapport étroit entre les causes et leurs effets perd de sa précision. Cette éviction du déterminisme absolu ne prouve pas, bien sur, que la possibilité de poser des actes libres existe; mais il est désormais devenu impossible de nier cette éventualité, à priori, au nom d'une omnisciente science déterministe.

4. *Hypothèses scientifiques récentes sur l'origine de notre liberté*

Après avoir vu les bases de la remise en cause du déterminisme strict, voyons quelques hypothèses scientifiques, en rapport avec l'indéterminisme quantique, émises au cours des dernières décennies.

Ces hypothèses ne forment pas un ensemble cohérent, mais représentent diverses approches, parfois convergentes, du problème.

4.1. *Pierre Auger: auteur de 'L'homme microscopique' (1966)*

Pierre Auger part du fait que le comportement des particules atomiques, régi par des lois strictes collectivement, reste imprévisible individuellement. La particule quantique individuelle semble donc jouir de ce qu'on pourrait appeler un certain degré de liberté. Elle échappe au déterminisme qui régit inévitablement les réactions de foules.

Selon Auger, cette autonomie de la particule peut se retrouver au niveau macroscopique (c'est-à-dire aux dimensions qui nous sont familières, des grands ensembles de particules, comme par exemple les organismes vivants).

La condition de cette activité autonome est que cet ensemble de particules atomiques qu'est un organisme, forme une individualité, c'est-à-dire réagisse en bloc, *comme un Tout*. Cette propriété se manifeste dès la formation d'une molécule d'hydrogène. Deux atomes mettent en commun leurs électrons et forment ainsi une molécule individualisée. Dans la totalité que forme la molécule, les propriétés de chacun des deux atomes ne peuvent plus être décrites qu'en fonction du 'tout' moléculaire auquel ils sont intégrés.. Ceci reste vrai pour les cellules, formées de molécules intégrées par milliards et les animaux pluricellulaires formés de milliards de cellules. Les propriétés de chaque cellule ou organe sont fonction du 'tout', c'est-à-dire de l'organisme où elles s'intègrent.

Selon Auger, c'est précisément ce qui caractérise la *matière vivante*.

Ceci est très important car c'est là toute la *différence entre un cerveau vivant et* un computeur artificiel, *un ordinateur*, dont les divers organes ne collaborent que superficiellement, comme les rouages d'une horloge et non pas en profondeur, à chaque étage de leurs composants, de la particule quantique à l'ordinateur total, en passant par le niveau atomique et moléculaire.

La conclusion de Pierre Auger, proche de celle de Teilhard est: *'L'être vivant se présente lui aussi comme un amplificateur qui amène l'indétermination fondamentale à l'échelle de la liberté'* (Auger 1966: 5).

4.2. *Bifurcations et émergence*

'La nouvelle alliance' est un hybride, né du croisement d'un physicien, Ilya Prigogine, prix Nobel de physique, et d'une philosophe, Isabelle Stengers. (Il s'agit bien sur, de l'interfécondation de leurs pensées.) Ce livre fait appel à deux notions importantes: celle de *bifurcation* et celle *d'émergence*.

L'instabilité que l'on constate au niveau microphysique de la matière peut, dans certaines conditions favorables, engendrer au niveau macroscopique, un nouveau régime de fonctionnement du système. Il faut pour cela que ce système se trouve éloigné de ses conditions normales d'équilibre énergétique. Dans ces conditions, une cause extérieure minime et fortuite, suffira à faire franchir au système un *point de bifurcation* où le choix entre l'un des nouveaux états possibles dépendra de la nature de cette cause déclenchante. Le nouveau régime de fonctionnement *'résulte de l'amplification d'une déviation microscopique qui, 'au bon moment' a privilégié une voie réaction-nelle au détriment d'autres voies également possibles'*. Rappelons que l'événement quantique déclenchant échappe individuellement au déterminisme strict. Ces notions se réfèrent également à la *théorie des catastrophes* du mathématicien René Thom (Prigogine et Stengers 1979: 1, 5, 6).

Prigogine n'hésite pas à parler d'un 'choix' opéré par le système, au niveau de la bifurcation. Non pas qu'il s'agisse 'd'une quelconque liberté subjective', mais parce que l'état du système après la bifurca-tion ne dépend plus seulement de son état antérieur, ni de l'agence-ment de ses parties constitutives. Ce nouvel état dépend d'une réaction du système *'en tant que Tout'*, d'un seul bloc. Dans un tel système réagissant globalement, tout se passe comme si chaque molécule était 'informée' instantanément de l'état de l'ensemble du système. Une cellule vivante qui réagit 'comme un tout ', ne se com-porte pas comme un mécanisme rigide. (J'ajouterais personnellement: comme un ordinateur). Elle comprend des myriades de molécules jouissant entre elles d'un nombre énorme de degrés de liberté. La réponse globale n'est donc plus prévisible.

Par ailleurs, chaque système ainsi globalisé possède une *'histoire' qui lui est propre*, faite de la succession des bifurcations plus ou moins aléatoires par lesquelles il est passé. Cette *'histoire'* de chaque système vivant, unique et tributaire du hasard, *joue un rôle* dans les choix opérés lors des bifurcations ultérieures.

Toutes ces propriétés des systèmes éloignés de leur état d'équilibre contribuent à affranchir progressivement la matière vivante du strict déterminisme imposé à la matière inerte de nos machines outils, ordi-nateurs ou autre robots. Cela amène Prigogine à admettre la possibi-lité *d'émergence* de propriétés *qualitativement* nouvelles, comme par exemple, la liberté, au niveau des formes complexes de vie, qu'il qualifie de 'supermoléculaires.

Mais ne nous y trompons pas; Prigogine ne voit dans l'émergence de propriétés qualitativement nouvelles, aucune intervention d'une quelconque transcendance. Le monde qu'il nous décrit reste cantonné dans le domaine de la matière. Il précise:

> Contrairement à la plupart des doctrines de l'émergence qui, comme nous le faisons, soulignaient la nouveauté qualitative du tout par rapport aux parties, cette 'émergence' d'un comportement supermoléculaire ne transcende en rien les méthodes de la science quantitative. (Prigogine et Stengers 1979: 1, 5, 6)

Et afin que nul doute ne subsiste, Prigogine récuse toutes ces interprétations 'qui nous présentaient comme sujets volontaires, conscients, doués de projets (…) citoyens d'un monde fait pour nous. Il est bien mort le monde finalisé…' (Prigogine et Stengers 1979: 1, 5, 6). Il n'en reste pas moins que les possibilités d'émergence d'actions libérées du déterminisme évoquées par Prigogine, fournissent à la pensée de Teilhard un arrière-fond plus fertile que le terrain desséché de la science mécaniciste classique.

4.3. *Approche systémique du réel*
La théorie de Prigogine a quelques points communs avec un courant scientifique assez récent, que l'on peut nommer *l'approche systémique du réel*. Celle ci est née de la physique quantique où l'immobilité, la solidité, sont remplacées par l'interaction, le dynamisme, la fluidité. Dans cette approche systémique, l'univers est considéré non pas comme un ensemble d'objets juxtaposés, mais comme un enchevêtrement de systèmes fonctionnels en interaction, où naissent des *boucles de rétroaction*. Ce terme de boucle de rétroaction, venu de la cybernétique, la science des robots, est le maître mot de cette approche systémique.

> Une telle boucle apparaît chaque fois que les résultats produits par une réaction quelconque, physique ou chimique, exercent à leur tour une influence sur les éléments qui sont en jeu dans cette réaction. Par exemple, dans notre corps humain, les hormones secrétées par un organe s'accumulent dans le sang et lorsque leur concentration atteint le taux souhaitable, leur présence freine la sécrétion de la glande qui reprendra lorsque le taux sanguin d'hormone aura suffisamment baissé. (Daleux 2002: 6)

Ce bouclage entre une cause et son effet entraîne l'apparition de propriétés nouvelles dans la nature, soit en jouant un rôle régulateur qui stabilise un phénomène, comme c'est le cas ici, soit en jouant un rôle amplificateur, la réaction ainsi bouclée s'accélérant d'elle-même ou un rôle amortisseur qui arrête peu à peu la réaction. Le point important est que, selon les systémistes, c'est le feutrage d'interactions en boucles de dynamismes énigmatiques qui engendre, par leur mouvement même, tout ce qui apparaît à nos organes sensoriels comme un ensemble d'objet solides et inertes.

Sans verser dans le concordisme, comment s'empêcher de noter la similitude entre la vision teilhardienne d'un monde de dynamismes spirituels, qui nous apparaît comme matière, avec le monde systémiste dont les objets solides ne sont que l'apparence engendrée par les interactions de dynamismes dont la nature intime nous est inconnue. Chacune des deux conceptions devant, bien sûr, rester sur son propre plan, matériel pour le systémisme, spirituel pour le monde de Teilhard.

4.3.1. *Henri Atlan.* Ce biologiste considère, dans son livre 'Entre le cristal et la fumée', que l'*hypercomplexité cérébrale* des êtres évolués, et notamment de l'Homme, laisse de plus en plus de place à l'aléatoire dans ses réactions au milieu ambiant. Mais notre cerveau a besoin pour cela, de s'associer à notre *mémoire*, cérébrale ou génétique où se trouve résumée toute notre histoire passée, ainsi que celle de notre espèce humaine (nous retrouvons ici la notion d'histoire individuelle liée aux bifurcations, évoquée par Prigogine). Selon Atlan, les éléments déjà mis en mémoire, influencent par la suite les processus cérébraux de réponse aux stimulations du milieu extérieur. La conscience capable d'actes volontaires serait donc un phénomène hybride, né de la conjonction de notre mémoire, tournée vers le passé et de notre faculté de prévision, qui contribue à construire l'avenir. Il y a là une boucle de rétroaction positive, dit Atlan.

Atlan considère donc que nous ne dépendons pas étroitement de notre programme génétique, comme le considéraient les scientifiques réductionnistes du siècle dernier. Selon lui, notre impression d'être autonomes, conscients et doués de volonté libre, n'est ni tout à fait vraie, ni l'objet d'une illusion. Mais notre volonté consciente n'a prise sur le futur des événements que pour le court terme. Le futur à long terme dépend des actions aléatoires du milieu extérieur sur notre organisme, qui sont par définition, imprévisibles.

Et Atlan conclut: 'Cette même vision des choses qui nous empêche d'accepter la vieille idée déterministe mécaniciste, nous empêche aussi de considérer la conscience et la volonté comme des espèces de forces extra-physiques, manifestations de pointe d'un principe vital ou humain' (Atlan 1979: 7, 9).

Atlan reste donc, lui aussi, au niveau des interactions matérielles.

4.3.2. *L'acte libre: une boucle dans le temps.* Joël de Rosnay, dans son livre *Le macroscope* (1965), utilise à son tour la notion de boucle cybernétique qui apporte des considérations originales sur les rapports entre *l'exercice de la liberté* et *l'écoulement temporel*.

Dans la causalité telle que l'envisage la science, la cause précède toujours son effet, dans le sens de l'écoulement temporel du passé vers l'avenir. Mais notre action intelligente se développe dans un écoulement inverse du temps, de l'avenir vers le passé. En effet, chacun de nos actes poursuit un but futur que nous désirons atteindre. Ce but futur étant précisé, nous remontons du futur vers le passé la chaîne des actions à accomplir pour l'atteindre.

La vie intelligents se situe donc au carrefour où se croisent deux écoulements temporels opposés: le temps de l'observation du monde, du passé vers l'avenir et le temps de l'action sur le monde, de l'avenir vers le passé.

Mais si nous inscrivons le rapport cause — effet dans une boucle de rétroaction où sans cesse l'effet rétroagit sur sa propre cause, il devient impossible de dire si c'est la cause qui précède l'effet ou l'effet qui précède sa cause. Nous aboutissons à une causalité circulaire. C'est un bouclage de ce type qui caractérise l'acte intelligent et libre. La flèche du temps se referme alors sur elle-même.

C'est pourquoi, selon Joël de Rosnay, la *liberté de l'action* serait totalement *contenue dans l'instant présent*. Ce qui la rend indétectable pour la science classique qui ne considère que l'aspect causal des phénomènes, qui s'écoulent du passé vers l'avenir (De Rosnay 1975: 7).

4.3.3. *Choisir ses choix*. Le sociologue Edgar Morin s'appuie, lui aussi, sur la notion de boucle rétroactive pour rendre compte de l'émergence de la liberté avec la montée de la vie. Ce qui l'amène à distinguer deux degrés de liberté: la liberté de *choisir ses actes* (Morin 1977) qui est celle des animaux face aux problèmes posés par le milieu ambiant. Mais l'homme accède à un second degré de liberté qui consiste non seulement à choisir ses actes, mais à *choisir ses choix* (Morin 1980: 7). C'est un échafaudage de plus en plus complexe de boucles rétroactives, qui élève le cosmos du simple indéterminisme quantique à la liberté humaine, en passant par la semi-liberté animale.

Toutes ces hypothèses émises par des scientifiques contemporains sur les origines et le mode d'émergence de la liberté humaine, ont un point commun. La liberté dont ils admettent l'existence reste relative et plus ou moins dépendante de l'enchaînement déterministe de cause à effet; elle n'a pas de réalité métaphysique spirituelle. Aucune de ces théories ne quitte le plan du matérialisme, avec cette nuance que la physique quantique introduit une conception nouvelle de la matière, beaucoup moins rigide que celle de la physique classique et auréolée d'une part d'inconnu et de mystère.

5. *La liberté selon Teilhard confrontée à ces diverses hypothèses*

Nous avons vu tout à l'heure que Teilhard ne s'est pas limité à l'affirmation péremptoire de l'existence de la liberté d'action de l'Homme. Allant plus loin que la plupart des théologiens, après avoir posé cette certitude intuitive, il a lui-même passé cette affirmation au crible de la critique rationnelle. C'est ce qui lui a permis de saisir dès sa racine, de façon prémonitoire, l'extraordinaire floraison actuelle d'interprétations et hypothèses scientifiques qu'éveille le problème de l'existence de la liberté humaine.

C'est ainsi que dès 1945 il a pu faire allusion, comme nous l'avons vu, à l'indéterminisme quantique comme précurseur de la liberté humaine, rattachant le *'rayon de choix accordé à chaque corpuscule élémentaire'*, à la *'sphère d'indétermination reconnue par la Science (…) comme un attribut particulier de l'Infime'* (Teilhard de Chardin 1963: 2, 3, 5, 8).

Teilhard avait compris l'importance de la notion de niveaux hiérarchiques successifs au cours du mouvement évolutif, 'dans la mesure où l'arrangement qu'il engendre s'élève en direction de groupements à la fois toujours plus astronomiquement compliqués, plus physiquement organisés, et plus psychologiquement indéterminés' (Teilhard de Chardin 1963: 2, 3, 5, 8), c'est-à-dire plus libres.

Teilhard enfin, a lui aussi utilisé la notion d'*émergence* de propriétés nouvelles telles que la vie ou la liberté, par la formation d'ensembles d'éléments, à la fois 'composés et centrés', c'est-à-dire capables de réagir aux incitations du milieu extérieur, en bloc, comme un tout formant une unité. Parmi ces ensembles centrés, Teilhard range l'atome, la molécule, la cellule, l'être vivant.

Mais au delà de ces points communs, gardons-nous d'oublier le caractère essentiel qui distingue la pensée teilhardienne de celle des divers scientifiques, que nous venons d'évoquer. Teilhard dépasse le niveau purement matériel des interactions physiques. Sa pensée profondément spiritualiste voit en l'Esprit le fondement et le support des éléments matériels, qu'il sous-tend. Pour Teilhard, cette montée vers la liberté, liée au mécanisme évolutif, est animée et soutenue par l'attraction d'un 'Centre divin', Oméga, Source de toute spiritualité et de toute liberté.

De tout cela retenons que Teilhard de Chardin a su pressentir l'importance des découvertes scientifiques du début du XXe siècle et les inclure dans une vue synthétique et prémonitoire de notre univers en cours de maturation évolutive, en marche vers l'Esprit et la Liberté.

Bibliographie

Atlan, Henri
 1979 *Entre le cristal et la fumée* (Editions Seuil).
Auger, Pierre
 1966 *L'homme microscopique* (Editions Flammarion).
Bohr, Niels
 1961 *Physique atomique et connaissance humaine* (Editions Gonthier).
Brillouin, Léon
 1959 *Vie, matière et observation* (Editions Albin Michel).
Capra, Fritjof
 1979 *Le TAO de la physique* (Editions Tchou).
Daluex, André
 2001 *Teilhard de Chardin, science et foi réconciliées?* (Edition Gabriandre).
 2002 *Teilhard de Chardin, permis de croire en l'au-delà* (Editions Gabrian-
    dre).
Heisenberg, Werner
 1967 *Science et synthèse (Ouvrage collectif) Coll: Idées* (Editions NRF).
Morin, Edgar *La Méthode: La nature de la nature* (Editions Seuil).
 1980 *La Méthode: La vie de la vie* (Editions Seuil).
Prigogine, Ilya, and Isabelle Stengers
 1979 *La nouvelle alliance* (Editions Gallimard).
Rosnay, Joël de
 1975 *Le macroscope* (Editions Seuil).
Teilhard de Chardin, Pierre
 1955 *Le Phénomène humain* (Editions Seuil).
 1962 *L'Energie humaine* (Editions Seuil).
 1963 *L'Activation de l'énergie* (Editions Seuil).
 1969 *Comment je crois* (Editions Seuil).
 1965 *Lettres à Léontine Zanta* (Editions Desclée de Brouwer).
 1965 Le Milieu divin (Editions Seuil).
 1965 *Science et Christ* (Editions Seuil).

Part II

TEILHARD AND MYSTICISM

3

AN OVERVIEW OF TEILHARD'S COMMITMENT TO 'SEEING' AS EXPRESSED IN HIS PHENOMENOLOGY, METAPHYSICS, AND MYSTICISM*

John A. Grim and Mary Evelyn Tucker

The deeper relationships of organic matter and human consciousness continue to challenge human understanding even as exclusively mechanistic models of physical matter lose their explanatory power. One vision that still reflects one of the most inspired examinations of these evolutionary questions is that of Pierre Teilhard de Chardin (1881–1955), French Jesuit and paleontologist. Teilhard grappled with novel questions for his day, namely, the meaning and significance of traditional religions and their cosmologies in light of the scientific story of an evolving universe. Moreover, as his personal life story brought him into encounters with Asian cultures he had to assess the relationships, if any, of Western-based science to the religions of the world. Certainly, there were limits to his awareness of Asian religions and cultures, as well as historical constraints on his scientific knowledge, but the ongoing significance of Teilhard's thought is that it extends into current discussions regarding the relationship of religion and science, religion and evolution, and spirit and matter.

During the twentieth century many thinkers have pondered the relationship of human consciousness to material reality. From the standpoint of the empirical sciences, consciousness appears as an emergent phenomena having come from nothing but inert, non-conscious matter that composes the known universe. Religious-oriented

*   This article is based on the 'Introduction', by John Grim and Mary Tucker, to Arthur Fabel and Donald St John (eds.), *Teilhard in the 21st Century: The Emerging Spirit of Earth* (Maryknoll, NY: Orbis Books), pp. 1-12 (copyright: The American Teilhard Association, 2003, ISBN 1-57075-5078).

thinkers have often framed their inquiry in terms of divine and human interactions — that is, religious revelations in which a divine mediation is seen as having broken into the separated worlds of the human and created matter. Consciousness is imaged as having been extended from the divine realm to the human as if God reached across space to impart psychic vitality to the languid body of Adam.

Secular humanistic thinkers have emphasized a second, or human, mediation by highlighting the significance of personal interactions with other humans. Human agency is considered primary, divine agency is discounted. In these anthropocentric perspectives matter often occupies a subservient, secondary position as epiphenomena in which the non-human life-world is seen largely as of service to, or use by humans.

Teilhard took a different approach from either of these predominantly traditional religious or modern secular emphases. He offered a more holistic vision by situating consciousness as integral to the emerging universe. Teilhard proposed that the increasing complexity and consciousness of the evolution of the universe is manifest in the appearance of humans. Complexity-consciousness, for Teilhard, is an emergent property of matter itself that directly involves his position on spirit also. Using the phrase, 'the spirit of the Earth', he focused on the quantum of matter that successively evolves into the layered envelopes encircling the planet from the lithosphere of rock, the hydrosphere of water, and the biosphere of life. This 'spirit of Earth' subsequently evolves into the consciousness humankind now displays in the thought sphere or noosphere surrounding the globe. Unwilling to separate matter and spirit, he understood these linked spheres as differential and interrelated dynamics operative within the same emergent reality. For Teilhard, the plural, diverse matter of the universe in the process of evolutionary change is ultimately pulled forward by the unifying dynamics of spirit.

Teilhard dedicated his life work to fostering an active realization by humans of their evolutionary roles in relation to emergent matter-spirit. This he framed as the challenges of *seeing*. To assist this seeing Teilhard articulated a phenomenology of the involution of matter, metaphysics of union with spirit, and a mysticism of centration of person (Teilhard de Chardin 1975: 205). This article investigates this challenge of 'seeing' by means of brief reflections on Teilhard's phenomenology, metaphysics, and mysticism. It concludes by highlighting some of the contributions and the limitations of Teilhard's thought.

Teilhard's Life Question: Seeing

Born into a Catholic family in the Auvergne region of southern France, Teilhard entered the Jesuit religious order where he was encouraged to study early life forms or paleontology. It is not surprising that his readings in evolutionary theory and his field studies of fossils brought him to question the traditional Genesis cosmology of the Bible. As Teilhard in his late twenties came to understand an emerging universe that had changed over time the Genesis story of creation in seven days became a less satisfying cosmology. The challenge, as Teilhard saw it, was to bring Christianity and evolution into a mutually enhancing relationship with one another. The path to this rapport was first to wake up to the dimensions of time that evolution opened up: 'For our age, to have become conscious of evolution means something very different from and much more than having discovered one further fact... It means (as happens with a child when he acquires the sense of perspective) that we have become alive to a new dimension' (Teilhard de Chardin 1968a: 193).

Teilhard struggled to extend contemporary science beyond an analytical, demystifying investigation of the world towards a means of seeing the spiritual dimensions of space and time in the evolutionary process. In so doing his efforts became entangled in the Modernist controversy. Within the Roman Catholic Church this controversy was especially intense from the late nineteenth century into the first two decades of the twentieth century. It involved in part an ongoing conflict between the conservative Curia in the Vatican and contemporary ideas especially articulated by French theologians and philosophers that were perceived as threatening to Catholic orthodox thinking. This included, in particular, the Darwinian theory of evolution and critical methods for interpreting the Bible. Caught in these tensions, Teilhard struggled throughout his life to remain loyal to the teachings of the Catholic Church at the same time as he articulated an unfolding vision of what he saw as a vast creative universe.

At the very outset of his major work, *The Human Phenomenon*, Teilhard spoke of the challenge for humans to see into the deep unity of evolution:

> Seeing. One could say that the whole of life lies in seeing—if not ultimately, at least essentially. To be more is to be more united—and this sums up and is the very conclusion of the work to follow. But unity grows, and we will affirm this again, only if it is supported by an increase of consciousness of vision. That is probably why the history of the living world can be reduced to the elaboration of ever more perfect eyes at the heart of

> a cosmos where it is always possible to discern more. Are not the
> perfection of an animal and the supremacy of the thinking being measured
> by the penetration and power of synthesis of their glance? To try to see
> more and to see better is not, therefore, just a fantasy, curiosity, or a
> luxury. See or perish. This is the situation imposed on every element of the
> universe by the mysterious gift of existence. And thus, to a higher degree,
> this is the human condition. (Teilhard de Chardin 1999: 3)

For Teilhard evolution was a unific movement. Thus, he identified
the perceived separation between matter and spirit as a central problem in comprehending the unity of evolution. This was evident, he
observed, in the mechanistic, Cartesian science of his day that viewed
matter as dead and inert. However, a split was also evident in dualistic religious worldviews that saw God as transcendent and apart
from created matter. Thus, Teilhard sensed the deeper dualisms of
the Western worldview manifest in both scientific and religious fields
though he did not articulate the full cultural dimensions of his insight.
He sought to unite his scientific affirmation of the world of matter
with his formative Catholic faith in the divine. This unity, he felt, was
manifest in evolution. In one of his most striking statements Teilhard
put forward an apologetics, or defense, of his personal belief that
boldly proclaims his faith in the world (see Henri de Lubac 1967: 129-
43). He writes:

> If, as the result of some interior revolution, I were to lose in succession my
> faith in Christ, my faith in a personal God, and my faith in spirit, I feel that
> I should continue *to believe* invincibly *in the world*. The world (its value, its
> infallibility and its goodness) — that, when all is said and done, is the first,
> the last, and the only thing in which I believe. It is by this faith that I live.
> And it is to this faith, I feel, that at the moment of death, rising above all
> doubts, I shall surrender myself (Teilhard de Chardin 1971b: 99).

Rather than leading away from Christianity, Teilhard argued that the
scientific investigation of evolution would actually lead one toward a
profound sense of a cosmic Christ in the universe whom he saw as
drawing evolution toward a greater personalization, and deepening
of the spirit. Teilhard coined the term 'christic' as an expression of his
experience of the Cosmic Christ of evolution. That is, the 'omnipres-
ence of transformation' in evolution centrated in complexity-consciousness and drawing matter forward (Teilhard de Chardin 1978:
94). The separation of spirit from matter so prevalent in the science
and religion of his day according to Teilhard overlooked this deep
unitive quality of the emergent universe.

As evolutionary science since Darwin had reported, the universe,
is a cosmogenesis, namely, in a state of continual development over

time. This is in stark contrast to two major cosmological positions in the West, namely, the one-time creation of all existence as presented in the biblical book of Genesis, or degeneration from a once perfected cosmos as in classical Neo-Platonism. Evolution displays dynamic, self-organizing processes from the atom to the galaxies. Thus, a new cosmology was emerging at the turn of the twentieth century that described atoms as eventually forming into cells that evolved into multicellular organisms and on into higher forms of life. This is the process over which Teilhard puzzled when he noted that with greater complexity of life comes greater consciousness until self-reflection emerges in humans.

Disintegration, change, and suffering are, for Teilhard, inevitable dimensions of the evolutionary process in which the plurality of matter resists unity with spirit. 'Christ is he', Teilhard writes, 'who structurally in himself, and for all of us, overcomes the resistance to unification offered by the multiple, resistance to the rise of spirit inherent in matter' (Teilhard de Chardin 1971b: 85). Progress to higher states of complexity and consciousness required, according to Teilhard, a deficit as the flow of energy decays to unusable entropy. Corresponding to the individual person, an entropy of suffering has a redemptive function integrated into the larger transformations related to creative, universe processes.

As individuals 'see' they will come to realize how they are participating in larger evolutionary dynamics and thus contributing to the flourishing of the Earth community. For Teilhard the ultimate human act was to bind one's energies with evolution and to unite one's personhood with that animating center which is drawing forward all of creation to a culmination of evolution in the christic, or Cosmic Christ.

Phenomenology: The Significance of Complexity-Consciousness

Teilhard attempts his fullest telling of the story of evolutionary processes in *The Human Phenomenon*, completed in 1940. This comprehensive synthesis first appeared in English in 1959 and a new translation was published forty years later in 1999. There he suggests that any consideration of physical mass in the world entailed at least 'three infinites'. The first two 'infinites' were the realms of the infinitely large and the infinitely small. While scientific studies emphasized cosmos and atom (the large and the small), Teilhard proposed a third axis of biological complexity that provided a link to consciousness.

This axial law of complexity-consciousness for Teilhard moves through matter and acts as its basis for organization. The evolution of matter in this perspective proceeds as an involuting, or inward-turning, progression that moves from a simple cellular stage toward greater complexity and conscious reflection. From particles and molecules to atoms, from single cells to multi-cellular organisms, from plants and trees to invertebrates and vertebrates, evolution displays a movement towards more complex organisms and toward greater sentience.

Teilhard accepts the idea of initial creation in the great flaring forth of the primal fireball. However, he clearly could not accept a biblical, literalist view of a completed seven-day creation in the form as presented in Genesis. The facts of science stand in question of such a literal, textual explanation of the appearance of life. Moreover, it was his understanding of evolution and his explanation of evil as resulting from the energy-entropy flows of life's progression that brought him into conflict with the Church (Lukas and Lukas 1997: 87-96).

From Teilhard's perspective all of matter was evolving toward higher forms of complexity-consciousness. Matter, then, could not be regarded as simply evil in the gnostic sense. Nor could matter be conceived as emanations from a higher consciousness into lower worlds of intelligence and form as in neo-Platonism. Instead, in Teilhard's view matter is inexorably associated with spirit in which both work as a unified, vital instrument towards the growth of consciousness. This process culminates, for Teilhard, in the personalizing force of hominization, that is, the conscious reflection of the universe in the human.

In *The Human Phenomenon*, Teilhard posits three qualities of matter: plurality, unity, and energy (Teilhard de Chardin 1999: 12). Plurality implies an endless degradation or breaking apart, a downward movement of things. Thus, there is in the universe an infinite possibility for differentiation. Unity arises in relation to plurality in that the different volumes of matter are co-extensive and bound to one another. Paradoxically, union differentiates into increasingly identifiable entities. Energy resides in the dynamic interaction of things, the power of bonding. It indicates an upward movement, a power of building up. While complexity-consciousness is an emergent property, Teilhard also saw that the cosmos is being held together and drawn forward from above and ahead.

Teilhard emphasizes the wholeness of all of matter rather than its fragmentation. It is exactly that vision of wholeness in evolutionary processes that he strives to outline in *The Human Phenomenon*. He sees

matter as differentiated by plurality, yet, simultaneously, an interconnected whole by unity — a quantum infused by energy.[1] An essential principle of this total system is the second law of thermodynamics that specifies the dissipation and the loss of usable energy. This
basic dialectic of spirit-matter is at the root of the entire evolutionary
process according to Teilhard. This dialectic is central for understanding how entropy or dissipation is a necessary corollary of forward movement.

In explaining the internal and external dimensions of spirit-matter
Teilhard spoke of the psychic and physical dimension of things. His
justification for such a view lies in inductive observation in which
human consciousness is not situated as an evolutionary aberration or
addendum, but as its defining emergent quality. He asserts:

> Indisputably, deep within ourselves, through a rent or tear, an 'interior'
> appears at the heart of beings. This is enough to establish the existence of
> this interior in some degree or other everywhere forever in nature. Since
> the stuff of the universe has an internal face at one point in itself, its
> structure is necessarily *bifacial*; that is, in every region of time and space, as
> well, for example, as being granular, *coextensive with its outside, everything
> has an inside* (Teilhard de Chardin 1999: 24).

For Teilhard, then, evolution is both a psychic and physical process; matter has its within and its without. Teilhard describes two
kinds of energy as involved in evolution, namely, *tangential* and *radial*.
Tangential is 'that which links an element with all others of the same
order as itself in the universe'. Radial energy is that which draws the
element 'toward ever greater complexity and centricity in other
words, forwards' (Teilhard de Chardin 1999: 30). Teilhard observes
that there are self-organizing principles or tendencies evident in
matter that result in more intricate systems:

> Left long enough to itself, under the prolonged and universal play of
> chance, matter manifests the property of arranging itself in more and more
> complex groupings and at the same time, in ever deepening layers of con-
> sciousness; this double and combined movement of physical unfolding
> and psychic interiorisation (or centration) once started, continuing, accel-
> erating and growing to its utmost extent (Teilhard de Chardin 1965: 139).

He suggests, then, that the evolution of spirit and matter are two
phases of a single process: 'Spiritual perfection (or conscious

---

1.   This holistic view of evolution is currently being documented in the systems sciences and science of complexity. See, in particular, the annotated
bibliography of these sciences done by Arthur Fabel, 'The Emerging Discovery of
a Self-Organizing Universe' available on the Forum on Religion and Ecology web
site <http://environment.harvard.edu/religion>.

'centricity') and material synthesis (or complexity) are merely the two connected faces or parts of a single phenomenon' (Teilhard de Chardin 1999: 27).

Teilhard thus saw the deep weave of matter and spirit from the early formation of the universe to the emergence of life on Earth and into the appearance of the human. Matter is in a state of complex development that passes through certain critical phases of trans-formation. The first of these phases is that of granulation in which matter gives birth to constituent atoms and molecules are formed. Eventually, mega-molecules arise and, finally, the first cells. In all of this, Teilhard assumes vast spans of time as opposed to the seven-day creation story of Genesis. While Teilhard would clearly not have known the most current date for the age of the earth, namely, 13.7 billion years, he was abreast of the latest thinking of his scientific colleagues on many issues regarding evolutionary theory.

The thresholds of the evolutionary process as outlined by Teilhard are: first, *cosmogenesis* – the rise of the mineral and inorganic world. The second is *biogenesis* in which organic life appears. Gradually, there is an increase in cephalization (development of a more complex nervous system) and cerebration (more complex brain) until *anthropogenesis* is reached. This third phase implies the birth of thought in humans and for the first time evolution is able to reflect upon itself. Humans become the heirs of the evolutionary process capable of determining its further progression or retrogression. This is an awe-some responsibility and much of Teilhard's later work explicates how humans can most effectively participate in the ongoing creativity of evolutionary processes.

The importance of greater personalization, or 'hominization', of the individual and the species joins the cosmological and ethical dimensions in Teilhard's thought. The florescence of humans around the planet has resulted in natural processes being adapted into the human realm or noosphere. For example, the hominization of natural selection now results in humans deciding in many instances what forms of life will survive in fragile ecosystems. As the mathematical physicist, Brian Swimme, notes it is another natural process, namely, neotony, or the observed characteristic of an extended juvenile stage among mammals that encourages play, which is hominized into an extended youth among humans manifest in such social expressions as celebrations and sports (Swimme 2001).

At our present stage of evolution humans join with the interior pull of complexity-consciousness resulting in an affection that draws forward all of evolution. Thus, a greater spiritualization of the universe is affected which Teilhard calls the transforming power of love, the amorization of things. By the increase of amorization and personalization in the individual, there arises a collective spirit of thought encompassing the globe that Teilhard terms *noogenesis*. The final threshold is when evolution moves towards its highest form of personalization and spiritualization in the Cosmic Christ of the universe. Having come to that which has been drawing evolution forward through all its millennia of movement, spirit-matter simultaneously arrives at the end that was its beginning, namely, the Omega point.

The implications, then, of Teilhard's phenomenology for human action can be summarized as follows:

> The essential phenomenon in the material world is life (because life is interiorized).
> The essential phenomenon in the living world is the human (because humans are reflective)…
> The essential phenomenon of humans is gradual totalization of humankind (in which individuals super-reflect upon themselves). (Teilhard de Chardin 1975: 175)

Within this perspective the human plays a vital part in the evolutionary process through increased socialization, and broadened planetization. This is because the human is that being in whom evolution becomes conscious of itself and looks back on the unfolding universe process. While significant questions can be raised regarding Teilhard's hierarchical arrangements of life on seemingly more progressive levels, still the force and insight of his thinking about evolution are remarkable for his time.

The collective consciousness and action of humans now emerging in the noosphere were something that Teilhard realized had enormous potential for creating a global community. Thus, Teilhard sees a need for increased unification, centration, and spiritualization. By unification, he means the need to overcome the divisive limits of political, economic, and cultural boundaries. By centration, he means the intensification of reflexive consciousness, namely, a knowing embrace of our place in the unfolding universe. By spiritualization he means an increase in the upward impulse of evolutionary processes that create a zest for life in the human. In all of this he sees the vital importance of the activation of human energy so as to participate more fully in the creative dynamics of evolution. Human creativity, for Teilhard, derives from a passionate dedication to meaningful work and productive research informed by the renewing dimension of the arts and cultural life.

As the human currently makes itself felt on every part of the planet the challenge now is to enter appropriately into the planetary dimensions of the universe story. As Thomas Berry has suggested in drawing Teilhard's thought forward, this requires new roles for the human — ones that enhance human-Earth relations rather than contribute to the deterioration of the life systems of the planet (Berry 2003: 77-80). Because humans are increasingly taking over the biological factors that determine their growth as a species, they are capable of modifying or creating themselves. The full range of ethical issues in such a progress-oriented view of human cultural evolution was not considered by Teilhard. Teilhard's contributions, however, do lead to a fuller realization that as we become a planetary species by our physical presence and environmental impact, we need also to become a planetary species by our expansion of comprehensive compassion to all life forms.

Metaphysics: The Dynamics of Union

Teilhard realized that his speculations regarding the inherent nature of the universe were preliminary (Teilhard de Chardin 1975: 192). Yet, what he sought was a 'universe-of-thought' that would increasingly build toward a unified center of coherence and convergence. Thought, as a form of animated movement, carries forth complexity-consciousness. Though Teilhard was aware of the work of Henri Bergson, and did not significantly draw on the later work of the phenomenologists, he exhibits a tension similar to that between Edmund Husserl and Maurice Merleau-Ponty. That is, Teilhard's understanding of the evolutionary dynamics responsible for human thought as well as the role of thought in drawing evolution forward are similar to the hold that the transcendent self of Kantian thought had on Edmund Husserl even as he called for a return to 'the things themselves'. Merleau-Ponty was deeply influenced by Husserl's call to return to the immediacy of experience of the world, yet he broke with Husserl by locating human thought and consciousness not in a transcendent realm but in the human body perceiving the world. In a related sense, Teilhard argued that, 'the moving body is physically engendered by the motion which animates it' (Teilhard de Chardin 1975: 193). Teilhard seems to have been influenced by Bergson's sense of the inherent vitality, or *élan vital*, of evolution yet rejected

Bergson's interpretation of that vitality as aspiritual and random. Rather, Teilhard connects evolutionary vitality to later phenomenological emphases on the shaping of the knowing body through the cosmological evolution of the world. Unique to Teilhard, however, is his religious analogy of the Omega point as that which both allures and is positioned as the culmination of the evolutionary process. Teilhard describes this point as a pole of consciousness that is both immanent and transcendent. He sees the Omega point as: '…an ultimate and self subsistent pole of consciousness, so involved in the world as to be able to gather into itself, by union, the cosmic elements that have been brought to the extreme limit of their centration – and yet by reason of its *supraevolutive* (that is to say, transcendent) nature enabled to be immune from that fatal regression which is, structurally, a threat to every edifice whose stuff exists in space and time' (Teilhard de Chardin 1975: 185).

Such an animating and alluring center Teilhard recognizes is not directly apprehensible to humans, but its existence can be postulated from three points. The first is the *irreversibility* of the evolutionary process – once put into motion, it cannot be halted. Furthermore, there must be a supreme focus towards which all is moving or else a collapse would occur. The second point is that of *polarity*. This implies that a movement forward necessitates a stabilizing center influencing the heart of the evolutionary vortex. This center is independent but active enough to cause a complex centering of the various cosmic layers. The final principle is that of *unanimity*. Here, he suggests that there exists an energy of sympathy or love that draws things together, center to center. However, the existence of such a love would be lost if focused on an impersonal collective. Thus, there must exist a personalizing focus – 'If love is to be born and to become firmly established, it must have an individualized heart and an individualized face' (Teilhard de Chardin 1975: 187).

Teilhard calls this the 'metaphysics of union' for he claims that the most primordial notion of being suggests a union (Teilhard de Chardin 1975: 193). He describes the active form of being as uniting oneself or uniting with others in friendship, in marriage, in collaboration. The passive form he sees as the state of being united, or unified by, another. He then describes the successive phases of the metaphysics of union. The first is that God in his triune nature contains his own self-oppositions. Thus God exists only by uniting himself. Second, at the opposite pole of the self-sufficient First Cause (God) there exists the multiple of matter. This is the passive potentiality of arrangement, yearning for union with the pole of Being. Finally, the creative act of God takes on a significant meaning — creation reflects the creator. The emergence of increasing complexity in matter and the participatory reflection of humans is an echo to the deepest personalization towards which the divine moves. 'To create is to unite' thus by the very act of creation the divine becomes immersed in the multiple. This implies that the scope of the incarnation extends through all creation. Teilhard regards his metaphysics as being linked with the essential Christian mysteries. That is, 'There is no God without creature union. There is no creation without incarnational immersion. There is no incarnation without redemption' (Teilhard de Chardin 1975: 198; King 1989) Interestingly, Teilhard presents here a formidable challenge to the traditional anthropocentric Christian emphasis on redemption exclusively for humans by extending redemption into the cosmological context.

Mysticism: The Centering of Person in Evolution

The challenge for Teilhard of integrating his religious and scientific commitments placed him in a personal crucible that forged a creative, unitive vision. Traditional mysticism in the world's religions, as Teilhard surveyed this spiritual perception, was generally understood as an interior experience that demanded a de-materialization and a transcendent leap into the divine. Teilhard, however, realized a radical re-conceptualization of the mystical journey as an entry into evolution, discovering there an immanental sense of the divine.

As a stretcher-bearer during World War I, he had intuited the inherent directions of this call when he wrote, 'There is a communion with God, and a communion with the earth, and a communion with God through the earth' (Teilhard de Chardin 1968b: 14). Eventually, Teilhard came to realize that human participation in this communion experience brought one into the depths of mystery. As Teilhard expressed it, 'I see in the World a mysterious product of completion and fulfillment for the Absolute Being himself' (Teilhard de Chardin 1978: 54). The process of communion is for Teilhard the centration and convergence of cosmic, planetary, and divine energies in the human.

Teilhard defines mysticism as 'the need, the science and the art of attaining the Universal and the Spiritual at the same time and each through the other' (Teilhard de Chardin 1975: 12). To become one with a larger whole through multiplicity was the goal of his mysticism. He sees mysticism as a yearning of the human soul towards the cosmic sense evident in many of the world's religions (Teilhard de Chardin 1971a: 82). Teilhard understands mystical union as the deepest interiority that leads to a cosmic sense of being pulled forward into the whole without losing the personal. For Teilhard, this union is found at the heart of all art, poetry and religion.

Teilhard sees the mysticism that is needed for the future as the synthesis of two powerful currents — namely that of evolution and that of human love. 'To love evolution' is to be involved in a process in which one's particular love is universalized, becomes dynamic, and is synthesized. As with all mystical visions a paradoxical challenge unfolds in trying to relate the particular character of human love to the sense of an all-embracing, divine love. Teilhard extends this challenge to love without hesitation into the larger human family, but also into an increasingly expanding awareness of spirit and matter throughout nature. By universalized, then, Teilhard means 'the Real is charged with Divine Presence' (Teilhard de Chardin 1968a: 167; 1970: 120) This mystical experience reaches back to those earlier experiences Teilhard understood as 'communion'. He wrote:

> As the mystics felt instinctively, everything becomes physically and literally lovable in God; and God in return becomes intelligible and lovable in everything around us…as one single river, the world filled by God appears to our enlightened eyes as simply a setting in which universal communion can be attained (Teilhard de Chardin 1968a: 168).

This view embodies not simply an anthropocentric or human-centered love, but a love for the world at large. Teilhard's mysticism is activated, for example, in scientific investigation and social commitment to research as well as in comprehensive compassion for all life. Mysticism is something other than simply passively enjoying the fruits of contemplation of a transcendent or abstract divinity. For Teilhard love is always synthesized in the personal. Here lies the point of convergence of the world for Teilhard — the center in which all spiritual energy lies. By means of this personalizing force at the heart of the universe and of the individual, all human activities become an expression of love. It is in this sense Teilhard conjectures that, '…every activity is amorized' (Teilhard de Chardin 1968a: 171).

For Teilhard the mystical path leads to a sense of evolution in which individual personalization converges from the meridians of overwhelming plurality toward centration on a powerful intuition of the whole. This whole, for Teilhard, is the Divine Milieu within which we live, and breathe, and have our becoming.

Contributions and Limitations in Teilhard's Thought

Teilhard's particular legacy, then, for the twenty-first century includes a vastly deepened sense of an evolutionary universe that can be understood as not simply a cosmos but a cosmogenesis. This dynamic emergent universe can now be viewed as one that is intricately connected: from the great flaring forth of the original fire ball and the first hydrogen and helium atoms to the appearance of life in the original replicating cells and the gradual development of the myriad life forms. Teilhard shows us again and again how this process is at once unified and diversified (Swimme and Berry 1992).

The legacy of Teilhard's vision of cosmogenesis affirms the extraordinary interrelationship and interconnection of the whole. Teilhard describes the irreversible flow of increasing complexity in cosmic evolution and thus provides empirically documented evidence for seeing the profound relationality between and among all parts of the universe.

This interconnectivity changes forever the role of the human. We can no longer see ourselves as an addendum or something 'created' apart from the whole. We are, rather, that being in whom the universe reflects back upon itself in conscious self-awareness. The deepening of interiority in the mind-and-heart of the human gives us cause for celebration and participation in the all-embracing processes of universe emergence (Berry 1988: 22, 219). The implications for a greatly enlarged planetary consciousness and commitment to ecological awareness are clear.

Such a perspective leads to a subtle but pervasive sense for Teilhard that the universe is threaded throughout with mystery and meaning. This is in distinct contrast with those who would suggest (often dogmatically) that the universe is essentially meaningless, that evolution is a completely random process, and that human emergence is a result of pure chance. For Teilhard, however, the evolving universe is not one he would describe as due to 'intelligent design'. Rather, evolution for Teilhard is dependent on an intricate blending of the forces of natural selection and chance mutation, on the one hand, along with increasing complexity and consciousness on the other. This does not lead automatically to a teleological universe, but one nonetheless that holds out to the human both a larger sense of purpose and promise.

This promise at the heart of an innately self-organizing evolutionary process is also the lure toward which the process is drawn (Haught 2002). With this insight Teilhard provides a context for situating human action. This context of hope is indispensable for humans to participate with a larger sense of meaning in society, politics, and economics as well as in education, research, and the arts. A primary concern for Teilhard was the activation of human energy that results in a zest for life. The existentialist despair that pervaded Europe between the two world wars was something he wished to avoid. For Teilhard the spirit of the human needed to be brought together with the spirit of the Earth for the flourishing of both humans and the Earth.

In the face of enormous odds from a conservative religious opposition and from a materialist scientific perspective, Teilhard provided the human community with novel ways of understanding creation apart from the static cosmos pictured in the Genesis story. He dramatically shifted Christian theological agendas from an exclusively redemptive focus on the historical person of Jesus of Nazareth toward one cognizant of the dynamic picture of creation given by the evolutionary sciences. His sense of the Cosmic Christ embedded within and drawing creation forward constitutes a creative reading of the Gospels, the epistles of Paul and the Church Fathers. As Thomas Berry suggests, his perspective moves from a preoccupation with redemption to a concern for creation, namely, an understanding of the universe at large (cosmology) and of Earth in particular (ecology). Rather than situating the human as an aberration in the random processes of evolution, Teilhard argued that consciousness was an integral component of the axes of complexity evident in evolution. This is because his comprehensive incarnational spirituality affirms an increasingly centered, personalized universe radiating a numinous interiority. Teilhard struggled to understand this 'within of things' in light of his scientific work and came to profound reflections on the mystical character of science itself in exploring the universe that are among his most original contributions.

Some limitations of Teilhard's thought might be noted along with his contributions (Berry 1982). Teilhard inherited the modern faith in progress that was a particular legacy of the French Enlightenment. This accounts for his optimism with regard to human's ability to 'build the Earth'. This led to Teilhard's over-emphasis on technological achievements as the sign of progressive evolution. There is a tendency toward an overstated anthropocentrism in his descriptions of the human as the culmination of universe evolution. This led to his overemphasis on scientific discoveries and technological achievements as signs of progressive evolution. In this sense, Teilhard's eloquent reflections on scientific research as a mode of contemplation makes us aware that he inadvertently affirmed applied science without considering its implications for disrupting earth processes. For example, Teilhard appears unwilling or unable to consider the implications of nuclear waste and pollution when he wrote about the marvels of nuclear power in the late 1940s and early 1950s (Teilhard de Chardin 1968a). Likewise, with regard to genetic engineering, Teilhard seemed unaware of the potential deleterious consequences of intrusion into the genetic patterning of matter itself. As a corrective to this overly optimistic faith in science and technology to create a better future, many suggest that our current environmental challenges call for the engaged natural and social sciences as well as alternative technologies that promote flourishing life on this planet.

Despite his intense commitment to a communion with the Earth, Teilhard had no developed sense of that ecological insight into what we now call 'bioregions', or local ecosystems and watersheds. Profoundly committed to a vision of cosmic interdependence, he was in some ways unable to fully appreciate that vision unfolding in the particularity of bioregions and the complex fluorescence of ecosystem life on Earth. His Christian sensibilities often led him to collapse the diversity of life into a plurality of matter brought to higher convergence in the Cosmic Christ. For example, his Mass on the World in the *Hymn of the Universe* is a striking cosmic liturgy that celebrates matter as the vehicle of the holy. It thus can be appreciated for its advancement in Christian thinking. Yet, what language of sacrifice might Teilhard have expressed had he known of the looming assault of current extractive economies on the planet and the scale of global demands for limitless consumer goods? In addition to human achievements through science and technology he might have considered particular ecosystems and life forms as part of the creative diversity of evolution that have meaning in themselves and are valuable in their interdependence.

Like most people of his time, Teilhard was also limited by his understanding of the world's religions. For example, he discusses Hinduism largely through the lens of Upanishadic/Vedantic monism. This typical colonial emphasis on a seminal trunk of the tree on South Asian religious thought did not adequately consider the other equally significant varieties of regional, philosophical, and devotional Hinduism. In addition, Teilhard had little developed textual or anthropological understanding of Confucianism, Daoism, and Chinese Buddhism even though he spent several decades living in China. Finally, he had a stereotypical Western view of indigenous traditions as 'static and exhausted' (Teilhard de Chardin 1971a: 25). While it is not helpful to substitute one stereotypical view for another, namely, a romanticized view of indigenous traditions as simply 'first ecologists'. Still, the diversity of cultural reflection on the human condition, and depth of intimacy with local bioregions evident in indigenous environmental knowledge recommends more serious considerations. Teilhard, on the other hand, positioned Christianity as the vehicle for a rich spirituality that would foster and direct the evolutionary process. Thus, he privileged Christianity as a major axis of evolution rather than affirming it as *his* entry into reflection and contemplation of evolution.

Despite these limitations, what emerges in any consideration of the life and thought of Teilhard is an appreciation of his grace under pressure, his steadfast commitment to a vision that challenged many of his deepest values, and his efforts to align a life of science with his religious journey. He has provided us with one of the few intellectual and affective syntheses that draw on science and religion in such profound and novel ways. His vision of universe emergence and of the role of the human in that emergence stands as one of the lasting testimonies of twentieth-century thought.

Conclusion

Teilhard's sweeping evolutionary perspective provides a context for understanding the human in a universe far larger and more complex than we had imagined. Teilhard realized that the evolutionary perspective requires a shift in thinking and in moral commitment. Realizing that we are in an unfolding, changing, developing universe, he understood that the human mirrors a dynamic cosmogenesis, not simply a static cosmos. A primary question for Teilhard was how to valorize human action and inspire the zest for life amidst inevitable human suffering and the travail of natural disasters, as set within a picture of evolutionary space and time as indifferent to life.

Teilhard presents a phenomenology of evolution as dynamic process in which the psychic character of physical matter evolves into ever greater complexity and consciousness. He posits an ever-present unifying center drawing forward a creative process that culminates in the divine reality from which it emerged. Teilhard was aware of the mystical character of his vision of reality and he groped for the language that would accord with his deep commitment to Catholicism. Simultaneously, he sought a language that would also speak to nonbelievers. Personhood appealed to him as a metaphor that satisfied his concern lest he be misunderstood as advocating a monistic pantheism or favoring the impersonalizing tendencies of certain political ideologies. In his view, the mystical union was not a collapse of the individual into a cosmic void. Rather, human participation in the evolutionary process was, for Teilhard, a centration of person in the cosmic turn towards increasingly complex organization and conscious in-dwelling. For these profound insights into evolutionary dynamics and our particular role in them we are indebted to Teilhard. His legacy has been taken up from a variety of disciplines that is testimony to his enduring influence half a century after his death.

References

Berry, Thomas
    1982   *Teilhard in the Ecological Age* (Teilhard Studies, 7; Chambersburg, PA: American Teilhard Association for the Future of Man).
    1988   *The Dream of the Earth* (San Francisco: Sierra Club Books).
    2003   'The New Story', in Arthur Fabel and Donald St John (eds.), *Teilhard in the 21st Century: The Emerging Spirit of the Earth* (Maryknoll, NY: Orbis Books): 77-88.
Haught, John
    2002   *In Search of a God of Evolution: Paul Tillich and Pierre Teilhard de Chardin* (Teilhard Studies, 45; Chambersburg, PA: American Teilhard Association for the Future of Man).
Lubac, Henri de
    1967   *Teilhard de Chardin: The Man and His Meaning* (New York: New American Library).
Lukas, Mary, and Ellen Lukas
    1997   *Teilhard: The Man, The Priest, The Scientist* (Garden City, NY: Doubleday).
King, Thomas
    1989   *Teilhard, Evil and Providence* (Teilhard Studies, 21; Chambersburg, PA: American Teilhard Association for the Future of Man).
Teilhard de Chardin, Pierre
    1965   *The Appearance of Man* (New York: Harper & Row).
    1968a   *Science and Christ* (New York: Harper & Row).
    1968b   *Writings in Time of War* (New York: Harper & Row).
    1970   *Let Me Explain* (New York: Harper & Row).
    1971a   *Human Energy* (New York: Harcourt Brace Jovanovich).
    1971b   'How I Believe', in *Christianity and Evolution* (trans. R. Hague; New York: Harcourt Brace Jovanovich): 96-132.
    1975   'My Fundamental Vision', in *Toward the Future* (trans. R. Hague; New York: Harcourt Brace Jovanovich): 164-208.
    1978   'The Christic', in *The Heart of Matter* (trans. R. Hague; New York: Harcourt Brace Jovanovich): 80-102.

1999   *The Human Phenomenon* (Bristol: Sussex Academic Press). This work is a new translation by Sarah Appleton Weber of the original French manuscript.

Swimme, Brian
    2001   'Interview', *What is Enlightenment?* 19 Spring/Summer.

Swimme, Brian, and Thomas Berry
    1992   *The Universe Story* (San Francisco: HarperSanFrancisco).

4

ONE PLANET, ONE SPIRIT:
SEARCHING FOR AN ECOLOGICALLY BALANCED SPIRITUALITY*

Ursula King

Our New Consciousness of One Planet

Our experience of nature—of the whole natural world or the *bio-sphere*—is today very much the experience of *one planet,* in terms of our scientific knowledge, but also in terms of our perception of the living world as a great, wondrous, and ever so vulnerable habitat threatened by many a disaster and wanton human destruction. I think the general awareness of the history of the earth, of the history of life and the great biodiversity of the planet is far greater today than it has ever been in the past, in spite of earlier nature poets and mystics. This profound change in perception is largely due to the environmental movement and to the scientific knowledge on which it is based, but also to the huge impact of the media. We only need to think of some television documentaries and widely popular nature films such as the well-known *Blue Planet* TV series or the Channel 4 documentary on *The Day the Earth Was Born,* but also the publication of such stunning pictures as *The Earth from the Air* by Yann Arthus-Bertrand which are known around the world.

We all live on one and the same planet; we form one humanity, however different and torn apart. We share a common destiny and a

*   This is a revised version of my American Teilhard Association Annual Lecture, given in New York on 3 May 2003. I dedicate it with much gratitude to Mary Evelyn Tucker and John Grim who invited me to this event, and who have done so much through their conferences and publications for the development of the field of ecology and religion, and also for the development of Teilhardian studies.

common responsibility for the future of life on earth and for our own, human future. In the history of our planet it is an appropriate moment to reflect on the transformative potential of spirituality, for we can perceive in our current geo-political situation the outlines of what has been called a 'world civilization', the consciousness of one world — a world of terrifying, but also hopeful complexity.

The word 'globalization', so often used in this context, has for many primarily negative associations since the process of globalization is all too often only criticized for its excesses and harmful effects, whether those of global market capitalism, industrial militarism or excessive consumerism. Yet it is perhaps too often forgotten, especially among theologians and critical ethicists, that the consciousness of the *global*, of one planet as one world, also has important positive features in terms of a greater sense of belonging together, and has produced the remarkable growth of a new sense of global responsibility which tries to address global problems through concerted human effort, through a growing consensus and the search for a shared ethic grounded in the same intentions and spirit.

The increasing use of the word 'global' does not carry the same meaning as what was previously simply referred to as 'the world' — for example in *world* literature, *world* history, *world* economy, *world* geography or *world* religion. The word 'global' sometimes functions in this way too, but it primarily indicates a different kind of consciousness, a different awareness altogether — of the world and of ourselves. This consciousness relates to a new order of complexity wherein the particular and universal, the local, regional and international interact in quite a new and previously unknown way. There is a search for new identities, both transnational and personal, some times described as a 'critical, corporate consciousness' which seeks a new unity and expresses itself in the search for a new collective will and for a new global order. Teilhard de Chardin began to reflect long ago on 'the planetisation of humanity' and 'the formation of the noosphere', presented as 'a biological interpretation of human history' (Teilhard de Chardin 1964a: 155).

The word 'globe' in the sense of a body in the form of a sphere has existed in the English language since the middle of the sixteenth century. Derived from the Latin 'globus', it refers to a round body or mass; this word 'globe' was in the sixteenth century applied to the earthly, terrestrial globe — to our world, which Marshall McLuhan described in the 1960s as a 'global village'. Although the word 'globalization' was first recorded in the 1961 edition of *Webster's New*

Dictionary, the idea of new, global processes of change had been around for at least thirty years by then, and in the 1980s the thought of globality was mostly expressed in the language of economics and ecology. Globalization has been defined as 'the process by which the world becomes a single place' and 'the consciousness of the globe as such' (Robertson 1987). This involves a high complexity of newly emerging relationships between individuals, communities, national societies and international groups and organizations — affecting humanity as a whole (Steger 2003).

The process of globalization has highlighted in a new way the countless local, regional, historical, cultural and religious differences in the world, the particularity of different ethnic groups and communities of faith. Among the potential responses to the growth of global perspectives is that of deep-seated fear and hatred, of a retrenchment into one's own position, as is evident from the widespread rise in religious and political fundamentalisms around the globe, which reveal the profound ambivalence of contemporary social, political and religious changes. Yet in spite of such entrenchment religious groups and institutions also foster an international outreach — like other organizations around the world they have to place themselves not only internationally, but also globally. Such new global positioning has a reflexive effect on their internal thinking, teaching and action. This is paralleled in interfaith dialogue where dialogue *between* members of different faiths also leads to a new dialogue *among* members of the same faith — *interreligious* dialogue is paralleled by *intra-religious dialogue, which* in turn has profound implications for a newly emerging global spirituality.

Conceptions of the world as a whole and of the organic unity of humankind — moreover, of the intrinsic unity of humankind and the planet — are not alien to the religions of the world, for such universality of common belonging, of a shared origin and destiny, is often deeply enshrined in their original vision and teachings. We only have to think of the concept of the *'oikoumene'* — the whole inhabited world — that the early Christians took over from the Greeks and Romans. We also possess numerous religious teachings about the inclusiveness of creation and salvation. Such visions are inclusive and universal in their intentionality, but little of this universality has ever been fully put into practice. Today there are many genuine attempts to make such global perspectives become a reality. Many writers now provide definitions of global culture, one of which is 'The emergence of a new set of universally shared images and practices…and thus, *an altered condition of universality*' (Franklin *et al.* 2000: 2). Already more than ten years ago, the Club of Rome published its much discussed report on *The First Global Revolution* (Club of Rome 1991) which stressed that our world possesses a promising opportunity, one unlikely to be provided again, to shape a new understanding and new attitudes towards the *world as a whole*. The Club of Rome report argued that while contemporary societies are much confused about morals and ethics, and while we experience much social, educational, personal and environmental chaos, it is essential for humanity to respond to this unique opportunity for a global revolution and find the *wisdom* needed to deal with the problems and opportunities in the right way. But how can we find such wisdom? How can we deal with our personal, social and ecological predicaments? Traditionally, religions have fostered wisdom and morality, have shaped individuals and groups, and yet their teachings have shown few outward signs of success because their loftiest ideals have rarely been fully realized in practice.

This task is impossible to achieve if humankind does not creatively draw on what Thomas Berry in his seminal book, *The Great Work* (Berry 1999) calls the 'four wisdoms': (1) the wisdom of the classical traditions, that is to say the wisdom of traditional religions and philosophies; (2) the wisdom of native peoples; (3) the wisdom of women; and (4) the much more recent and newer wisdom of science. The convergence of traditional spiritual perspectives with some of the spiritual insights that modern science can yield is a truly exciting development since the spiritual resources of science in relation to our attitudes to nature have been little explored so far. Since the dawn of time human experiences of nature have often included an awareness of a presence in nature as well as an experience of a deeper unity with nature, but these have not been closely interrelated with a systematic scientific knowledge of the natural world as we possess it today.

Berry has argued that while 'we have more scientific knowledge of the universe than any people ever had, it is not the type of knowledge that leads to an intimate presence within a meaningful universe' since, with the rise of the modern sciences, 'we began to think of the universe as a collection of objects rather than as a communion of subjects', so that 'we no longer hear the voice of the rivers, the mountains, the sea. The trees and meadows are no longer intimate modes of spirit presence.' This sense of the sacred dimension of the universe has to be recovered. While it exists in Native American and other religious traditions, Berry thinks that it is less available 'from our modern western religions' (Berry 1999: 15, 16, 17, 23) So the question arises: how can we relate ecology, spirituality and the global heritage of the world faiths?

Connecting Ecology, Spirituality and the World

Ecological concerns are at the top of many contemporary agendas but what does the growth in ecological awareness really imply? Ecology is often simply described as a practical discipline concerned with the study of organisms in their environments or 'homes'. The term 'ecology' thus seems to refer to both our external environment and to nature as a whole, of which we as human beings are a part. The words *as a whole* are of decisive importance here, for scientists study different ecosystems from micro- to macro-level. These are never isolated but interconnected within a greater whole, so that ultimately the whole planet is understood as one vast ecosystem. The interconnectedness of this system as a living whole which we call Earth must be made explicit whenever possible. Such a perspective leads to ecology as a philosophy, as a way of thinking about the world which must also include thinking about spirituality as our way of being *in* and *part of the world as a whole*, of our acting within and through it, and in connection with other people. I refer here particularly to the views of *deep ecology* and do not mean a shallow environmental approach that remains merely external without doing away with the traditional separations between nature, humanity and the earth. An all-inclusive ecological approach breaks down hierarchical divisions and is grounded in *biocentric equality*. Humans are living as part of nature on this planet; we study humanity as part of nature, and this ultimately means that the spiritual dimension of human experience is also embedded in the natural world of our planet, that spirit is in the world, and that the world opens up to us ever new encounters with the divine spirit.

But what is spirituality? How to define it? Although widely used today, the word 'spirituality' is surrounded by much conceptual confusion. For some people it seems more connected with the fuzzy, weird or occult than with something ultimate, sacred, or with being at home with God in the world. The subject matter of spirituality is a perennial human concern, but the way this concern finds concrete expression varies greatly from culture to culture and from one religion to another. We all know that there are different schools of spirituality, and that past and present spirituality are not necessarily the same, even within the same religious tradition. The concept of spirituality has its origin in the Christian tradition, but its usage has become so universalized that the word is today found in connection with all religions, in a comparative and interfaith context, but also in a secular setting outside religious institutions altogether.

From a historical point of view, different spiritualities are different cultural forms or the expression of different religious ideals. From the point of view of a person of faith, spirituality forms part of the history of divine-human interaction, a breakthrough of the spirit into history, a piercing through beyond history. Spirituality, not as an idea or concept but as *praxis*, is resonant with the longings of the human spirit for the permanent, eternal, everlasting—for wholeness, peace, joy and bliss, which have haunted human beings throughout history and for which many persons on our planet are seeking today.

Ewert Cousins, in his preface to the series *World Spirituality: An Encyclopedic History of the Religious Quest* (Cousins 1985) describes spirituality as being concerned with the inner movements of the human spirit towards the real, the transcendent, the divine. Spirituality is understood as wisdom intended to help one follow a path, guiding one on a journey towards the goal of spiritual realization. Cousins also emphasizes that following such a path today must include dialogue with other spiritual traditions in the world, and that it has to occur in a global context. He even speaks of the emergence of a new discipline, 'global spirituality', which intends to study spirituality 'not merely in one tradition or one era but in a comprehensive geographic and historical context' (Cousins 1985: xiii-xiv).

There is a great burgeoning of interest in spirituality, although much of this is rather unwholesome and not at all connected with ideas about the *world as a whole*. Much spirituality is too past-oriented and far too individualistic by being primarily focused on a person's inwardness. This goes together with the modern emphasis on individual self-development and personal fulfillment, based on trends in contemporary psychology. But this is not understanding spirituality *ecologically*, as a dynamic process and vivifying energy connected with *all of life*. Nor is the traditional Christian understanding of spirituality always helpful here, even though it was grounded in community. But far too much of it developed in the cloister, in separation from the world, and consisted of ascetic and monastic practices. Thus traditional spirituality is often cast in a strongly patriarchal, hierarchical and dualistic mode. It was often considered a primarily male domain, where the search for holiness was built on the contempt of the body and the world, and even more on the contempt of women. It was a spirituality that connected less than it separated — separating men from women, and from the world.

Past spiritual advice was often based on dualistic notions of dividing the ordinary world of work and matter from that of the spirit. Today we need a different kind of *'spirituality-of-being in-the-world'*, a *spirituality of being connected* to the ordinary life in the world with its daily relationships and responsibilities, a spirituality that makes sense of our environment without and within. Such a perspective is not without its precedents in earlier religious teachings, but on reading many spiritual 'classics' today, one is often struck by the one-sided emphasis on renunciation and asceticism, sometimes developed to pathological extremes. One is equally struck, especially as a woman, by the discovery that what first appears as gender-neutral spiritual advice addressed to apparently asexual beings, in practice often turns out to be the advice of male spiritual mentors to their male disciples, so that spiritual writings throughout world religious literature contain many sexist and antifeminist passages, which cannot promote the balanced wholeness and interpersonal connections we seek and need today.

Given our contemporary global context and environment, how can spirituality actively help to shape persons and planet? Or to put it differently, how can we arrive at an ecologically balanced spirituality? A true *'spirituality-of-being-in-the-world'* has to address itself to the practical problems of our world, including the great environmental tasks of species conservation and ecologically sustainable development. Many traditional spiritualities are neither connected to the *world as a whole* nor to the *every-day world* of our lives. From a contemporary planetary and personal perspective much of traditional spirituality has to be reconceived and re-visioned in order to become a true leaven of life, relating to humans, nature and planet. How can we re-vision spirituality ecologically?

Re-Visioning Spirituality Ecologically:
The Mutual Embeddedness of Biosphere and Noosphere

The relationship between people and planet is fragile and complex. The question of how to live in harmony and ecological balance is not an easy one and although there are historical instances of scholarly discussion of the issue, the contemporary ecological crisis with its unprecedented species destruction and pernicious greenhouse effect calls for radical spiritual transformation (Ridd 2003). Ridd mentions that the word 'ecology' was first used by the biologist Ernst Haeckel in 1866, that the 'greenhouse effect' was first mentioned in 1863, and that Carl von Linné wrote a book on *The Oeconomy of Nature* as long ago as 1749 (Ridd 2003: 42).

Certain spiritual attitudes of the past linked to beliefs about the domination and exploitation of nature are in many ways part of the inherent ecological problems we face. For this reason a new and radically re-oriented spirituality must also be part of the solutions we seek. The contemporary science of ecology certainly has an ethical and moral dimension to it, but it often mistrusts traditional religions and spiritualities or simply ignores them. Together with others I take the view that the spiritual arises out of and is strengthened by the mutual embeddedness and contemporary co-evolution of the biosphere and noosphere. In turn, an ecologically grounded and harmoniously balanced spirituality can heal many wounds of our world and ourselves.

In saying this, I am greatly inspired by *The Biosphere and Noosphere Reader,* subtitled *Global Environment, Society and Change,* edited by the environmental scientists Paul R. Samson and David Pitt (Samson and Pitt 1999). This important collection of papers by western and Russian scientists reveals clearly the considerable intellectual lineage and diffusion of the two related concepts of the biosphere and noosphere as well as their diverse interpretations by contemporary scientists. I can only mention some of the key ideas here.

The Austrian scientist Eduard Suess first suggested the term *'biosphere'* in 1875 in his book *The Origin of the Alps* and wrote more about this new concept in *Das Antlitz der Erde* (1883 1901) translated as *The Face of the Earth* (1909–24). Pierre Teilhard de Chardin used the very title of this book as the title of a long article he contributed to *Les Etudes* in 1921, where he described this face as one of mountains, continents and oceans. He wrote:

> The title at the head of these pages is that of the Austrian geologist Suess's book in which he drew the portrait of our planet, the general relief of which he came to understand as a marvellous effort of synthesis. My reason for using these words 'The Face of the Earth' is that they admirably express and resume the results reached by geological science in the last half-century. The earth has a physiognomy, a countenance, a face. (Teilhard de Chardin 1966a: 26)

Although Suess had expressed the solidarity of all life, he never expanded much on the term *biosphere*, which was soon taken up by other scientists. According to Samson and Pitt, Teilhard de Chardin was an early promoter of the biosphere concept, although they are wrong in saying that he actually reviewed Suess's book *The Face of the Earth*, as stated in their *Reader*; one must conclude that they cannot have consulted this article if they mistook it for a book review of Suess's work (Samson and Pitt 1999: 15).

Suess's book primarily inspired Teilhard de Chardin to think of the interrelations of the living world rather than of randomly distributed altitudes, lands and waters. At the same time he was already working on his concept of the noosphere as is evident from the following passage with which the 1921 essay closes:

> Having given its 'personality' to the iron and stone earth before our eyes, we have come to feel a contagious desire to construct, in our turn, from the sum total of our souls, a spiritual edifice as vast as that on which we gaze; as vast as the earth that was born from the labour of geogenical forces. All around the rocky sphere whose physical vicissitudes he described with such mastery, Suess…saw the biosphere stretching like a veritable stratum of animated matter, the stratum of living beings and humanity. The great educational value of geology consists in the fact that by disclosing to us an earth, which is truly *one*, an earth, which is in fact, but a single body since it has a face, it recalls to us the possibilities of establishing higher and higher degrees of organic unity in the zone of thought which envelops the world. In truth it is impossible to keep one's gaze constantly fixed on the vast horizons opened out to us by science without feeling the stirrings of an obscure desire to see people drawn closer and closer together by an ever-increasing knowledge and sympathy until finally, in obedience to some divine attraction, there remains but one heart and one soul on the face of the earth. (Teilhard de Chardin 1966a: 45)

To say just a little about the emergence of the *noosphere* concept, it is important to remember that Teilhard de Chardin's consciousness of the immensity of the earth and its peoples, their common origin and destiny and their place in nature, developed through his geological and biological studies, his extensive travels in North Africa and Asia, especially in China, but also through his experience of the war of the trenches. Reflecting on his experiences during his night watches in the trenches of the first world war, the whole world appeared to him as one great 'thing', as if perceived from the moon. He described the globe as surrounded by a layer of blueness which for him symbolized the density of thought, and later, during the mid-1920s, he coined the word *noosphere* in collaboration with his philosopher friend Edouard Le Roy. Derived from the Greek word *nous* or mind in the sense of integrating vision, the noosphere describes the layer of mind, thought and spirit within the layer of life covering the earth. Many years later, the image of our globe floating against a blue background became familiar all over the world through the famous photograph taken of the earth from the moon — the picture of our bluish-green planet suspended in space and surrounded by blackness, so aptly named 'Earth Rise'.

As Bernice Marie-Daly rightly pointed out:

> For…decades, we humans have viewed this marvelous sight, and it has impacted our psyches with deep images of interconnectedness and beauty. This picture has become for many of us a mandala of spiritual renewal and hope, an image of our evolution toward oneness and global awareness that Teilhard foresaw… However, for all its beauty, stillness, and simplicity, this earth portrait does not convey the existence of the particulars: the varied racial, ethnic, religious, economic, and cultural diversities among humans, as well as the variety and splendor of myriad species of our planet. (Marie-Daly 1991: 1)

To allow for the latter, we have to think of the immense diversity of the *biosphere* and *noosphere* — the sphere of life on earth and the sphere of human thought and will, of love and action, which were so closely interwoven and interdependent for Teilhard de Chardin. Samson and Pitt maintain on one hand that Teilhard described the noosphere as a 'new layer', the 'thinking layer' *outside* and *above* the biosphere; on the other hand they also say that Teilhard's description of the noosphere seems to be more spiritual than that of Le Roy, underlining 'a "psycho-biological" dimension linking mind and spirituality to the physical nature of living systems'. According to them, Teilhard 'draws attention to the idea of an emerging globally reflexive consciousness… The human phenomenon is seen as a manifestation of the universe unfolding on itself and becoming aware of its own existence — akin to a baby seeing itself in the mirror for the first time' (Samson and Pitt 1999: 5). A marvelous image!

Edouard Le Roy was the first to publish on the noosphere in 1927, referring extensively to Teilhard de Chardin. The Russian scientist Vernadsky, who lived in Paris during the 1920s, also took up the concept and diffused it through his own writing in Russian, and thereby influenced a whole generation of Russian scientists who continued the discussions about biosphere and noosphere in their own writings which mostly became known in the West only after the fall of the Soviet Union. The Russian environmental scientist Nikia Moiseev wrote about his reflections on the noosphere in a 1989 piece for UNESCO where he describes the noosphere as 'the concept of a new humanism' (Samson and Pitt 1999: 168).

Frequently, the term 'noosphere' is mentioned by authors in the contemporary literature without giving any explanation of its meaning (Mooney 1987) or it is, quite wrongly, 'spiritualised' as in Mary

Midgley's comment about 'a developing spiritual cosmos called the Nöosphere' (Midgley 2002: 68). Far more helpful and to the point is theologian John Haught's description:

> Our own hominised planet is now developing a noosphere (a new geologi-
> cal stratum consisting of tightening webs of mind, culture, economics,
> politics, science, information and technology), thus moving evolution in
> the direction of a new level of complexity-consciousness. Apparently, and
> in spite of the protests of many biologists to the contrary, a cosmological
> perspective shows that there is a net overall advance or 'progress' in
> evolution after all. Teilhard abstractly refers to the ultimate goal of this
> advance as 'Omega'. (Haught 2002: 3)

The Biosphere and Noosphere Reader documents four different understandings of the noosphere, its usage by several scientists, and also
the resistance to this concept over the years as well as its affinity
with, and difference from, contemporary Gaia theory. The editors
describe the noosphere as the realm of mind or intellect which 'lies at
the intersection where science and philosophy meet...an interdisciplinary domain of wide interest and high relevance that remains outside
the purview of most specialists, but is of major significance for the
future of humankind and the biosphere...the noosphere is neither
pseudo-science nor new age nirvana, but rather a "vision of the possible" based on the combination of physical parameters and human
potential' (Samson and Pitt 1999: xi).

When Samson and Pitt started working on their *Reader* in April
1998, a simple *Alta Vista* search on the Internet revealed 1,955 refer-
ences for the term noosphere, whereas Harvard University's multi-
library database *Hollis* revealed only six documents using a similar
keyword search. They concluded from this, first, an enormous interest in the noosphere among those active on the Internet, 'many of
whom claim it as a useful concept to describe the ultimate evolution
of the World-Wide–Web into an unprecedented form of super-con-
sciousness', and second, that the use of the term noosphere occurs
more in secondary titles rather than in the titles and keywords of
more traditional databases (Samson and Pitt 1999: xi).

Although Samson and Pitt do not discuss spirituality in relation to
the noosphere, they quote authors who do and point to developments of considerable significance for an ecological spirituality.
Reflecting on the noosphere in relation to contemporary global issues,
they affirm that,

> Regardless of which world view is taken, the noosphere represents an
> essential phase in the history of our planet. In essence, it involves the
> 'coming of age' of a species — in this case, *Homo sapiens* – which, in *reflect-
> ing* on itself and its environment, fundamentally alters the evolutionary

process and future development on Earth… What matters is that the noo-sphere is an unprecedented event on Earth and that society appears to be entering a critical period in this phase. In many senses, the Earth has become a single system, an interwoven relationship of global mind and global action.' (Samson and Pitt 1999, 181)

They also speak of 'noospheric institutions' (the UN and increasingly Non Governmental Organizations, and new guidelines such as the *Earth Charter* which Gorbachev has called the new ten command-ments) and noospheric structures 'which are rather of a network nature, where there is a convergence of forces rather than a Cartesian diversification' (Samson and Pitt 1999: 185). They refer to many Teil-hardian ideas and stress the holistic vision of the noosphere concept while including pluralistic and flexible approaches, together with the notion of balance. They conclude:

> If the unity of humankind will prove to be a crucial factor in human devel-opment, community with nature will be at least equally important. The environmental movement is therefore central to the noosphere, alongside the preservation of cultural heritage. This complementarity of diversity is not a contradiction, since the unity and holism of the noosphere—as with the biosphere—is made up of a mosaic of different, and sometimes con-flicting, components. It is not unlike Lovelock's notion of the living planet with its diverse elements, interactions and species that produces an emer-gent sense of the whole. (Samson and Pitt 1999: 186)

In the light of these comments it would be most rewarding to under-take a close study of Teilhardian texts which affirm the close interlink, dare I say the organic embeddedness, of biospheric and noospheric developments. I cannot undertake this here, but I think such a study would throw new light on Teilhard's understanding of spirituality, religion and mysticism. Until now most discussions of his concept of the noosphere, including my own, have treated it as too separate from the biosphere, from the vast cosmic web of life. Let me give a few quotations from Teilhard de Chardin's own works. In his 1925 essay on 'Hominization' he writes: 'Let us…understand the biosphere by the Noosphere' (Teilhard de Chardin 1966a: 67). He also proposes:

> to regard the thinking envelope of the biosphere as of the same order of zoological (or if you like telluric) magnitude as the biosphere itself… Unless we give up all attempts to restore man to his place in the general history of earth as a whole without damaging him or disorganizing it, we must place him above it, without, however, uprooting him from it. And this amounts to imagining…above the animal biosphere a human sphere, the sphere of reflexion, of conscious invention, of the conscious unity of souls (the Noosphere, if you will) and to conceiving, at the origin of this new entity, a phenomenon of special transformation affecting pre-existent life: *hominization*. (Teilhard de Chardin 1966a: 63)

In 1947 Teilhard published his article on 'The Formation of the Noo-sphere. A Biological Interpretation of Human History' in the *Revue des Questions Scientifiques* (Teilhard de Chardin 1947; 1964a: 155-84), where he discusses the noosphere in terms of biology (birth, zoologi-cal structure, anatomy, physiology), and only when reflecting on the future phases of the noosphere, he turns at the end to 'the problem of God'. He writes of the need first to give place 'in the mechanism of biological evolution to the special forces released by the psychic phenomenon of hominisation', and second, 'to encompass the formation...arising out of this factor of hominisation, of a particular biological entity such as has never before existed on earth—the growth, outside and above the biosphere, of an added planetary layer, an envelope of thinking substance, to which, for the sake of convenience and symmetry, I have given the name of the Noosphere.' In a footnote he comments that Vernadsky interprets Suess's term 'biosphere' in the sense of the 'terrestrial zone containing life', whereas Teilhard means by it 'the actual layer of vitalized substance enveloping the earth' (Teilhard de Chardin 1964a: 157). One could not have a clearer statement about the parallelism and connections between biosphere and noosphere.

As Teilhard explains elsewhere, through modern science and technology, especially modern means of communication, humanity is ever more closely being drawn together through external forces, but the human community is not yet moved by the same spirit, it is still searching a centre, a heart. The success of a search for such a synthe-sis is by no means assured. If the pressure of the earth forces human beings into coming closer together, it is not at all certain that what he calls 'ultra-hominization' will occur, that a balanced human and earth community can be created. Certain external and internal conditions have to be met for human and natural life to remain in balance, and these conditions are a tremendous challenge to humanity. Life on earth will fail if certain external conditions are not met, as he states in *Man's Place in Nature*:

> Should the planet become uninhabitable before mankind has reached maturity; should there be a premature lack of bread or essential metals; or, what would be still more serious, an insufficiency, either in quantity or quality, of cerebral matter needed to store, transmit, and increase the sum total of knowledge and aspirations that at any given moment make up the collective germ of the noosphere: should any of these conditions occur, then, there can be no doubt that it would mean the failure of life on earth; and the world's effort fully to centre upon itself could only be attempted again elsewhere at some other point in the heavens. (Teilhard de Chardin 1966b: 118)

As to the internal conditions needed, these are bound up with the full exercise of human freedom: 'a *know-how to do*' to avoid various traps and blind alleys such as 'politico-social mechanisation, administrative bottle-necks, over-population, counter-selections' and, most important 'a *will to do*', not to opt out, not to be discouraged by difficulties or fears (1966b: 118).

Teilhard de Chardin was much concerned with 'building the earth', with developing 'the spirit of one earth', of seeing the whole world and all people within it as one. Much more could be said about this global earth spirituality (King 1989), which is also a profoundly ecological spirituality. Mary Evelyn Tucker has devoted an entire number of the American series, *Teilhard Studies*, to this theme (Tucker 1985), and has written on the subject herself (Tucker 1993). Mark McMenamin has also contributed a monograph on the evolution of the noosphere (McMenamin 2001) to the same series. Following Mary Evelyn Tucker's train of thought, I think Teilhard de Chardin's work provides many examples of 'listening to the voices of the earth', and for developing the much needed 'earth literacy' among our contemporaries. Teilhard repeatedly pointed out that we assess the material energy resources of our planet but do not give the same attention to our spiritual energy resources. Yet these are indispensable for sustaining persons and planet, for the world's religious and philosophical traditions possess irreplaceable resources, which can nourish the biosphere and foster the growth of the noosphere. Many aspects come together here, not only the importance of biodiversity, but also what I call the 'noospheric diversity' of our global cultural and religious heritage. A further healthy development of the noosphere requires the convergent encounter and dialogue between people of different faiths in East and West, North and South. This brings me to the question of what contribution our global religious heritage can make to the re-visioning of spirituality so as to become more ecologically balanced.

Resources of Our Global Religious Heritage
for an Ecologically Balanced Spirituality

We have to ask ourselves in what way the deepest insights of our global religious heritage can contribute to the spiritual transformation of the contemporary world, to an ecology of the mind as well as to an ecology of the environment. If one considers the natural and social world — cosmos and humanity — as undergoing a vast process of development which at present often appears to be chaotic and destructive, one must ask to what extent a more holistic, ecological way of looking at the whole world as *one* makes it imperative for members of different faiths to come closer together and cooperate in a new spirit. What the world needs most of all is a new global order and a new global ethics on whose fundamentals we can all agree. By way of example one may think of how much could be achieved if all Muslims and Christians, who represent half the global population, worked closely together for the well-being of the whole human community.

It is worth quoting here the eminent Harvard biologist E.O. Wilson who in his book *The Future of Life* (Wilson 2002) underlines the great ethical task for ensuring a future life for all species, including the human species. He is just as optimistic as Teilhard de Chardin, not only by advocating *biophilia* or the love of life, but he says that 'science and technology are themselves reason for optimism', for since the 1990s there has been 'a true revolution in global conservation', and a further reason for cautious optimism is,

> the growing prominence of the environment in religious thought. The trend is important not only for its moral content, but for the conservatism and authenticity of its nature. Religious leaders are by necessity very careful in the values they choose to promote. The sacred texts from which they draw authority tolerate few amendments. In modern times, as knowledge of the material world and the human predicament has soared, the leaders have followed rather than led the evolution of ethics. First into the new terrain venture saints and radical theologians. They are followed by growing numbers of the faithful and then, warily, by the bishops, patriarchs, and imams.
>
> For the Abrahamic religions, Judaism, Christianity, and Islam, the environmental ethic is compatible with belief in the holiness of the Earth and the perception of nature as God's handiwork. (Wilson 2002: 156, 172, 157)

Wilson devotes three pages of his book to discussing the efforts of religious groups for conservation and is of the opinion that if the two powerful sources of science and religion could unite, then some of the environmental problems could be quickly solved. At the same time concrete measures, such as examining the ecological footprint and the Living Planet Index, can provide a basis for wiser economic planning while the global technology of worldwide on-line information 'will allow people everywhere to see the planet as the astronauts see it, a little sphere with a razor-thin coat of life too fragile to bear careless tampering' (Wilson 2002: 157).

Another pressing environmental concern is the violence and destruction wrought by continuous wars on our planet. No other period in human history has been so deeply marked by a confrontational war culture than ours; the twentieth century has been called the most murderous century in which an estimated 187 million human beings have been killed in the numerous terrible wars since 1914 — that is to say ten per cent of what the world's population was in 1913 lost their lives through war (Hobsbawm 2002). In our global situation today it is an imperative to promote peace if we want to achieve a truly ecological balance. Religious leaders in the interfaith movement have long been aware of this. For example, already the first World Parliament of Religions, held in Chicago in 1893, stated that one of its explicit objectives was the aim 'to bring the nations of the earth into a more friendly fellowship in the hope of securing permanent international peace'.

Nobody has more emphasized the decisive role of religions in the process of global peace-making than the Christian theologian Hans Küng who has repeatedly said: 'No human life together without a world ethic for the nations; no peace among the nations without peace among the religions; no peace among the religions without dialogue among the religions' (Küng 1991). His work was instrumental in creating the *Declaration Toward a Global Ethic* at the Chicago Parliament of the World's Religions in 1993.

The first section of this *Declaration* deals with our urgent need for a culture of non-violence and respect for life. It speaks of the infinite preciousness of human beings, but also the protection, preservation and care which the lives of animals and plants deserve. It categorically states:

> We are *all intertwined together* in this cosmos and we are all dependent on each other. Each one of us depends on the welfare of all. Therefore the dominance of humanity over nature and the cosmos must not be encouraged. Instead we must cultivate living in harmony with nature and the cosmos. (Küng and Kuschel 1993)

To some, this may not be a strong enough expression to bring about the necessary transformation in our attitudes to the environment. As is the case with any declaration, the demands are too vague and not sufficiently specific to be of much help. The ecological crisis needs to be spelled out in considerable detail to shock people into greater awareness and influence their will to change their habits.

The need to promote a radical agenda for positive change is strongly argued by the report of the Independent Commission on Population and Quality of Life, *Caring for the Future. Making the Next Decades Provide a Life Worth Living*. It makes the important point that the 'carrying capacity' of our planet is strictly limited, while the 'caring capacity' of humanity has no limits. But at present the human community lacks the political will to act at a global level and take care of 'the global commons', such as water and oceans, the atmosphere and forests, for the good of all. The Commission,

> believes that we must transcend a narrow focus on the material basis of survival. We need now to establish our psychological, spiritual, and political capacities to care for each other as a determinant of progress and survival. The ethic of care—defining us as human beings—surmounts economic rationale: it can counteract individualism and greed. Caring for ourselves, for each other, for the environment is the basis upon which to erect sustainable improvement of the quality of life all around us. The care ethic now requires a drastic shift in paradigm.
>
> …We seek a new humanism to promote human rights not only in terms of legal guarantees but, more importantly, in the context of dignity. *Care* can provide the foundation for such a humanism. (Independent Commission Report 1996: 296)

Such a care ethic is part of an ecologically balanced spirituality. To change our world means that we have to develop the commitment and will to change our ways. Only then can we create a new global order animated by a different, a new spirit. This will not be possible without a spiritual renewal and return to the values of life, and a common commitment to a qualitatively better life for all. Religious and spiritual renewal are now occurring in a secular, pluralistic context, and religions must relate and speak to that context. Both the study of different religions and the practice of interreligious encounter can help to foster a new spirit among different believers, so that religious people can learn to foster peace rather than violence, and can aim for ecological and spiritual balance. For this to happen, renewal and reform have to take place within each of the different religions themselves. In addition, the whole human community can draw on the globally accessible resources of the world's religious heritage to develop a more holistic, an ecologically more balanced spirituality for humanity and the planet.

The transformation of humanity's relationship to the earth—of the awareness of one planet, one spirit—has two different aspects. On one hand people need to develop a greater spirit of caring for the earth; on the other hand, this spirit cannot develop in full without a change in the awareness of our connection with, and dependence on the earth and its products. Today the religious spirit is drawing great strength from this discovery of our rootedness in the earth and the awakening of a new sense of the cosmic. Many Christians feel inspired by a new approach to the whole of creation and reappropriate a powerful *creation spirituality*, which has numerous antecedents in the Christian tradition. Others speak of an ecological spirituality embracing the earth and assuming a new religious responsibility for the fate of the earth — an ability to respond with integrity and profound concern to our critical ecological situation. Carolyn Merchant, in writing about *Radical Ecology* (Merchant 1992), speaks about 'spiritual ecology' among one of several kinds of ecology rather than about 'ecological spirituality'. The main project of such a spiritual ecology:

> is to effect a transformation of values that in turn leads to action to heal the planet. Whatever religion or form of spirituality one practices, it is possible to find a connection to the earth and to the political work that needs to be done to change the present way of managing resources. Some religions are more radical than others and some envision a more radical political transformation than others. (Merchant 1992: 129)

The radical reflections on ecology are of immense importance for the future of humanity and planet earth. Their impact on all forms of contemporary spirituality has led to the emergence of a new ecological spirituality, which is gradually affecting all faiths. But current ecological concerns are also bringing about the revival of very different, ancient religious beliefs and practices, and are important within new religious movements. There is talk about a new *ecotheology*, and a new *ecospirituality*, which is more bound up with the development of the earth in the light of contemporary ecological concerns than is the case with creation spirituality (Hallman 1994). There exist quite a few attempts to develop a stronger ecological spirituality, not least in ecofeminism, where the concerns of the women's movement come together with those of the ecological movement.

These are all new developments which can help to re-vision spirituality ecologically. For developing such an ecological spirituality among members of different faiths, and through interfaith dialogue, important resources are provided by the *Forum on Religion and Ecology* organized by Mary Evelyn Tucker and John Grim. They have edited a series on *Religions of the World and Ecology* published by Harvard University Press. The journal *Earth Ethics* is important in this context as is the article by Mary Evelyn Tucker on 'The Emerging Alliance of Religion and Ecology' in *Worldviews* (1997). There are considerable resources in each faith tradition for developing more harmonious relations to our earth and cosmic environment. In addition we need to rediscover the seeds for peacemaking in our different religious traditions, but also recognize the many harmful seeds, which can nurture violence and hatred rather than harmony and peace.

A planetary, ecological vision together with a commitment to a culture of non-violence and peace also undergirds the principles of

The Earth Charter, developed through an international consultation process and approved at UNESCO Headquarters in Paris in March 2000. It is a declaration of fundamental principles for building a just, sustainable, and peaceful global society in the twenty-first century, drawing its inspiration among others from 'the wisdom of the world's great religions and philosophical traditions'. Several religious organizations were part of its consultation process, and some religious groups have already issued statements in response to the Earth Charter. Its call for action includes the promotion of 'a culture of tolerance, nonviolence and peace' (IV.16), and it underlines the need for 'sustainability education' (IV.14b) and 'the importance of moral and spirituality education for sustainable living' (IV.14d). This is a profoundly spiritual statement which draws on all religious and secular sources available to meet the greatest challenge humankind has ever met: to create a new peace culture on earth.[1]

To renew the earth as 'a bio-spiritual planet' we need to draw creatively on all available spiritual disciplines, use all educational resources and energies in an effort that crosses the traditional boundaries between different religions, spiritualities and cultures. Thinking of ecological spirituality also means that spirituality is understood in an evolutionary sense. Spirituality itself develops and unfolds so as to articulate the human condition in a way that is commensurate to a particular time and age. Contrary to an earlier instrumental attitude, which explored and exploited nature, the ecological attitude approaches the natural world as our home and as a sanctuary which needs to be treated with responsibility, care and reverence, and which discloses to those of faith the lineaments of divine revelation. Studying the epic of evolution, the history of an evolving universe, the history of our planet and its living forms, can create a new kind of religiousness, a deep sense of wonder and mystical awareness of oneness which links up with earlier mystical experiences, yet also contains something new. The biologist, Ursula Goodenough, has movingly written about *The Sacred Depths of Nature* (Goodenough 2000) where she articulates a 'covenant with Mystery' and a profound gratitude for being part of the immense web of life. The cosmologist, Brian Swimme, speaks about *The Hidden Heart of the Cosmos*, and says 'that science now enters its wisdom phase' (Swimme 1996: 3). These

---

1.   More information on the Earth Charter is available on its website, <http://www.earthcharter.org> or by contacting The Earth Charter International Secretariat c/o Earth Council, PO Box 319-6100, San Jose, Costa Rica. Email <info@earthcharter.org>.

are fine contemporary examples of a spirituality that seeks to be ecologically balanced, grounded in a sense of presence in, and oneness with, nature of which nature mystics, visionaries and poets spoke in earlier ages, and which we now experience anew within a larger ecological and global context.

People all over the globe dream of a different world than the one we live in. They hope, work and pray for a better world, a more just and peaceful world freed from wars and tensions, where humans can live in harmony with nature. More people are developing a new awareness of 'one planet, one spirit', especially through the ecological movement and through new scientific approaches which are revealing to us a new sense of earth and cosmos. To nurture a truly balanced, new spirituality appropriate for our ecological age is a scientific, educational and mystical task presenting the human earth community with a tremendous challenge, but a challenge, which holds great hope and promise for our world.

The transformative dynamic of an ecologically balanced spirituality, which arises out of the mutual interplay of biosphere and noosphere, can be greatly strengthened by the global spiritual resources of humankind. Only when all these resources are conjoined and converging together can we hope to develop the sound ecological spirituality our planet so urgently needs, and which some scientists and religious thinkers are wise enough to perceive. Pierre Teilhard de Chardin was one of them and he saw love as essential to such a spirituality. I have discussed the role of unifying love as the greatest source of energy in the noosphere in another article, in which I have compared Teilhard's views on love with the extraordinarily parallel but completely independent ideas of Russo-American sociologist Pitirim Sorokin (King 2004).

Teilhard's powerful vision of 'communion with the earth', of 'the spirit of the earth', of the human place in nature and the emergence of the noosphere as a conscious sphere of unification and love within the great epic of life, still provides many seeds for thought and action for creating a truly ecological spirituality, and a better, more just and peaceful world for all.

References

Berry, Thomas
    1999   *The Great Work* (New York: Bell Tower).
Club of Rome Report
    1991   *The First Global Revolution* (New York: Simon & Schuster).

Cousins, Ewert (ed.)
    1985–   *World Spirituality: An Encyclopaedic History of the Religious Quest* (New York: Crossroad Publishing Company).
Fabel, Arthur and St John, Donald (eds.)
    2003   *Teilhard in the 21st Century: The Emerging Spirit of the Earth* (Mary-knoll, NY: Orbis Books).
Franklin, S., C. Lury and J. Stacy
    2000   *Global Nature, Global Culture* (London: Sage).
Goodenough, Ursula
    2000   *The Sacred Depths of Nature* (New York: Oxford University Press).
Hallman, David G.
    1994   *Ecotheology: Voices from South and North* (Geneva: WCC Publications; Maryknoll, NY: Orbis Books).
Haught, John F.
    2002   *In Search of a God for Evolution: Paul Tillich and Pierre Teilhard de Chardin* (Teilhard Studies, 45; New York: American Teilhard Association for the Future of Man).
Hobsbawm, Eric
    2002   'War and Peace', *The Guardian* (23 February).
Independent Commission Report
    1996   Independent Commission on Population and Quality of Life: *Caring for the Future, Making the Next Decades Provide a Life Worth Living* (Oxford/New York: Oxford University Press).
King, Ursula
    1989   *The Spirit of One Earth: Reflections on Teilhard de Chardin and Global Spirituality* (New York: Paragon House).
    2004   'Love—A Higher form of Human Energy in the work of Teilhard de Chardin and Sorokin', *Zygon: Journal of Religion and Science* 39/1 (March): 77-102.
Küng, Hans
    1991   *Global Responsibility: In Search of a New World Ethic* (London: SCM Press).
Küng, Hans, and Karl-Josef Kuschel
    1993   *A Global Ethic: The Declaration of the Parliament of the World's Religions* (London: SCM Press).
Le Roy, Edouard
    1927   *L'exigence idéaliste et le fait de l'évolution* (Paris: Boivin).
Marie-Daly, Bernice
    1991   *Ecofeminism: Sacred Matter/Sacred Mother* (Teilhard Studies, 25; New York: American Teilhard Association for the Future of Man).
McMenamin, Mark A.S.
    2001   *Evolution of the Noosphere* (Teilhard Studies, 42; New York: American Teilhard Association for the Future of Man).
Merchant, Carolyn
    1992   *Radical Ecology* (London/New York: Routledge).
Midgley, Mary
    2002   *Evolution as a Religion* (London/New York: Routledge).
Mooney, Christopher
    1987   'Teilhard de Chardin', in M. Eliade (ed.), *The Encyclopaedia of Religion* (Chicago: Macmillan Publishing Company), XIV: 366-68.

Ridd, Kevin
2003 'Beyond Stewardship: The Search for a Truly Ecological Christian Spirituality' (University of Bristol PhD thesis).

Robertson, Roland
1987 'Globalization Theory and Civilisational Analysis', *Comparative Civilisational Review* 17: 20-30.

Samson, Paul R., and David Pitt (eds.)
1999 *The Biosphere and Noosphere Reader: Global Environment, Society and Change* (London/New York: Routledge).

Steger, Manfred B.
2003 *Globalization: A Very Short Introduction* (Oxford: OUP).

Suess, Eduard
1875 *Die Entstehung der Alpen (The Origin of the Alps)* (Prague: F. Tempsky).
1904–24 *The Face of the Earth* (Oxford: Clarendon Press).

Swimme, Brian
1996 *The Hidden Heart of the Cosmos* (Maryknoll/New York: Orbis Books).

Teilhard de Chardin, Pierre
1921 La Face de la Terre *Études:* 585-602 (5–20 décembre 1921) (reprinted in Volume III of *Oeuvres, La Vision du Passé* [Paris: Édition du Seuil, 1957]: 41-69; English translation in *The Vision of the Past* [London: Collins, 1966]: 26-48).
1964a *The Future of Man* (London: Collins).
1964b 'The Formation of the Noosphere. A Biological Interpretation of Human History', in Teilhard de Chardin 1964a: 7-35; first published in *Revue des Questions Scientifiques* (Louvain, 1947): 7-35.
1966a *The Vision of the Past* (London: Collins).
1966b *Man's Place in Nature* (London: Collins).
1986 *Hymn of the Universe* (London: Collins Fount Paperbacks).

Tucker, Mary Evelyn
1985 *The Ecological Spirituality of Teilhard* (Teilhard Studies, 13; New York: American Teilhard Association for the Future of Man).
1993 *Education and Ecology: Earth Literacy and the Technological Trance* (Teilhard Studies, 28; New York: American Teilhard Association for the Future of Man).
1997 'The Emerging Alliance of Religion and Ecology', *Worldviews: Environment, Culture, Religion* 1: 3-24.

Tucker, Mary Evelyn, and John Grim
2003 'Introduction', in Arthur Fabel and Donald St John (eds.), *Teilhard in the 21st Century: The Emerging Spirit of Earth* (Maryknoll, New York: Orbis Books): 1-12.

Wilson, Edward O.
2002 *The Future of Life* (London: Little, Brown).

5

Teilhard: A Mystical Survivor!

Diarmuid O'Murchù

Teilhard de Chardin was a visionary figure of the twentieth century that has passed on to posterity several seminal insights of theological and scientific import. Some of these seminal ideas are outlined below. After the posthumous publication of his major written works in the 1960s several Teilhardian associations were formed around the world. Their membership consisted largely of scholars and academics committed to promoting his vision in various fields of learning. This scholarly cohort is now an aging group, with a dwindling membership. Some regret that younger people seem reluctant to pick up Teilhard's vision and promote it as they did.

But Teilhard was not merely a formidable scholar, in scientific and spiritual terms; he was also a mystic, and as Thomas M. King (1988) suggests, it is his mystical vision more than anything else that undergirds the originality of his thought and the passion of his commitment. Whereas scholarly research on Teilhard requires successive generations of specialists to promote his vision, his mystical insights, like all mysticism, has a tendency to wriggle its way in and out of the fissures of life, somewhat like the living Spirit of God that blows where it wills. In this essay I wish to suggest that it is the mysticism of Teilhard more than anything else that is thriving in our time.

The Mystical Teilhard

Mysticism is a wisdom denoting different things to different people (cf. Cupitt 1998; Horgan 2003; Johnston 2000; McIntosh 1998). It carries a popular and somewhat misguided interpretation of an enraptured intimacy with the divine, granted only to the exceptional few. According to this understanding, the mystic has largely transcended human need and aspiration, and in a sense lives beyond creation rather than within it. This, in fact, may be quite a distortion of mystical illumination, because as Walter Stace (1960) highlights in his seminal work on this topic, what characterizes the mystic more than anybody else is a deep sense of immersion in the divine energy at work in creation itself.

Perhaps, nobody is more at home in this world than the mystic; the last thing on earth the mystic aspires to is to flee the world. For the mystic, the divine radiates in every fiber of creation, sometimes leading to intense ecstasy, and at other times to a rending sense of pain and suffering. This is the quality of mystical engagement that characterizes Teilhard's life and work. I suggest it is a dominant feature of all mysticism, often overlooked, or unnoticed, precisely because the major religions, to one degree or another, succumb to dualistic splitting between the sacred and the secular, spirit and body, heaven and earth.

In his various writings, Teilhard (1975: 209-10) distinguishes between the first and second roads. The first refers to the apprehension of a common stuff underlying the variety of concrete beings. It is the common ground which provides a shared context for the multiplicity of creatures. It provides a global sense of identification, but for Teilhard one that is devoid of true love.

The second road embraces the fundamental mystery inherent within all creation, the divine energy animating and sustaining everything in being, the circle of energy which in its deepest meaning is a circle of Spirit (cf. King 1996: 62-63). This engenders a sense of *unification*, built and sustained by the power of love, the primary energy of God.

Teilhard also seems to contrast Eastern and Western (Christian) mysticism, suggesting that the former requires individual dissolution for the sake of the common wholeness whereas the Western, Christian approach affirms individual and personal uniqueness while pursuing ultimate wholeness. The unifying power of Spirit both underpins and animates creation in the diversity and range of its diffuse elements. Christian mysticism offers a unified vision that otherwise eludes our grasp. For the different senses in which Teilhard understands the notion of mysticism, see Teilhard (T. King 1988: 13-19, 65).

Although Teilhard distinguishes between the Eastern and Western approaches, one detects a sense of evolution from the one to the other rather than any kind of dualistic separation. The Christian form brings to greater fulfillment and transparency that which is perceived to be inchoate in the Eastern form. This inclusive approach can be gleaned from a key passage in *Le Milieu Divin*:

> Christian mysticism extracts all that is sweetest and strongest circulating in all the human mysticisms... It shows an astonishing equilibrium between the active and the passive, between possession of the world and its renunciation, between a taste for things and an indifference to them. But there is really no reason why we should be astonished by this shifting harmony, for is it not the natural and spontaneous reaction of the soul to the stimulus of a milieu which is exactly, by nature and grace, the one in which that soul is made to live and develop itself? (Teilhard 1960: 119)

Perhaps, the true genius of Teilhard for our time is that his mystical comprehension has transcended boundaries he himself probably never envisioned. Even in contexts where his name is never cited, his vision flourishes. This is particularly apparent in contemporary movements like creation-centered spirituality (Fox 1984); the new cosmology (Swimme & Berry 1992; Brockelman 1999); the ground-breaking work of the micro-biologist, Lynn Margulis (1998); and the post-Darwinian attempts at a more coherent theory of evolution (Chaisson 2001; Eldredge 1999; Haught 2000; Laszlo 1993, 1996). Teilhard set a flame ablaze, one that now illuminates some of the most pioneering and controversial research in a number of important fields.

Teilhard, and the Sacred in Creation

To the church and world of his day Teilhard was an enigma. His vision was large, expansive, inclusive and liberating, largely devoid of the dualisms that characterized his time. His formation at every stage of his life would have included a strong suspicion of the created world, with a tendency to dismiss it as irrelevant, dangerous and sinful. The language of fleeing the world, abandoning the world, and even hating the world would have featured strongly in his priestly formation and training. By some wonderful gift of grace, insight, and one thinks no small measure of courage, Teilhard transcended all that, and while being acutely aware of the pain, contradiction and sin in the world, he nonetheless appropriated in his life, writings and personal faith a deep comprehension of the divine at work in creation.

Long before creation spirituality and the new cosmology gained their current popularity Teilhard regarded cosmic creation as the primary revelation of God for all of us. Not merely did he sense the divine at work in the intricacies of nature itself, but his evolutionary research endowed him with a breadth of vision in which he could see the hand of God at work across aeons which mainstream religion only vaguely comprehends. Teilhard was a nature mystic, with an integrated spiritual vision, which the church and culture of his day seemed unable to comprehend or appreciate. Indeed, the churches and religions in our time still struggle on how best to honour the ecological challenges that now face us (see Geering 2001).

Teilhard the Evolutionist

Scholars have made various attempts to categorize Teilhard as an evolutionary theorist. He certainly does not fit the classical or neo-Darwinian categories, with their emphasis on the survival of the fittest. Parallels are often drawn with the vision of Comte de Lamarck (1744–1829), who was one of the first to suggest a lower-to-higher sequence in the evolutionary line. I guess a Teilhard of our time would show a keen interest in the theory of punctuated equilibrium but obviously would want to extend its frame of reference to include spiritual and theological considerations (O'Murchù 2002). Of all the modern renditions of Evolutionary Theory perhaps the one that best represents Teilhard's vision is that of Brian Swimme & Thomas Berry (1992), in their rendition of the universe story.

For Swimme and Berry (1992), evolution thrives on three interrelated movements: *differentiation, interiority and communion*. Differentiation refers to the unique individuality of every entity in creation from the tiniest cells to the galactic structures. Interiority, is very much the new notion that Teilhard brings to all previous attempts at an evolutionary theory: that the movement of evolution is both 'forward' and 'upward' inspired by a spiritual driving force that defies human rationality. Communion, naming that foundational interrelatedness whereby everything in creation needs everything else to grow and flourish, also owes a great deal to Teilhardian thought. For Teilhard, the Noosphere is a type of cosmic intelligence, capable of gathering into one, the diverse energies on which creation thrives. And Christogenesis, as the omega point of evolution, is postulated as an ultimate state of communion in which all is gathered as one under God.

Teilhard, having himself lived through two world wars was acutely aware of the reality of suffering in the world, and often refers to it in his writings. In the Christian culture of his day, the suffering Christ, and the symbol of the Cross, were the primary signs of hope in the face of meaningless suffering. Teilhard went a step further by highlighting the central place of the Resurrection as the ultimate answer to the meaning of suffering and anomie. If Teilhard were alive today, no doubt he would endorse the insights of Swimme and Berry (1992), suggesting that suffering needs to be viewed within the cyclic paradox of creation and destruction that permeates the evolutionary process at every stage of its unfolding.

Where Teilhard would be most at home in the new cosmology is in it's foundational emphasis on creation as an evolving story, forever being narrated in the divine–human partnership of co-creation. Beyond the reductionism of classical science and the anthropocentric preoccupation with hard fact, Teilhard detected a global creative process more akin to a drama; perhaps, more accurately, a dramatic liturgy. A powerful story, imbued with the prodigious creativity of the divine, requires a powerful medium to captivate and celebrate its ceaseless unfolding. Science, particularly the new physics, offers some engaging insights, but fails to weave the web that begets the trans-formative narrative. Teilhard was one of the first in our time — indeed for many centuries — to articulate the story in its divine cosmological grandeur. And his influence has been significant, although only infrequently acknowledged by scientists and theologians of our time.

Teilhard the Christian

Teilhard is often hailed as a hero who remained loyal to the Catholic Church despite the rather harsh limitations imposed upon his life's work and his writings. One wonders what would be his response if he were alive today. The Christian faith community today espouses an understanding of faith considerably different from that of Teil-hard's day. Following Christ is not so much about loyalty to a Church, or formal religion; it is much more about engaging our faith in dialogue with the major political and economic questions of our age. The vision of the Gospels, focussed on the Kingdom of God, takes on a radically new significance in the Christian consciousness of our time.

In the past, the vision of the Kingdom was often domesticated and even suppressed, because it evoked Christian faith of a type that stretched and transcended the specific issues of a particular church or denomination. The Kingdom of God evokes a global invitation and commitment to right relationships based on justice, love, compassion and liberation. It is addressed to all people of good will and not merely to denominational Christians. This depth of vision and concern is precisely what inspired and animated Teilhard. Although, in his writings he rarely alludes to the notion of the Kingdom of God, his vision is certainly congruent with that enlarged horizon to which every Christian is called.

For Teilhard, the world rather than the Church was the primordial sacrament in which we celebrate God's creative presence and the divine call to new life. In every movement of nature, in every evolutionary outburst, often endowed with paradox and even contradiction, Teilhard saw the divine unfolding. His was a faith inspired by the living Spirit; a hope that could not be eroded, and a love pointing us all in the direction of those right, just and life-sustaining relationships that constitute the New Reign of God.

Today, the churches and denominations still struggle to make sense of these enlarged horizons, and in several cases respond cautiously and fearfully. Meanwhile a new spiritual hunger breaks upon our landscape throwing many conventional believers into confusion and uncertainty. It seems to me that we are on the threshold of a new mystical revolution, and perhaps nothing less is required if we are to be spared from the perdition that awaits us as we continue to exploit and torture creation, often in a thoughtless and reckless fashion.

Globalization rules the world today, the colonialism of our age, reaping havoc on the resources of creation and plunging the poor as well as the suffering earth itself into anguish and anomie. Socially and economically, the perilous consequences are becoming all too apparent, and voices of protest arise whenever corporations and their representative bodies gather in forum. Valid though the protests are, they often lack prophetic vision without which deeper transformation is unlikely to take place. That vision, to which Teilhard gave birth in our time, is what is now needed to push the human species beyond greed and exploitation toward a global vision of sustainability and holistic growth.

Teilhard attempted to awaken an ecological sensitivity and environmental responsibility for the world of his time. Conditions for nature and the planet were then a great deal more benign and sustainable than they are today. The intransigence at the Earth Summit in South Africa in the Fall of 2002, painfully illustrates the cavalier attitude of many Western governments to the sufferings of our time endured by both the human and earth bodies. Were Teilhard among us today, he would have much harsher things to say, and would be condemned and ridiculed, I suspect, not merely by the religions, but by secular governments as well. One trusts that his living spirit is alive and well and awakening in other human souls the prophetic contestation our world needs so desperately at this time.

Teilhard the Mystical Scientist

In some circles the debate between science and religion seems as rigidly divided as it ever has been. Each side accuses the other of intransigence and ideology. Deane-Drummond (2001) suggests that there is a greater openness for science to interrogate theology, while theologians are rarely given the opportunity to speak first. As the debate continues, there is evidence to suggest that theologians will not alone participate more fully, but indeed are more likely to voice the critical questions that concern the wider human family. Although Teilhard's name is unlikely to be invoked, I suspect his vision will continue to be honoured even in a salient way.

In the human community generally, where growing numbers of people read about theology and science, and many attend conferences on the ensuing dialogue, the sense of openness and mutual engagement is a great deal more vibrant. In these forums one often hears Teilhard's name, and one encounters several people who claim they were first introduced into the interdisciplinary mode through their contact with Teilhard's writings. It is in this emerging new amorphous network that I detect the spirit of Teilhard to be most alive, vibrant and prophetic.

I wish to make three observations on this networking constituency which help to illustrate how the mystical vision of Teilhard has percolated through this wider group of people:

1.   There are those who to varying degrees are disillusioned with mainstream church or religion. This includes many Christians who have deeply loved the Church but are now undergoing a process of inner transformation whereby they know intuitively they are outgrowing their need for formal Church or religion in its conventional mode. Something deep within is calling them to a larger sense of God, and a more generic sense of connection with the God who engages them in the flourishing of creation. In my experience, women feature more strongly than men in this category.

2.   For others, the starting point in a new spiritual exploration is creation itself. These tend to be people who have always loved nature and found deep meaning within the creative universe itself. Their pain tends to be that of being unheard or misunderstood — by the scientist who ridiculed them, the theologian who warned them about the dangers of pantheism, or the priest who accused them of being post-modernist

or 'new-age'. Their personal and pastoral dilemma frequently is one of 'Where do I turn next?' I meet these people at virtually every Conference I attend.

3.   And there are the folks of the third age, usually over 60 and sometimes well into their 80s. In the USA, these constitute the single largest group attending workshops and conferences on the New Cosmology. No longer burdened with the responsibilities of family and work, they devote their time and energy to 'more serious' things. I find them deeply inspiring people to work with. And I suspect that they have always carried these deeper insights and convictions about the divine at work in creation, but somehow had to wait for 'old age' before they could engage more creatively with this inherited wisdom. As more elderly folks join this cohort, indeed one realizes that Theodore Roszak (2001) may well be right in suggesting that it is the elderly, and not the young, who will offer a more sustainable prospect for our threatened creation.

Academically, the evolutionary ideas of Teilhard enjoy a certain acceptance in our time thanks in particular to the pioneering vision of people like Erwin Laszlo, Niles Eldredge and Lynn Margulis (all referred to above). I guess Teilhard's concern for this time would be around the ethical sphere relating to genetic engineering and the relentless movement to gain more and more control over human life and the reproductive process. While he would rejoice at the benefits that have accrued for human well-being, I guess he would contest quite vociferously the manipulative and invasive orientation in contemporary genetic research.

And I am sure he would laud the interest in his work and vision as it has spread into the wider human community, far beyond the Catholic faith community of his background, transcending the academic institutions from within which he initially explored his insights. Like all great visionaries, vision outpaces even the luminary himself; truth has its own way to grow and evolve; gratefully, the Spirit continues to blow where she wills!

References

Brockelman, Paul
    1999   *Cosmology and Creation* (Oxford: Oxford University Press).
Chaisson, Eric J.
    2001   *Cosmic Evolution: The Rise of Complexity in Nature* (Cambridge, MA: Harvard University Press).

Cupitt, Don
    1998   *Mysticism after Modernity* (Oxford: Basil Blackwell).
Deane-Drummond, Celia
    2001   'Wisdom: A Voice for Theology at the Boundary with Science',
              Ecotheology 10: 23-39
Eldredge, Niles
    1999   *The Pattern of Evolution* (New York: W.H. Freeman).
Fox, Matthew
    1984   *Original Blessing: A Primer in Creation Spirituality* (Santa Fe, NM:
              Bear & Co.).
Geering, Lloyd
    2001   'An Ecological Faith for the Global Era', *Ecotheology* 6: 12-22.
Haught, John F.
    2000   *God After Darwin: A Theology of Evolution* (Oxford: Westview Press).
Horgan, John
    2003   *Rational Mysticism* (New York: Houghton Mifflin Co.).
Johnston, William
    2000   *'Arise My Love': Mysticism for a New Era* (Maryknoll, NY: Orbis
              Books).
King, Thomas M.
    1988   *The Way of the Christian Mystics: Teilhard de Chardin* (Wilmington,
              DE: Michael Glazier).
King, Ursula
    1996   *Spirit of Fire: The Life and Vision of Teilhard de Chardin* (Maryknoll,
              NY: Orbis Books).
Laszlo, Ervin
    1993   *The Creative Cosmos: An Unified Science of Matter, Life and Mind*
              (Edinburgh: Floris Books).
    1996   *Evolution: The General Theory* (Cresskill, NJ: Hampton Press).
Margulis, Lynn
    1998   *The Symbiotic Planet: A New Look at Evolution* (London: Weidenfeld
              & Nicolson).
McIntosh, Mark
    1998   *Mystical Theology* (Oxford: Basil Blackwell).
O'Murchù, Diarmuid
    2002   *Evolutionary Faith* (Maryknoll, NY: Orbis Books).
Roszak, Theodore
    2001   *The Longevity Revolution: As Boomers Become Elders* (California:
              Berkeley Hills Books).
Stace, Walter
    1960   *The Teaching of the Mystics* (New York: New American Library).
Swimme, Brian, and Thomas Berry
    1992   *The Universe Story* (San Francisco: Harper).
Teilhard de Chardin, Pierre
    1960   *Le Milieu Divin* (London: Collins/Fontana).
    1961   *The Prayer of the Universe: Selected from Writings in Time of War*
              (London: Fontana).
    1975   *Towards the Future* (New York: Harcourt Brace Jovanovich).

Part III

TEILHARD AND ECOTHEOLOGY

6

Cosmic Communion:
A Contemporary Reflection on the Eucharistic
Vision of Teilhard de Chardin

Mary Grey

Introduction: Reading Teilhard with New Eyes

There is a double meaning to my expression, 'Reading Teilhard with new eyes'. I have to confess that my first reading was deeply prejudiced. In 1960 I was an Oxford undergraduate reading philosophy when the reaction to *The Phenomenon of Man* broke out in university circles (Teilhard de Chardin: 1955, 1959). Although many of us initially read this text excitedly, the current fashion in Oxford philosophy was logical positivism, which judged any statement as meaningless that was not capable of empirical verification or falsification. My Christian faith struggled hard to maintain some kind of survival strategy in such a climate. But what dealt the death knell to our being able to appreciate Père Teilhard's vision, was a review of *The Phenomenon of Man* in *Mind* 1961 by Sir Peter Medawar (Medawar 1961).[1] This condemned the book as written by a scientist of a third-rate discipline (such was his dismissal of palaeontology) whose only contribution was to make a wholly unjustified assumption on the basis of evolution, that the world would continue to evolve until it reached 'omega point'. Such was the influence of Medawar that, given also the positivist philosophical climate, there was no way a mere undergraduate could get away with an appreciative evaluation.

I was not aware at the time, but now I think that the dismissal and condemnation of Teilhard by Church authorities must indirectly have had something to do with this. I cannot believe that it was a *direct*

---

1. Robert Speaight describes this as 'eight pages of sustained invective' (Speaight 1967: 273).

influence, because the pre-Vatican II progressive climate in which I moved at this moment was desperate for change, and very supportive of the views of many theologians like Père Yves Congar who were silenced and 'exiled' by the Church.[2] But Père Teilhard's silencing was to be very effective. Ursula King tells a chilling story that took place just after his death in 1955, at a public enquiry into theological and scientific aspects of his work at the Catholic University in Montreal, Canada. The enquiry was chaired by the University Vice Chancellor — and the story is told by Julian Huxley in his *Memories*:

> One by one the theologians and the professors got up and said their piece. Was Père Teilhard a good scientist? No, he was not. Was he a competent philosopher? No, he was not. Was he a sound methodologist? No, he was not. People call him a geologist, but he was only an amateur. People call him a theologian — but was he? Finally, the Dominican rose to sum up. He spoke in beautiful French and went through all the arguments. The audience sat spell-bound. The Abbé in his sculptural white robes studied all the faces turned towards him, awaiting his verdict. He raised his hand from the ample folds of his cassock. Père Teilhard, he said, was a poet. 'Ses paroles sumptueuses sont un piège. Prenez garde de ne pas y tomber'.[3] He sat down in profound silence. Teilhard and all his works had been condemned. (Huxley 1973: 29; King 1997: 140)

The irony of the story is that Teilhard's reputation on this occasion was saved by Huxley's defence of his friend, much to the enthusiasm of the audience. Huxley, the atheist, praised the priest and mystic for his reconciliation of scientific fact and religious belief along evolutionary lines. Yet, the sting of the Vatican condemnation would also prevent others, like Thomas Merton, the great spiritual writer, from reading and appreciating Teilhard: it seems as if religious and scientific circles alike combined in erecting a barrier of suspicion around his legacy.

What made a new reading possible for me was my deepening involvement in the ecological movement and the emergence of eco-theology, followed by the burgeoning of ecofeminist spirituality on a global level. The awareness of the earth as a delicately balanced organism of interconnecting ecosystems, the fragility of the entire web of life, the dependence of humanity on all other life systems and the resistance to anthropocentrism (in some circles!) all drew me back to the side-lined cosmic vision of Teilhard de Chardin, where the whole of nature is permeated with a spiritual energy, where matter and spirit are but two sides of the same reality. I began to see that,

2.   I say 'exiled' because Père Congar was sent to Cambridge!
3.   'His sumptuous words are a trap. Take care not to fall into it'.

even if his scientific achievements were less significant than had been claimed (perhaps due to his working in such isolation?), yet this hardly warranted his total rejection. So I welcome this opportunity to set the record straight.

My question in this paper focuses on the promise of the Eucharistic vision of Père Teilhard. In his texts *The Mass on the World*, *Christ in the World of Matter* and *The Spiritual Power of Matter* (among others) a vision is articulated that makes a narrow spiritualising view of the Eucharist impossible (Teilhard de Chardin 1965). Here we are offered a way of changing hearts and minds of believers into a different practice with regard to nature, a transformation that was at the heart of Teilhard's own life-prayer. But how could this vision be effective now, given the fact that Teilhard wrote without any awareness of our contemporary context of disaster that threatens to engulf nature? (As I began this article, *The Guardian* newspaper in London carried a report of a scientific survey of the threat of extinction to the world's bird and insect species on a qualitatively different scale, on a level with the scale that once destroyed the dinosaurs [*The Guardian* 2004]). This is one of the reasons for the accusation of an unjustifiable optimism with regard to the future in his work. So my first step is to anchor Teilhard's work in the new context in which ecotheology finds itself. Only then can I reflect on how his eucharistic vision could be developed in a fruitful response to the gravity of our context.

Père Teilhard and the New Creation Story

It is not only the seriousness of the exploitation of nature that defines our context, but the remarkable re-defining of the contours of the relationship between science and religion. Here Teilhard de Chardin is now regarded as prophetic—as Huxley's comment has already shown. The great visionary of 'the new universe story' is widely recognized as being Thomas Berry, a Catholic priest of the Passionist Congregation—although he has now inspired a great following. In his first book, *The Dream of the Earth*, he acknowledges his debt to Père Teilhard (Berry 1988: 22). While recognizing that scientists like Lynn Margulis and James Lovelock have brought our attention to the fact that the earth is a living organism, the idea has been around for much longer, and Berry traces its influence to Vladimir Vernadsky and Teilhard de Chardin:

> The more scientific term *biosphere* was used in 1875 by an Austrian professor of geology, Edward Seuss (1831–1914). Later, also, he used the term in his 4 volume study, which was completed in 1909—it was translated into

English as *The Face of the Earth*. According to Jacques Grinevald, in an unpublished paper entitled 'The Forgotten sources of the concept of Bio-sphere', Teilhard read the work of Seuss in its French translation in 1920 and wrote a review of it in 1921. Already in the 1920s Vernadsky, Eduard Leroy and Teilhard were in contact with one another in Paris. Of these Vernadsky was the one who wrote the first extensive treatise, entitled *Le Biosphère*, in 1929. The term was quickly associated with *noosphere*, which was invited by Leroy, but popularised by Teilhard. (Berry 1988: 22)

Not only does Berry build on this idea of *noosphere* as the *thinking earth*, to which humanity must learn to listen, but others have devel-oped a far wider notion of consciousness from its inspiration (Abram 1996; Clarke 2002). Thomas Berry, all too aware of the conflicts and tensions that beset the planet and whose whole project is to summon us to the 'great work' of saving it from extinction, sees Teilhard as offering a method towards the resolution of these conflicts:

> As Teilhard suggested, we must go beyond the human into the universe itself and its mode of functioning. Until the human is understood as a dimension of the earth, we have no secure basis for understanding any aspect of the human. (Berry 1999: 219)

Not only does Berry agree with Teilhard in understanding the impor-tance of evolutionary progress, but he takes Teilhard seriously in stressing the importance of 'being present to the earth', accompany-ing it in its next stage of transformation:

> A concern for will does appear in the work of Pierre Teilhard de Chardin, particularly in *Human Energy*. He saw quite clearly that we must con-sciously will the further stages of the evolutionary process. Almost imme-diately this responsibility became too much for us to carry. We live now in a moment of indecision, carrying the world in our hands, afraid of trip-ping over our own feet and letting it fall to its destruction. (1999: 173-74)

Berry takes heart from the fact that people are learning to receive 'the total spiritual heritage of the human community as well as the total spiritual heritage of the universe, immersed as we are in a sea of energy 'beyond all comprehension'. In its call to a deeper commun-ion with all life forms — even though Berry does not, sadly, develop the *theological* potential of this in his subsequent work, in fact his focus becomes entirely different — this language is pure Teilhardian. It is also reminiscent of T.S. Eliot's lines:

> We must be still and still moving
> Into another intensity
> For a further union, a deeper communion,
> Through the dark cold and the empty desolation,
> The wave cry, the wind cry, the vast waters
> Of the petrel and the porpoise. In my end is my beginning. (Eliot 1959: 32)

This communion with cosmic life was a hallmark of Père Teilhard's spirituality from his youth. One of his earliest essays, 'Cosmic Life' written in the horrors of the First World War at Dunkirk, Easter 1916, already links his passionate love of nature with the love of God:

> I am writing these lines from an exuberance of life and a yearning to live; it is written to express an impassioned vision of the earth, and in an attempt to find a solution for the doubts that beset my action- because I love the universe, its energies, its secrets, and its hopes, and because at the same time I am dedicated to God, the only Origin, the only Issue, and the only Term. I want to express my love of matter and life, and to reconcile it, if possible, with the unique adoration of the only absolute and definitive Godhead. (King 1996: 56)

It is from this passionate love of all life and profound faith in the vibrant presence of God that permeates it, that Teilhard's key ideas emerge. First, God's presence in the world is a Christic presence, a cosmic presence and a transforming or transfiguring presence. It is not so much focused on the person of Jesus of Nazareth, but on God incarnate in Christ. And just as the world is in becoming (a concept developed by Process theologians) we can also speak of Christ-becoming. As he expressed it in 'The Total Christ':

> Since Jesus was born, and grew to his full stature, and died, everything has continued to move *forward because Christ is not yet fully formed:* he has not yet gathered about him the last folds of his robe of flesh and love which is made up of his faithful followers. The mystical Christ has not yet attained to his full growth; and therefore the same is true of the cosmic Christ. Both of these are simultaneously in the state of being and becoming; and it is from the prolongation of this process of becoming that all creativity ultimately springs. Christ is the end point of evolution, even the *natural* evolution, of all beings; and therefore evolution is holy. (Teilhard de Chardin 1965: 133)

This passage is important in showing us the saving significance of the cosmic Christ—a concept developed in contemporary spirituality in the context of the New Universe story. Matthew Fox, in his *The Coming of the Cosmic Christ,* acknowledges a debt to Père Teilhard—along with Meister Eckhart. Although his own Creation Spirituality develops in an entirely different way—and the mainlines of his thought cannot be described as Teilhardian—Fox appreciates the fact that Teilhard drew to our attention what most theologians failed to see:

> Teilhard de Chardin thought that 'besides his mystical body, Christ also has a cosmic body spread through the universe. And just as the mystical Christ has to attain his full growth, so too has the cosmic Christ'. (Fox 1988: 137)

Secondly, 'Christ is the end point of evolution' is sometimes described by Teilhard as 'Omega point' and this has sometimes acted as a stumbling block to his thought. Omega point was certainly a turn-off for Oxford philosophy, as I noted earlier! It is a very condensed notion. First, for Teilhard it represents the point at which the 'Universal and the Personal grow in the same direction and culminate simultaneously in each other' (Teilhard de Chardin 1959: 260). Secondly, he sees Omega as a distinct Centre radiating at a core of a system of centres. Here, in a passage that prefigures the contemporary critique of individualism, he is critical of the egoistic attempt to separate from others, maintaining that it is in the direction of convergence that we advance toward the other:

> According to the evolutionary structure of the world, we can only find our person by uniting together. (Teilhard de Chardin 1959: 263)

In the Omega point, he thinks, we can explain the march of things toward greater consciousness and the end of the process, the final convergence will take place in peace. At this point Teilhard introduces his Christian vision. God, the Centre of centres, coincides with Omega Point. The energy pushing toward it is Christic energy:

> Christ invests himself organically with the very majesty of his creation. And it is in no way metaphorical to say that man finds himself capable of experiencing and discovering his God in the whole length, breadth and depth of the world in movement. (Teilhard de Chardin 1959: 297)

In another essay, 'My Fundamental Vision', published posthumously, he wrote:

> In Christ-Omega, the universal comes into exact focus and assumes a personal form. Biologically and ontologically speaking, there is nothing more consistent, and at the same time nothing bolder, than this identification we envisage, at the upper end of *noogenesis*, between the apparently contradictory properties of the whole and the element. (Teilhard de Chardin 1975: 203)

Even if Omega point is not a strictly verifiable concept, it has evoked much appreciation and is recognized as a contribution within the New Universe story. As I have indicated, Thomas Berry emphasizes the idea of communion with creation. The theologian Jay McDaniel discusses Teilhard de Chardin's idea of creation as an adventure towards Omega point in relation to panentheism.[4]

---

4.   Panentheism is the view that all creation exists within God. It differs from pantheism in not limiting God to material creation.

> The major difference between panentheism and the Omega point dis-
> cussed by Teilhard de Chardin is that for the panentheist, the Omega point
> is not distant at all. It is near at hand. It is the ongoing interiority of God.
> (McDaniel 1995: 110)

This I find helpful, yet only if we do not limit the process to interiority, but, as McDaniel himself concludes, in words reminiscent of
the Eliot poem cited above,

> This Holy Being is itself Holy Becoming. It is an End that is always a
> Beginning, an Omega that is always an Alpha. Such is the continuing care
> of a 'new heaven' that is always green, always fresh, and steadfast in its
> love of the earth. (McDaniel 1995: 112)

The reason for this focus on Omega point is also to show that the
evolutionary process in Teilhard's thought is integral to the transfiguration of the universe, and this is close to what traditional theology
would call redemption. I stress this, as one of the heaviest criticisms
against him has been that there is no room for original sin and the
Fall in his thought, and that his whole scheme is mind-boggingly
optimistic. (Here there is a parallel to be made with the thought of
Matthew Fox.) Yet, we need to bear in mind two things: first, that the
early visionary texts are literally written from the trenches of Verdun
and other battle grounds in France, where Teilhard worked as a
stretcher bearer and was even decorated for his heroism. As the war
poets created their despairing laments, he was deepening his faith in
the incarnate God of creation and in the midst of the slaughter was
still able to believe in the triumph of beauty. Secondly, his theology is
grounded in the primacy of incarnation. But we should not separate
this from God's redemptive work. As the Process theologians say,
these are two movements within one great activity. Teilhard understood an organic pattern between these concepts:

> No God (up to a certain point…) without creative union. No creation with-
> out incarnational immersion. No incarnation without redemptive repay-
> ment. In a metaphysics of union, the three fundamental mysteries of
> Christianity are seen to be simply the three aspects of one and the same
> mystery of mysteries, that of pleromization (or unifying reduction of the
> multiple). (Teilhard de Chardin 1975: 198)

But incarnation for him undergirded his entire thought and spirituality. Christ as word made flesh had a cosmic significance, so that:

> The whole universe 'is seen to be flesh'. The universal, cosmic Christ is the
> centre of the universe, the centre of humanity, and the centre of each per-
> son. This is why he speaks of 'the heart' — the heart of matter, the heart of
> the world, the heart of humanity. (King 1997: 156)

With this in mind let us now revisit the eucharistic vision of Teilhard.

The Eucharistic Vision of Teilhard de Chardin

All that I have been describing has been a prelude to understanding the significance of the Eucharist for Teilhard: his pan-Christic mysticism, his understanding of his mission as a priest, his belief in the Divine transfiguration of matter, and its importance for the future of the universe — all are ingredients in what we could call the sacramentality of the entire cosmos.

This notion had many expressions, from early texts like '*Mystical Milieu*' (1917) '*Mass of the World*' (1923) through to '*Le Milieu Divin*' (1957)[5] and his autobiographical '*Heart of Matter*' (1950). It is above all, *Le Milieu Divin,* written in all the pain of condemnation by the Vatican that is held to be his finest achievement.

First, 'Mass of the World' is striking in its setting: in the midst of the steppes of Asia, without bread, wine or altar, Teilhard de Chardin offers to God all the labours and sufferings of the world (1965: 19-37). It is possible that it was written in the Feast of the Transfiguration. This is an intensely mystical text. It does not fit easily into any category. It is offering, communion, prayer for transformation and unity all at once. Here the amazing symbolism of fire blazes out as a primeval force in addition to *power* and *word*. For Père Teilhard, the whole universe was aflame. Fire is the symbolic means of achieving cosmic unity:

> Blazing Spirit, Fire, personal, super-substantial, the consummation of a union so immeasurably more lovely and more desirable than that destructive fusion of which the pantheists dream: be pleased yet once again to come down and breathe a soul into the newly-formed, fragile film of matter with which this day the world is to be freshly clothed. (Teilhard de Chardin 1965: 22)

As the editor of the text painstakingly points out, this prayer in no way conflicts with the central action of the Eucharist, transubstantiation: for Teilhard de Chardin, matter is already suffused with Divine energy.[6] So far-reaching is his understanding of incarnation that he sees the entire universe as assuming a body and face — in Christ. Each microcosm of the universe has the potential to express the incarnation of Christ with different degrees of intensity. This prayer shows us that the point of fire descending into the heart of the world is for the believer (= Père Teilhard)

5. It was published posthumously.
6. 1965: 23 n. 1. He cites from the text, *Le Prêtre*: 'The central mystery of transubstantiation is aureoled by a divinisation, real thought attenuated, of all the universe'.

> To consent to the communion which will enable it to find in me the food it has come in the last resort to seek. (Teilhard de Chardin 1965: 29)

This communion with the bread of Christ, filled with an impassioned love of Christ, will be lifted up and enabled to contemplate the face of God. It will be a surrender, a surrender to the processes of ageing and death, even the death of the entire earth, because at the same time a surrender to the exalted future to which God is leading the earth. But advancing and experiencing the earth is at the same time penetrating further and further into God, because Teilhard's basic vision is the union –or developing convergence — between God-in-Christ and the universe. The *Mass* ends with a prayer of dedication.

Such a vision was made possible by the high regard that Père Teilhard held for matter itself. Well aware that matter is subject to dissolution and decay, he can still write:

> Without you, without your onslaughts, without your uprootings of us, we should remain all our lives inert, stagnant, puerile, ignorant of both ourselves and God. (Teilhard de Chardin 1965: 69)

Matter — the necessary precondition for the appearance on earth of spirit — was vital for him as the power of uniting million of monads on their way to convergence in the Spirit. This Eucharistic vision was the burning heart of his spirituality:

> The Eucharist must invade my life. My life must become, as a result of the sacrament, an unlimited and endless contact with you, — that life which seemed, a few moments ago, like a baptism with you in the waters of the world, now reveals itself to me as communion with you throughout the world. (Teilhard de Chardin 1960: 126-27)

But this was in no way an automatic communion: Père Teilhard's eucharistic spirituality was one to be maintained with ascetic discipline, in purity, faith and fidelity. He saw the Divine cosmic milieu as a moving centre that each person must follow as the Magi followed the star (Teilhard de Chardin 1960: 139).

Eucharistic Vision/Threatened Earth

We can no longer share Teilhard's optimism. The convergence of all things he so passionately believed in, if it happens at all, lies in God's hands. How then can his eucharistic vision, offered to us with no awareness of the serious ecological disasters that threaten to overwhelm us, be of any relevance today?

First, his insight in condemning any flight from the earth, in seeing the redemptive process as a this-worldly activity inclusive of all life

forms has now been developed by many others. It is a great summons to overcome anthropocentrism. (Some will argue that the process described is still heavily anthropocentric if dependent on human
consciousness as we know it. But I imagine that if Teilhard was alive
today and participating in the many discussions broadening the
notion of consciousness he would find his ideas at home within
them.) Secondly, even if what Teilhard de Chardin described as
convergence in Omega point is dismissed, the idea of God drawing
the world into God's own future has been taken up by many theologians. This idea is very congruent with the work of Process theology
and indeed it is to be regretted that Teilhard had no dialogue with
this stream of thought which could have proved fruitful for him. John
Haught writes:

> ...God is the reality into which all events in the universe are finally synthe-
> sized and preserved as they aim toward a continually more expansive
> beauty. (Haught 1993: 35)

For the German theologians Jürgen Moltmann (b. 1926) and Wolfhart
Pannenberg (b. 1928), whose context is the second rather than the
first World War, what God achieves in the future through actual
historical events is crucially important. Pannenberg refers to God as
'the Power of the future' (Toolan 2003: 149-50). Moltmann—who
stands very close to Karl Barth in the belief of the revelation of Christ
as Word in history, believes the mode of divine presence is in the
form of promise directed to the future. Christ's death and resurrection were proclaimed as God's promise of a future Kingdom of right-
eousness. The future can be said to be present by evoking hopes and
resistance to the present situation (Grenz 2004: 76-77):

> The 'future' must be considered as the mode of God's being. (Moltmann
> 1970: 10)

Like Moltmann, Pannenberg also sees the unity of God as emerging
from this eschatological future. But rather than seeing the Word as
such as revelatory, he sees revelation as located in the:

> 'history of traditions', that is, in the events of history as understood within
> their historical context climaxing in the eschatological event. (Grenz 2004: 76)

This is a very different approach from the ideas of Teilhard. The focus
of the two German theologians is Divine presence revealed in the
events of history, somehow anticipating its fulfilment. For Teilhard
de Chardin it is the very stuff of matter itself that bears the spark of
the Divine, a God who is somehow moving matter to a glorious fulfilment.

But it is in the insights of the late David Toolan that I find both a congruence with Père Teilhard's ideas and a way to develop them further. David Toolan was also a Jesuit priest. Not only did he write in sympathy with Teilhard but his book, *At Home in the Cosmos*, was dedicated to him. Toolan's universe is consciously post-Einsteinian. He wrote in full consciousness of the ecological crisis, the dynamics of sustainability that are being violated and the numerous cultural assumptions of the west that have contributed to the death of nature. He is all too well aware that because of the magnitude of the problem, it is difficult for either science or religion to come up with a solution.

Toolan, like Teilhard, offers a cosmic eucharistic vision that is also based on the idea of transformation. But he earths this vision more concretely than Teilhard in the context of Jewish Passover as well as in the context of the looming death of Jesus:

> There are no theatrics here, no magic, simply the highly-charged action of a man who knows he will die on the morrow and must make every word and gesture count. Two great movements converge in what Jesus shows us here: the everlasting desire of cosmic dust to mean something great and God's promise that it shall be done. There is first a centripetal movement. We the followers and the disciples center in on Jesus, identify, become one with him. Then there is the centrifugal, decentralising movement. Jesus, both conduit of Spirit-Energy and cosmic dust himself, freely identifies himself with us and with the fruits of the earth — the ash of a dying star present in bread and wine — and converts these gifts of earth, the work of human hands, into another story than the nightmarish one we have been telling with them. (Toolan 2003: 210)

This other story is the fact that Jesus — in a context of unconditioned love and forgiveness — transforms, transmutes and breathes new meaning into all life forms. Jesus, as Toolan says, is 'bidding us to take in, to discover in our own soul-space the same Spirit that works in and through him' (2003: 211). I think that Toolan emphasizes a dimension that Teilhard needed to stress, that the redeeming work of Jesus, is in fact the saving work of the whole Trinitarian Godhead:

> In effect, Jesus is saying that the whole work of transfiguring earth stuff in accord with the creator's dream is not his solitary work but fundamentally the work of the Father in heaven…
>
> Swallow this, Jesus declares, I am God's promise for the elements, the exemplary inside of nature, its secret wish fulfilled. Swallow my words, let them resonate in the marrow of my bones, and you will tap into the same current of spirit that moves me. Swallow me and you will have taken in what God imagines for matter: that it be spirited, that justice be done to all, according to the vision of the great rainbow covenant. (Toolan 2003: 212)

Here there is an incipient theology of redemption as the work of the entire Trinity in a context of justice that is almost entirely missing from the texts of Teilhard and one of the major criticisms of his theology. As Emile Rideaux writes:

> Nevertheless, he (= Teilhard) seems to be inclined to merge the mystery of the redemption in that of Incarnation: he sees the cross primarily as the supreme means, used by Christ more effectively to urge on the world to its term. ... There is no trace in Teilhard of the Pauline dialectic of death, of death through the death of God, and the final of a fundamental alienation and a collective regeneration through Christ's priestly act. (Rideaux 1967: 225-26)

Toolan ends with a poetic and evocative picture of what our human role and vocation is in this context:

> We are great mothering nature's soul-space, her heart and vocal chords — and her willingness, if we consent to it, to be spirited, to be the vessel of the Holy One whose concern reaches out to embrace all that is created. When we fail in this soul work, fail in extending our own reach of concern, nature fails/falls with us. But when it happens, when we say yes to the Spirit who hovers over our own inner chaos, the mountains clap their hands, the hills leap like gazelles...we are nature's black box, her vessel of soul-space — and hence her last chance to become spirited, to be the vessel of God... (Toolan 2003: 215-16)

Toolan's stirring vision gives a new urgency to Teilhard's thoughts in our contemporary context. He has a more robust idea of the role of the Spirit in renewing broken creation. For it has to be admitted that Teilhard's pan-Christic vision has little space for the healing and transforming work of the Spirit. He writes of the Spirit as almost identical with God, with Omega point:

> Rich with the sap of the world, I rise up towards the Spirit whose vesture is the magnificence of the material universe but who smiles at me from far beyond all victories. (Teilhard de Chardin 1965: 27)

Or, in another passage, the Spirit as another word for the God of evolution:

> It is in fact God, God alone, who through his Spirit stirs up
> into a ferment the mass of the universe. (Teilhard de Chardin 1965: 79)

But there is a far wider role for the Holy Spirit other than as evolutionary energy. John's Gospel spoke of the coming of the Spirit who would teach us all the things that are to come (Jn 16.13). In our time the prophetic spirit as green face of God communicates a language linking human and non-human, revealing the false logic on which this split is built. As Spirit of truth, the Spirit attempts to lead us into a truth that builds just practises enabling flourishing for all life-forms. Thus the power of the Spirit's energy, is the power of being re-vitalized by being put in touch once again with the truth of sustaining forces of life, the truth of God's redeeming action.

Elsewhere I argued that the symbol of the Spirit as 'The Wild Bird who heals', responds to our contemporary crisis (Grey 2003: 103-21). In the call to protect the beauty of the wildernesses, the wetness, and all the creatures who live there, as well as to transform the urban deserts, deprived of meaningful contact with the earth, imaginations are awakened, as the Spirit creates healing connections and evokes commitment to creation. The Spirit's work here can also be seen as part of God's wisdom, Sophia- Hokmah, here understood as *redeeming* wisdom in a time of peril for the earth (Grey 1993; Deane Drummond 2000).

But if there is an argument for the effective role of liturgy and especially the Eucharist in a time of crisis, it must be found at this heart of God's redeeming and saving work *in its liturgical expression*. What Teilhard expressed as cosmic praise and thanksgiving needs to be placed in the wider context of faith in the God of broken creation, who will offer us redemptive possibilities even at this hour of danger.

The first obstacle is that this cosmological dimension is almost totally missing from official statements of the Roman Catholic Church. Sean McDonagh has made this clear:

> ...it is strange that, while the New Catechism of the Catholic Church is clear that the 'Eucharist commits us to the poor', it is silent on the relationship between the Eucharist and the imperilled creation. (McDonagh 1999: 196)

He argues that the covenant that the Eucharist recalls and re-presents is at the same time a cosmic covenant with the whole of creation, and that this has been forgotten. The liturgy as we experience it does not convey the truth of the earth's woundedness and the suffering of thousands of life forms, many of which are threatened with extinction. The urgency then is for the recovery of cosmic covenant as a movement of dedication to creation. Secondly, this is the *kairos* moment to re-think liturgy as a place of ethical commitment of the gathered community to the brokenness of creation for which we are largely responsible. Thirdly, it is a *kairos* moment for widening our understanding of sacrifice. In harmony with Toolan's imaginative eucharistic prayer in the words of Jesus,

> Swallow me and you will have taken in what God imagines for matter:
> that it be spirited, that justice be done to all,

partaking in *holy communion,* becomes exactly that, a communion with all Divinely-created life, and responding to God's purpose for it. It gives a Trinitarian understanding to Eucharistic communion. This means understanding sacrifice as a community act of solidarity with the suffering earth/suffering people. Fourthly, liturgy becomes a place where memory/Anamnesis becomes remembering what we were once, what we have been, what can now never be, given so much destruction. It is a place for the recovery of prophetic lament and grief for all that has disappeared, and the glory of God that can never be, because of what has been destroyed and what we are still destroying. It is time/space for repentance, for reconversion to the earth. And finally it is a time of new commitment and dedication to lifestyles geared to the flourishing and survival of threatened forms of life, human and non-human. *Leitourgia* is then reclaimed as the work of the people in the context of environmental catastrophe.

Conclusion

But how can this eucharistic vision claim to be inspired by Teilhard de Chardin, given his apparent unawareness of the need for ecological justice and lack of an explicit Trinitarian focus? I pondered this question, walking across the Common outside our cottage. I was feeling deeply troubled by many ecological issues – in particular the question of global warming and its effect on droughts and floods across the world. (I had just read of the growing numbers of people drowned in Haiti.) Despite these very real threats, I could not help being cheered by the sight of golden irises springing up by the streams, huge clumps of buttercups multiplying themselves exponentially, and birds singing their hearts out. I was reminded of what I had written some years ago, that prophetic action needs to go hand in hand with mystical experience (Grey 1997). It struck me that this is the gift of Teilhard for us today. I have argued that liturgy is the true home of ethical commitment for justice for the earth, seen as restored and redeemed creation. But activists will burn out eventually without being nurtured by a tangible experience of God's presence and *tangible* sustenance. What Teilhard – read through Toolan, who sets this firmly in Jewish and Christian core traditions – offers, is the *experience* of the Divine transformation of matter: but, more importantly, although he himself experienced the *Mass of the World* alone in the lonely Asian steppes, what is crucial today is for the community itself to become a mystic. That is, for the gathered people of God, to become transfused and transfigured with the experience of Divine presence in, and purpose for creation, and thus be energized to join the *great work*[7] of God's transformation of all life forms into the Trinitarian vision of new creation.

So in the spirit of Père Teilhard de Chardin, let us still celebrate the *Mass on the World*, but with humility, and with commitment to cosmic justice, in growing consciousness of what we have inflicted on Divine creation, but with his hope and his faith that God's redeeming action may still save this, the *milieu divin*.

References

Abram, David
   1996   *The Spell of the Sensuous* (New York: Random House).
Berry, Thomas
   1988   *The Dream of the Earth* (San Francisco: Sierra Books).
   1999   *The Great Work* (New York: Bell Tower).
Clarke, Chris
   2002   *Living in Connection* (Warminster: Creation Spirituality Books).
Deane Drummond, Celia
   2000   *Creation Through Wisdom* (Edinburgh: T. & T. Clark).
Eliot, T.S.
   1959   'East Coker' in *Four Quartets* (London: Faber & Faber).
Fox, Matthew
   1988   *The Coming of the Cosmic Christ* (San Francisco: Harper & Row).
Grenz, Stanley J.
   2004   *Rediscovering the Triune God* (Minneapolis: Fortress Press).
Grey, Mary
   1993   *The Wisdom of Fools?* (London: SPCK).
   1997   *Prophecy and Mysticism: the Heart of the Postmodern Church* (Edinburgh: T. & T. Clark).
   2003   *Sacred Longings: Ecological Theology and Globalisation* (London: SCM Press).
Guardian, The
   2004   'Shrinking Species', 20 March.
Haught, John
   1993   *The Promise of Nature: Ecology and Cosmic Purpose* (Mahwah, NJ: Paulist Press).
Huxley, Julian
   1973   *Memories*, II (London: George Allen & Unwin).
King, Ursula
   1980   *Towards a New Mysticism: Teilhard de Chardin and Eastern Religions* (London: Collins).
   1996   *Spirit of Fire: the Life and Vision of Teilhard de Chardin* (Maryknoll, NY: Orbis Books).

7.   The phrase is Thomas Berry's.

1997   *Christ In All Things: Exploring Spirituality with Teilhard de Chardin*
         (London: SCM Press).
McDaniel, Jay
1995   *With Roots and Wings: Christianity in an Age of Ecology and Dialogue*
         (Maryknoll, NY: Orbis Books).
McDonagh, Sean
1999   *Greening the Christian Millennium* (Dublin: Dominican Publica-
         tions).
Medawar, Sir Peter
1961   'Review of *The Phenomenon of Man*', *Mind* 70: 99-106.
Moltmann, Jürgen
1970   'Theology as Eschatology', in Frederick Herzog (ed.), *The Future of
         Hope: Theology as Eschatology* (New York: Herder & Herder).
Mooney, Christopher F.
1964   *Teilhard de Chardin and the Mystery of Christ* (London: Collins).
Rideaux, Emile
1967   *Teilhard de Chardin: A Guide to His Thought* (London: Collins).
Speaight, Robert
1967   *Teilhard de Chardin: A Biography* (London: Collins).
Teilhard de Chardin, Pierre
1917   'The Mystical Milieu', in Teilhard de Chardin (1968): 115-49.
1923   'The Mass on the World', in Teilhard de Chardin (1978): 119-34.
1950   'The Heart of Matter', in Teilhard de Chardin (1978): 15-79.
1955, 1959 *The Phenomenon of Man* (Paris, 1955; London: Collins).
1961, 1965 *Hymn of the Universe* (trans. Gerard Vann, OP; Paris: Editions de
         Seuil; London: Collins).
1963   *The Divine Milieu: An Essay on the Interior Life* (London: Collins/
         Fontana).
1966   *Man's Place in Nature* (trans. René Hague; London: Collins).
1968   *Writings in the Time of War* (London: Collins).
1975   'My Fundamental Vision', in *Toward the Future* (trans. René Hague;
         London: Collins): 164-208.
1978   *The Heart of Matter* (trans. René Hague; London: Collins).
Toolan, David
2003   *At Home in the Cosmos* (Maryknoll, NY: Orbis Books).

7

THE EXPLOITATION OF NATURE AND TEILHARD'S ECOTHEOLOGY OF LOVE

Robert Faricy

The Ecological Problem and the Theological Worldview

We find prevalent today, especially in the West, an exploitative model of the humanity-nature relationship. This model historically has acted, and acts now, to the detriment of the environment.

Lynn White's article, 'The Historical Roots of Our Ecological Crisis', in the periodical *Science* in 1967, precipitated a debate that has lasted up to the present (White 1967). White's hypothesis argues that our almost universally held attitudes towards the relationship between humanity and nature come from Christianity. With Christian arrogance we hold ourselves superior to nature, contemptuous of it. The roots of our exploitative attitude toward nature are essentially religious (White 1970, Appendix).

White and several authors after him hold that the contemporary aggressively exploitative attitude toward nature finds its origin in the Judeo-Christian doctrine of absolute human sovereignty over all other creatures. Christian tradition about human relationship with nature has depersonalized and disrespected nature. The first chapter of Genesis, in particular, gives humanity the mandate to dominate and to subdue nature (Marx 1970: 948; Erlich 1971: 129; Nicholson 1969: 264; Hardin 1980: 67). Empirical verification of the Lynn thesis can be found in a recent study that finds significant correlation between the Lynn thesis and belief in the Bible among mostly Reformation Protestant Christians (Eckberg and Blocker 1989: 509-17). The debate does not concern the morality of ruthlessly exploiting nature, but where the underlying perception of the humanity-nature relationship comes from. Does it really come from Christianity? Several theologians have defended Christianity against this accusation, pointing out that

Christian tradition about the humanity-nature relationship leads to stewardship of the earth rather than to its exploitation (Santmire, 1970; Sittler 1970; Hamilton 1970; Barbour 1970 and 1972 Derrick, 1972; Passmore 1974; Derr 1975; Marietta, Jr 1977: 151-66; Montefiore 1977: 199-211; Moss 1978: 89-103). Karl Braaten (1972), for one, is an exception; he finds it 'difficult to gainsay the Christian responsibility for the rape of nature' (p. 121). Richard Clifford (1988), shows convincingly that a Lynn White oriented interpretation of Genesis Chapter One is wrong. The point of Lynn White and those who follow him, however, is not the interpretation of Genesis One, right or wrong, but the origin of the western exploitative attitude toward nature.

It seems to me that not Christianity as such but rather the Christianity of the Protestant Reformation lies at the origin of our contemporary aggressively exploitative approach to nature. Here, one idea in particular has special importance: Martin Luther's theology of nature fallen and under God's judgment, and of human nature then as essentially sinful, and his resultant theology of the two kingdoms. In Lutheran theology, and in much Protestant theology in general, God and the world, the kingdom of Christ and the kingdom of the world, are perceived as in tension, in antithetical opposition. The Protestant tradition of the Reformation has read Genesis One's mandate to mankind in the framework of a humanity-nature antithesis. The result: our stewardship stands within a master–slave relationship in which we stand over nature as master over slave. And the order of creation stands under God's wrath, separated from the order of redemption. We need to deal aggressively with unruly nature in order to make it a good slave.

No one of course would deny that the Reformation tradition, and perhaps especially the Lutheran tradition, shows a deep appreciation for nature and of God's presence in nature. However, grace and nature, in general in the Reformation tradition, hold together in tension, in paradox, in some kind of opposition.

Obviously, the Reformation tradition has never encouraged irresponsible exploitation of nature. In fact, this tradition emphasizes not only divine sovereignty over nature but also the command to care for nature, to exercise stewardship towards nature — management with a strong sense of responsibility.

On the other hand, when grace and nature come together in synthesis, as in the Catholic tradition (for example in the Thomistic synthesis, in the Greek fathers of the Church, in the whole Orthodox tradition, in the Anglican tradition), then the relation between nature and humanity is understood more as more unitive, and with an attitude of working with nature rather than against it. The Catholic tradition puts greater emphasis on the principle of the incarnation. God has become truly human; matter is the proper vehicle of spirit; material reality in its present state is intrinsically good; human nature is radically and irrevocably good; and nature, although de-divinized, possesses religious value.

The problem with the Reformation view lies in this: responsible stewardship in obedience to the divine command is not enough, even in theory. The de-divinization of nature needs the balance that comes from an understanding of nature as rooted in Jesus Christ. This is how the Catholic view interprets the Pauline theology of the relationship between the world and the risen Christ.

To put the matter in different words: the Reformation worldview places the transcendent God over against nature, and immanent in nature as Creator. But not immanent as Redeemer. So the orders of creation and redemption find themselves separated. Nature is not at all object of redemption, and so it remains condemned under God's judgement. Genesis chapter one, understood in this context, leads to the exploitation of nature.

After the Reformation, the two great Catholic theologians and commentators on the works of Thomas Aquinas, Suarez and Cajetan, did the same thing. In trying to refute Reformation tenets, they perhaps inevitably took over the same assumptions, and chiefly that the orders of creation and redemption are separate. It took Pierre Teilhard de Chardin, Henri de Lubac, and Karl Rahner in the twentieth century to get the two orders, nature and grace, back together again for the Catholics.

Looking at the problematic in again a somewhat different way, we can follow Guy Swanson concerning immanence in post-Reformation Christianity.[1] In Swanson's analysis of the influence of social structures and their influence on belief systems, the Reformation rejected the idea of immanence. The gap of divine transcendence holds fast

1. See Swanson (1967) and various articles published since then. H. Paul Santmire (1985) posits a set of categories different from immanence and transcendence: that of 'the spiritual motif' and 'the ecological motif'. Unfortunately he places Pierre Teilhard de Chardin, perhaps the most incarnational and ecological theologian of the Christian tradition, in the 'spiritual' category, apparently under the impression that Teilhard views the world to come as purely spiritual. In fact Teilhard, an utterly orthodox Catholic theologian, holds the resurrection of the body and the transformation of this world at the parousia into the world to come. Teilhard is thoroughly eschatological. See Santmire 1985: 155-71 and 216-17.

for Protestants. God can and does act in the world, in nature, in human lives, across this gap; but the gap never diminishes. Catholics, on the other hand, see a certain strong radical immanence of God in Jesus Christ in the sacraments, especially in the Eucharist, and in the Church, especially in the mediation of divine teaching and disciplinary authority through Church hierarchy. Catholics hold a stronger incarnational immanence. We can find this Catholic view of incarnational immanence expressed in Catholic views of human nature (for example regarding abortion, contraception, and sexuality) as well as in Catholic understandings of nature in general (for example, in the offertory prayers of the Eucharist in the various liturgical rites). Without subscribing to Swanson's sociological theories, we can accept his ideas on immanence in Catholic and Reformation traditions.

Looked at in terms of immanence and transcendence, the problem with the Protestant Reformation world view is not that God's transcendence is exaggerated or overemphasized. The divine transcendence is absolute; we cannot possibly exaggerate it. The problem lies in not stressing sufficiently the immanence of Jesus Christ, of the Redeemer, in the world. Here too, a certain absoluteness holds true; God's transcendence and his immanence are, both, absolute and correlative; they go together.

The problem with not giving sufficient weight to the immanence of Jesus Christ in nature, in the world, in the cosmos, does not consist in understanding nature as secular instead of as sacred. Genesis, Chapter One, does desacralize nature, secularize it, take the sacred out of nature and put it where it belongs, in the transcendent God. Some writers, accordingly, want to resacralize nature so as to get more balance into our ecology. Because of the emphasis in the Reformation and general contemporary understanding of nature as secular, these writers feel that we need to rediscover the sacred in nature, and that we can learn from eastern religions a greater respect for nature.[2] This

---

2. The writings of Thomas Berry, for example, point Christianity in the direction of a nature mysticism that would at least partially sacralize nature, see nature with all its elements and all its species as a totality, the human species only one among many (Berry 1999). Thomas Berry, with the good intention of extending Teilhard's ideas, manipulates and twists them in order to make them useful in an ecospirituality that dismisses the idea of evolution and that diminishes the place of eschatology and of the cross and redemptive values — all fundamental to Teilhard's thought — in favor of a greater emphasis on creation. Berry wants to minimize the notions of evolution, progress, and development to bring out the desirability of a placid and peaceful present. He finds Teilhard's basic ideas, such as those of evolutionary development, progress, the cross in Christian life, and

kind of immanence does not really distinguish God from nature, and in the merging of God and nature finds a respect for nature as sacred, as possessing a certain divinity, as somehow sacred.

However, a truly Christian understanding of nature finds nature not sacred but holy, in no way divine but nevertheless full of God. The principle is that of Creator and creation. The Creator is closer to the creature than the creature itself. He gives it its existence. This makes the creature not God but itself.

The world is created in and through Jesus Christ. This makes it holy, somehow centered and sanctified in him.

Teilhard's Ecotheology of Love

Pierre Teilhard de Chardin is a hard man to classify; he fits into too many categories, many of them in apparent opposition. History has a difficult time knowing how to describe him. Scientist and poet, an original, but scrupulously obedient, critical of some churchmen but a lover of all things Roman Catholic beginning with the church herself, a man of deep prayer and a man of action, alone and lonely but a man who attracted friendship, cheerful and peaceful but sometimes deeply depressed or agitated, Teilhard was a man of too many parts to fit neatly into a classification system.

His thought, too, is a combination of many things, expressed in poetic language, in mystical language, in the language of science, and sometimes in words and phrases he invented himself. He was as complicated and as made up of contradictory elements as most of us are, and he needed many kinds of language to express his ideas.

Yet, Teilhard's thought is all of a piece, unified, coherent. The idea of love runs all through his theory of evolution and his ecotheology. The concept of love holds the entire edifice of his thought together. And this because, for Teilhard, love holds each element of reality, and all reality, together.

Teilhard died in 1955, long before the concept of ecotheology came into existence. And yet, his theology is, in fact, an ecotheology, an ecotheology of love.

the importance of science and technology, 'aggressive' (Berry 2003: 57-73, esp. 65-72; 1982). As opposed to Teilhard, Berry asserts that the ecological norm is not the human but rather the well-being and integral functioning of the whole earth community. Berry wants a return to the spatial and contemplative way of perceiving the world, and a turning away from the Western time experience of reality.

Evolution and Love

In one of his wartime journals Teilhard writes, 'Sometime I should gather all my ideas together in a synthesis built around the foundation of everything: love' (Teilhard de Chardin 1975: 186; see Trennert-Hellwig 1993; Faricy 1981: 13-33). However he never did write that synthesis. This article presents his thought in such a way as to show how love stands as the central and the synthesizing element of his Ecotheology of love.

In Teilhard's thought — and at every level of his thought: his theory of evolution that has love as its energy, his theology of Jesus Christ as the world's loving and animating center, his spirituality of love — love has the primacy. Love does everything. Love unites, not surface to surface but heart to heart, and therefore freely and strongly. Love creates. Love saves, love redeems. Love is the glue that holds everything together. Love holds the primacy: God's love for each of us and for the world in Jesus, the love of Jesus for each of us and for the world, our love for one another and for God.

For Teilhard, love is the great unifying force. Love is the energy of evolution (Teilhard de Chardin 1955: 293-303; 1962: 180-95; 89-105; 1965a: 99-102; 1956: 9; 1965b: 253-62; 378-79). At least in its most primitive forms, love exists at every level of evolution. Later in the evolutionary process, in mammals for example, love tends to take the forms of reproductive drives and of various kinds of bonding between members of the same species.

What binds creatures together is love. The interior mutual attraction that runs all through nature, that binds particles to make atoms, atoms to make molecules, cells to make bodily organs and whole bodies, when found at the level of human consciousness is what we most properly call love.

With the appearance in evolution of human beings, love enters the realm of reflexive consciousness, of the spiritual. In humans, love takes many forms: sexual love, love of friendship, larger friendships engendered by devotion to a common cause, patriotism, a sense of world unity. Love binds us together by a free mutual adhesion that comes from the interior, from the heart.

When a union is simply imposed from above, and does not take the form of a center-to-center union, the form of a free mutual adhesion of the persons united, then that union cannot hold. An imposed union does not hold; it is weak. A dictatorship, for example, has such weakness of union that it needs strong sanctions to create unity:

concentration camps, torture, death, for those who deviate from the plan imposed from on high.

But a union of love, love in some shape, some kind of love, holds because it has an interior strength. Love is the natural way of union, and the only bonding that truly holds the elements united together.

The highest and strongest and most human kind of love is love in the Christic zone of the world, the love poured into our hearts by the Holy Spirit, Christian love. By Christian love, Teilhard means not just love of one another, but love of the world and of all in it, love of everyone according to our relationship with each, love of all humanity, love of life, and love of the world itself.

Christian love is natural love elevated into the Christic zone of the universe where it shows its astonishing power to transform everything (Teilhard de Chardin 1959: 113-26).

Continuous Creation in Christ

Love is the energy, the force, of evolution and of human progress. The energy of all real growth, progress, evolution, is love. Growth, progress, evolution are the expression of God's continuous creative act. We receive, and perceive, God's creative activity in the world, in history, and in our lives as evolution, progress, and growth. The energy of creation, creation's force, is the love that God has for his creation in and through Jesus Christ risen.

Creation is not so much a divine act in the beginning as a now ongoing process. Jesus, the focal center of all history, the world's and mine, draws all things to himself, holding them in existence through his universal love. This process is creation: Jesus drawing the world to himself, reconciling all things in himself in whom everything holds together.

Teilhard tries to understand the mystery of creation in New Testament terms, and in dynamic and evolutionary terms. He wants to rethink the mystery of creation as the 'creation in Christ' that John's Gospel and the Pauline letters tell us about. How can we better understand all creation as 'made through him' [Jn 1.3], as 'created through him and for him' [Col. 1.16] in such a way that 'all things hold together in him' [Col. 1.17]? How can we rethink the dogma of creation so as to see that the risen Jesus 'is the head over all things' and that he 'fills all in all' [Eph. 1.22-23]? And how can we do this within the framework of a contemporary view of the world moving through history into a future?

Teilhard sees all of creation not as an act or a series of acts at the beginning of world history, but as a process going on now, a process that manifests itself in world history, as world history. God creates by uniting. Working through the risen Jesus, who stands at the future focal point of world history's convergence toward the ultimate future, God gradually draws all things toward some kind of unity in Christ, reconciling all things in him. The creative act in and through, and of, Christ draws all things toward a unity. The result is all of creation, the process of all things moving forward.

Creation as process includes, of course, suffering and death; it includes the cross. No multiplicity can move toward unification without some breakage, conflict, death, suffering, and — at the moral level — sin. Evil is statistically inevitable in any multiplicity moving toward a higher unity. The process of creation takes place in the structure of the cross.

The love of God, working through the love for all things in the heart of Christ risen, drawing all things to a unity in Christ, holds the world in existence and moves it into the future. This is creation in Christ, and it describes the relationship between Jesus Christ and creation. The risen Jesus stands as creation's future focal point; and, at the same time, his presence through his loving creative action permeates everywhere. The risen Christ is universally present, present to each creature and to all creation, through the creative love that sustains and unifies creation, and that draws it to himself.

Is this a kind of pantheism? No. A pantheistic religion regards all things as one; everything is God. The insight of pantheism is that it knows that God is present everywhere, more present to things even than they are to themselves. The mistake of pantheism is to think that therefore all creation is God. Pantheism misunderstands creation. 'To create' means to give the creature its own existence, to make it exist with an autonomous although dependent existence. God is creator. That makes each creature not God but itself. It makes creation not divine but existing in its own right, dependent on the Creator.

The Universal Christ

Through his love for all creation and for each element in creation, the risen Jesus makes himself present to all creation and to each element of it. He is everywhere, present to each part of the universe and to each person through his personal love for each. This idea has its origin in Teilhard's own religious experience.

After finishing his Jesuit studies in philosophy and theology, and after having taught for three years in a Jesuit secondary school in Cairo, and after having been ordained a priest, Teilhard found himself drafted into the French army at the beginning of the First World War in 1914. Assigned to a regiment of North African Zouaves, a unit especially active in fighting against the German army that had invaded Belgium, Teilhard lived through bullets and poison gas that took more than half the men in his regiment.

According to his conscience and the rules of the Catholic Church in France, he served as a stretcher bearer, not as a combatant. Of course, he continued to pray regularly, meditating at least an hour a day, to say Mass every day at least when that was possible, and to pray the Divine Office from the breviary as every Catholic priest does.

While serving at the front, amid the horrors of the war, Teilhard had some properly mystical experiences of Christ, probably beginning around March or April 1916. He understood, or rather experienced, the presence of the risen Jesus Christ in the world through his love, an intimate presence-through-love in the whole of creation. These experiences showed him the mystery of God's presence through Jesus Christ in the world, and they changed Teilhard forever. From then on, he had a new vision of reality, he saw things differently.

God was not 'up there', above, in some way distant. He was here, in Jesus risen, through the intense love that radiates out from the heart of Jesus, present to everything created, and to all of creation together, and to Teilhard, through the love of the risen Christ for each creature and for all creation. Teilhard described these experiences later in an essay, attributing the visions to a fictitious person, and writing about them as fiction ('Christ in the World of Matter', in *Hymn of the Universe* [1961: 39-51]). I know, however, from conversations with Jeanne Mortier, Teilhard's secretary for many years, that — far from made up — the experiences happened to Teilhard himself.

He kept notes on these experiences, and on his reflections on them, in small notebooks, the kind that French school children still use. These notes, in turn, became the basis of essays, the first descriptions of Teilhard's Christian understanding of reality and of his spirituality. He began to write his reflections on these experiences, in the form of notes and then essays, in the spring of 1916. At Verdun, east of the Meuse River, between Rheims and Metz, Teilhard recorded his mystical experiences, as fiction, in the form of three stories. The following comes from the first story, called 'The Picture'.

My mind was occupied with a problem that was part philosophical and part aesthetic. I thought: suppose Christ should choose to appear bodily here before me, what would he look like? How would he be dressed? Above all, how would he become material, and in what way would he stand out against the objects surrounding him? ...Meanwhile, my gaze fastened itself without any thought on my part on a picture of Christ offering his heart to us. This picture hung in front of me on the wall of a church into which I had gone to pray. ...My vision began. To tell the truth, I could not say exactly when it began, for it already had a certain intensity when I became conscious of it. As I allowed my gaze to wander over the picture I suddenly became aware that the picture was *melting*; it was melting in a special manner, hard to describe. ...The vibrant atmosphere which surrounded Christ like an aureole was no longer confined to a small space around him, but radiated outward to infinity... *The entire universe was vibrant!* And yet, when I looked at particular objects, one by one, I found them still as clearly delineated as ever and preserved in their individuality. All this movement seemed to emanate from Christ, above all from his heart. ...And I stood dumbfounded.

...When I was able to look at it again, the picture of Christ in the church had once again taken on its too precise outlines and its fixed features (Teilhard de Chardin 1961: 42-46).

Teilhard de Chardin's vision of Jesus risen who fills the whole world with his love, while a vision, represents a truth. Jesus's love *does* fill the world. And yet, he does not love all things indistinctly, sort of all grouped and merged together. He loves each thing, each part of nature, and in particular each person, individually.

Teilhard not only wrote this; he believed it and he lived it. His union in love with Jesus Christ risen, that Jesus Christ who is Lord of all (organically, not just juridically, present to everything holding it in existence by his love) was the center of his life.

Official Jesuit censors often refused Teilhard's writings approval for publication partly or wholly because the censors held Teilhard's ideas pantheistic and therefore heretical. The censors argued this way: If Jesus Christ is present everywhere in the way that Pierre Teilhard de Chardin claimed he was, then everything is Jesus. Individual creatures cannot be differentiated from their Creator present in Christ, and therefore all things are Jesus Christ; everything and everyone is God. The Jesuit censors did not and perhaps could not understand Teilhard's thought. They read him in the categories of Saint Thomas Aquinas and of the theology of their time, their own theology, and so they misread him.

In many places in his writings, Teilhard explains clearly the union of all things with Jesus Christ, and often he contrasts that union with the belief of pantheistic religions that hold all things to be one, and God. True union differentiates the elements united, and that differentiation takes place at the level of the union. For example, the organs of the human body are differentiated according to function. The five players on a basketball team are differentiated according to their team union; each does something a little different, plays his own position. Members of a surgical team have different specialties, do diverse things in the operating room. Union differentiates.

The error of pantheistic systems, like some eastern religions, lies here: they recognize God as more interior to creatures than the creatures are to themselves; and they conclude that therefore everything is God. Christianity has a doctrine of creation. The Creator makes creatures to be precisely not Him but themselves; he gives them existence. Teilhard explains creation as creation in Christ; existence comes from Jesus risen holding creatures in existence by his love for them, in a differentiating union that makes them to be not Him but themselves (Teilhard de Chardin 1969: 71-91).

When true union exists between persons, at the level of persons, then the differentiation produced by the union takes the form of a *personalization* (Teilhard de Chardin 1959: 137-56). The persons united in love are personalized, grow as persons because of the union. Union of persons personalizes. This is true of union with Jesus. Jesus unites me to himself in love. And that union is the main source of my personal growth. He creates me now, every day, every moment, through loving me.

We can find examples of personalizing love all around us: The love of a married couple that truly love one another and sacrifice for one another does not lead the couple to form one amorphous blob. On the contrary in that union of love lived out every day each grows as a person. Each becomes herself or himself. The same is true of the love of parents for their children; the children become themselves, their own persons, within that union of affirming love. Love creates us, makes us more ourselves, personalizes us.

This is true above all of union with Jesus. His love, accepted by me, received in me, helps me to be myself, to grow. It creates me more. The greatest saints have been the greatest persons and the greatest individuals. Francis of Assisi, so normal that many thought him unbalanced; Ignatius of Loyola, neurotic and with many psychological problems, but an outstanding person, close to Jesus Christ; Catherine of Siena, forceful, strong, dynamic, and loving and tender, a great person made that way through her prayerful union with Jesus. This is true too of people close to the Lord in our own times: Mother Teresa of Calcutta, Martin Luther King, and Pierre Teilhard de Chardin himself.

In Teilhard's theology, Jesus Christ risen is more present to creation through his creative love than creation is present to itself. His
creative love creates, makes creation to be created, not God, not Jesus
Christ, but itself (Teilhard de Chardin 1956: 2-11).

The Lord's creative loving presence to me makes me myself; he
creates me; his love creates me, holds me in existence, moves me
forward into the future. This is true of each of us and of every
creature and of all creation.

We co-create with God the Creator. Whatever we do in the direction of unification, of love, of building or maintaining toward Jesus,
toward the Kingdom, participates in the process of creation, of the
reconciliation of all things in Christ. We are co-creators with the
Creator. What I do or undergo has value, not just for this world but
for the world to come, and not only because I offer it to the Lord or
have a right intention in doing or undergoing it. What I do and what
I undergo is important in itself, does something, builds, prepares for
the time when this world will end and be transformed.

Through his love for all creation and for each element in creation,
the risen Jesus makes himself present to all creation and to each
element of it. He is everywhere, present to each part of the universe
and to each person through his personal love for each.

In his published writings and also in his spiritual journals and
retreat notebooks Teilhard speaks of 'the Universal Christ' (1976: 56-
60). He calls the Universal Christ 'the Universal Lover'.

The Universal Christ is the same Jesus of Nazareth, who died for
us and who has risen, understood according to his presence everywhere in the universe through his love. This is not however love 'at a
distance'. The risen Jesus transcends all time and space by reason of
his resurrected state, and so he can be fully present to every time and
every space, to me now. He is present, through his love, loving me
now.

The Lord of all who holds the world in existence, moving it forward by his love, holds me in his hand, in his heart, moves me
forward, gives me life and growth. Christ is the instrument, the
Center, the Term of all creation; by Him everything is created, sanctified, vivified. All things find their coherence in Christ. He is the First
and he is the Head. In him everything was begun and everything
holds together and everything is consummated. He is the Alpha and
the Omega, the beginning and the end, the foundation stone and the
keystone. Jesus is he in whom all things are created and he in whom
the entire world in all its depth, its length, its breadth, its grandeur,

its physical and its spiritual, comes to be, takes on consistence. The world is above all a work of continuous creation in Christ. The universal influence of Jesus Christ, far from disassociating things, consolidates them; far from confusing things, it differentiates them.

Only union through love and in love (using the word 'love' in its widest and most real sense of 'mutual internal affinity') because it brings individuals together, not superficially and tangentially but center to center, can have the property of not merely differentiating but also personalizing.

Teilhard's ecotheology is one of using nature responsibly and of caring for the environment because it understands all things, including human beings, as integrally united, together, in Jesus Christ risen.[3]

References

Barbour, Ian
  1970   *Science and Secularity: The Ethics of Technology* (New York: Harper).
  1972   *That Earth Might Be Fair* (New York: Harper).
Berry, Thomas
  1982   *Teilhard in the Ecological Age* (Teilhard Studies, 7; Chambersburg, PA: American Teilhard Association for the Future of Man).
  1991   *Befriending the Earth* (Mystic, CT: Twenty-third Publications).
  1999   *The Great Work* (New York: Bell Tower).
  2003   'Teilhard in the Ecological Age', in Arthur Fabel and Donald St John (eds.), *Teilhard in the 21st Century* (Maryknoll, NY: Orbis Books): 57-73 and especially 65-72.
Braaten, Karl
  1972   *Christ and Counter Christ* (Philadelphia: Fortress Press).

3.   For ecotheologies somewhat similar to, or at least compatible with, Teilhard's see Haught, 1993 and Edwards, 1995. Thomas Berry, who often writes and speaks of the great influence of Teilhard on his thought, an influence that no one would contest, nevertheless is not in his ideas really compatible with nor similar to Teilhard. Berry holds Teilhard to have an 'excessive optimism' (1991: 25). Teilhard, in fact, seems to have had no optimism at all; in his later years he was often anxious and depressed. He did however have great hope, hope in Jesus Christ risen, the very center of Teilhard's ecotheology. Although Thomas Berry writes: 'Basically my position is the theological position taken by Teilhard' (1991: 54), this does not seem to me to be true. The fundamental difference in theological positions, in my opinion, is this: Berry wants us to see the world spatially, as static but full of God. Teilhard sees the world in the existential structure of Jesus carrying his cross; the world is dynamic, progressing, developing, moving rapidly — not without great suffering — into a future that lies hidden in Jesus' heart. This calls not for a placid or contemplative optimism but for a dynamic and energizing hope that encourages us to help build, with and toward Jesus, our own particular crosses united with his, into that future.

Clifford, Richard
    1988   'Creation in the Bible', in R. Russell *et al.* (eds.), *Physics, Philosophy,*
                and Theology (Vatican City: Vatican Observatory).
Derr, Thomas S.
    1975   *Ecology and Human Need* (Philadelphia: Fortress Press).
Derrick, Christopher
    1972   *The Delicate Creation* (London: Devon-Adair).
Eckberg, D., and T. Blocker
    1989   'Varieties of Religious Involvement and Environmental Concerns:
                Testing the Lynn White Thesis', *Journal for the Scientific Study of*
                Religion 28.4: 509-17.
Edwards, Denis
    1995   *Jesus the Wisdom of God: An Ecological Theology* (Maryknoll, NY:
                Orbis Books).
Erlich, Paul
    1971   *How to Be a Survivor* (New York: Ballentine).
Faricy, Robert
    1981   *All Things in Christ* (London: Collins).
Hamilton, Michael
    1970   *This Little Planet* (New York: Scribner).
Hardin, Garrett
    1980   'Ecology and the Death of Providence', *Zygon* 15: 57-68.
Haught, John F.
    1993   *The Promise of Nature: Ecology and Cosmic Purpose* (New York:
                Paulist Press).
Marietta, Don E., Jr
    1977   'Religious Models and Ecological Decision Making', *Zygon* 12: 151-
                66.
Marx, Leo
    1970   'American Institutions and Ecological Ideals', *Science* 170: 945-52.
Montefiore, Hugh
    1977   'Man and Nature: A Theological Assessment', *Zygon* 12: 199-211.
Moss, Rowland
    1978   'God, Man, and Nature', *The Teilhard Review* 13: 89-103.
Nicholson, Max
    1969   *The Environmental Revolution* (London: Hodder & Stoughton).
Passmore, John
    1974   *Man's Responsibility for Nature* (London: Gerald Duckworth).
Santmire, H. Paul
    1970   *Brother Earth: Nature, God, and Ecology in Time of Crisis* (New York:
                Nelson).
    1985   *The Travail of Nature* (London: Fortress Press).
Sittler, Joseph
    1970   *The Ecology of Faith* (Philadelphia: Fortress Press).
Swanson, Guy
    1967   *Religion and Regime* (Ann Arbor: University of Michigan Press).

Teilhard de Chardin, Pierre
    1955   *Le phénomène humain* (Paris: Seuil).

1956   'L'apport spirituel de l'Extreme-Orient: quelques reflexions per-
          sonnelles', *Monumenta Nipponica* 12: 1-11.
1959   *The Phenomenon of Man* (trans. Bernard Wall; New York: Harper &
          Row).
1961   *Hymne de l'univers* (Paris: Seuil).
1962   *L'énergie humaine* (Paris: Seuil).
1965a   *L'activation de l'énergie* (Paris: Seuil).
1965b   *Ecrits du temps de la guerre* (Paris: Grasset)
1969   *Comment je crois* (Paris: Seuil).
1975   *Journal* (ed. N. and K. Schmitz-Moorman; Paris: Fayard).
1976   *Le coeur de la matière* (Paris: Seuil).
Trennert-Hellwig, M.
1993   *Die Urkraft des Kosmos* (Freiburg: Herder).
White, Lynn
1967   'The Historical Roots of Our Ecological Crisis', *Science* 155 (March
          10): 1203-1207; frequently reprinted, for example in F. Schaeffer,
          Pollution and the Death of Man (Wheaton, IL: Tyndale, 1970).

Part IV

TEILHARD AND ENVIRONMENTAL RESPONSIBILITY

8

Our Environmental Responsibilities in Light of Contemporary Cosmology: A Teilhardian Retrospect

Richard W. Kropf

1. *Introduction*

Despite his eye for both details of nature as well as his ability to grasp the broad lines of evolution, few would credit the Jesuit paleontologist Pierre Teilhard de Chardin (1881–1955) as having been an environmentalist or ecological pioneer. His view of the appearance of the human species at the 'summit' of vertebrate evolution, his celebration of reflective thought (apparently unique to humans) as the crossing of a threshold beyond the capacities of the rest of the animal kingdom, his optimistic acceptance of technology (including the advent of nuclear power), all this seems to place him squarely within the mood of modernity characteristic of the first half of the twentieth century. This seems in stark contrast to the disillusionment of the post-modern era which, after the failure of two wars 'to end all wars', has given rise to contemporary ecological consciousness.

The extent to which cosmology — defined as that branch of physics that has to do with theories about the origin, evolution, present state, and likely future of the Universe — may seem to have little immediate import to the subject of ecology, understood as 'the scientific study of the interactions of organisms with their environment, including the physical environment and other organisms living in it' (E.O . Wilson 1992: 380). But if we are to believe Martin Rees, Great Britain's current 'Astronomer Royal', cosmology has a great deal to say not only about the long term future of the universe, but also about the short term prospects for the continuation of life on Earth. In his 2003 book *Our Final Hour: A Scientist's Warning: How Terror, Error, and Environ-*

mental Disaster Threaten Humankind's Future – in This Century and Beyond, Rees sees us as almost certainly destroying the ability of earth to sustain life much beyond the year 2100 and that unless we begin to colonize the planet Mars by the year 2050, we shall surely be too late to prolong the existence of the human race.

However, even this adventuresome prospect raises troubling questions for us here on planet Earth. Recent discoveries, both by a European spacecraft orbiting Mars and by the US National Aeronautic and Space Agency (NASA) employing robot-operated vehicles on that planet's surface, appear to confirm that Mars at one time contained, at least in places, copious amounts of water. If so, this latest discovery would seem to help back up the claims made back in 1996, but which still remain disputed, of what some believe to be fossilized traces of primitive life in a Martian meteorite discovered in Antarctica.

A similar question looms regarding the planet Venus, our other nearest neighbor in planetary space. As a result of exploration by various orbiting vehicles and probes, some, according to *The Cambridge Atlas of Astronomy* (Adouze *et al.* 1988: 73-74), have theorized that Venus once had a considerable amount of water before a runaway greenhouse effect raised the temperature of that planet's surface to approximately 760°K, considerably hotter than Mars, which is much closer to the Sun (the Earth's mean temperature is about 250°K and Mars about 230°K). The present Venutian atmosphere is 97% carbon dioxide laced with considerable amounts of sulfur dioxide – the principal component of 'acid rain'. If so, the implications regarding the history of life, and its likelihood elsewhere in the Universe, are immense. If some form of life, no matter how simple, once existed on Mars, and perhaps even on Venus, and now no longer does, what might this have to say about the future of life on our own planet?

2. Cosmological and Theological Perspectives

That cosmology and theology have been often closely linked – much too closely for many scientists' comfort – is an historical fact of life. For a long period of time, before the advent of the scientific age, cosmological speculation was closely bound to cosmogenies or religious accounts or stories that accounted for the origin of the Universe. Ecology, if back then it existed as a 'science' at all, was clearly subsumed within the prevailing cosmo-theological outlook. Yet, as we shall see, there have always been, at least a few thinkers, even among theologians, who questioned the prevailing assumptions.

2.1. *Theological Speculations*

Despite the geocentric cosmogeny assumed by the author(s) of Genesis, particularly the anthropocentric view of nature given by the second (Jahwist) account of creation, at least some Christian theologians had long been speculating about the possibility of life elsewhere in the Universe. Indeed, one of the very earliest among them, Origen of Alexandria (c. 185–c. 254), thought that the stars might be the home of other intelligent beings, and although many similar ideas of Origen were long held in suspicion, Origen's views were not forgotten. How much Origen's speculations in this realm, but transposed into more angelic roles, are reflected in *The Celestial Hierarchies* and other mystical writings of the still unidentified (but probably a fifth or sixth century Syrian monk) author known to us as 'Pseudo-Dionysius' or incorporated into the *Periphysion* of the peripatetic ninth-century Irish scholar John Scotus Eriugena is hard to say, but by the fifteenth century, the Franciscan theologian William of Vaurouillon (1392–1463) was contesting the long-prevailing view, held by the Dominicans who followed their master Thomas Aquinas, that the Earth was the focal point of *all* of God's creative and redemptive activity.

However, following the implications of the arguments presented by the Polish cleric and mathematician Nicholas Copernicus (1473–1543), two other Dominican scholars, Giordano Bruno (1548–1600) and Thomas of Campanella (1568–1639), reversed course from their order's champion and declared their belief that the Universe may harbor life elsewhere (O'Meara, 1999: 6). However it was not this belief that cost Bruno his life at the hands of the Inquisition, despite the Church's condemnation of the Copernican theory in 1616 and the official silencing of Galileo in 1632. Although the trial transcripts are said to have been lost, it is much more likely that the heresies for which Bruno was executed were his pantheistic leanings and denial of the doctrine of the Holy Trinity.

Nevertheless, the issue raised by such speculations, of course, should be fairly obvious, at least in terms of specifically Christian theology. For more traditional Christians, the idea that God may have created life, especially intelligent life, elsewhere, raises serious questions about the adequacy of the whole Christian understanding of humanity's uniqueness, and especially the doctrine of the Fall (Original Sin) and the need for redemption, and hence, the belief in Jesus Christ as the universal Redeemer.

As a result, it should be no surprise that this latter issue seems to have been the principal concern raised in Teilhard's mind as far back as 1920 in his essay 'Fall, Redemption and Geocentrism' (Teilhard de Chardin 1971: 38, 44) and yet again, as late in his life as 1953 in a theological reflection titled 'A Sequel to the Problem of Human Origins: The Plurality of Inhabited Worlds' (1971: 229-36). This was in addition to the obvious difficulties presented by the doctrine of Original Sin to any evolutionary thinker. Teilhard's interest in this question had been increasing all along, especially after the confirmation by astronomer Edmund Hubble, in the 1920s, that many of the various 'spiral nebulae', long suspected as far back as the philosopher Immanuel Kant and by astronomers like William Hershel to be other galaxies similar to our own 'Milky Way', were indeed such. Even more astounding was the conclusion that these galaxies, generally speaking, are receding from each other at tremendous rates of speed, which was contrary to Einstein's (and practically everyone else's) view of a steady state universe. This confirmed the views of the Russian meteorologist Alexander Feinman and the Belgian cleric and mathematician Georges Lemaître, who independently but nearly simultaneously arrived at what has since been termed — somewhat derisively by Cambridge physicist Fred Hoyle — 'The Big Bang' version of the Universe. All these developments were followed by Teilhard with a great amount of interest (see the note added on pp. 47-48 of Teilhard de Chardin 1959), and to an extent not generally realized influenced a great deal of his own theological thinking — particularly his speculations, later in life, regarding a possible 'Third [i.e. Cosmic] Nature' of Christ.

2.2. *The Expanding Universe*

Since then the Big Bang scenario has been further refined first by Alan Guth's initial 'inflation theory' and confirmed by various other findings, for example, the evidence from the COBE satellite and other even more exact microwave background studies. In addition, further astronomical data, much of it collected during the 1990s from observations of Type 1A supernovae, have not only corrected much of Hubble's early estimates of the expansion rate of the Universe, but have even yielded data that seems to indicate that at present, some 13.7 (plus or minus 5%) billion years after the settling down of the expansion after the first few moments of initial inflation, the expansion rate of the Universe is increasing, all but eliminating the possibility of the Big Bang ever reverting into a 'Big Crunch'. This in turn eliminates the possibility that our Universe can ever be seen as recycling itself in some way to somehow prolong or repeat its existence. Although others have been toying with various 'multiverse' theories — as has the Russian-born physicist Andrei Linde, who has been proposing a new 'eternal chaotic inflation' model to supplement Big Bang theory in a way that might allow for the existence of both simultaneous or even sequential 'universes' (Alspach 2004: 1, 3) — it should be noted that many scientists, such as Eric Chaisson in his 2001 book, *Cosmic Evolution: The Rise of Complexity in Nature*, still reject such 'multiverse' ideas as 'bizarre' and belonging to the realm of 'science fiction' (Chaisson 2001: 9-10). Nevertheless, could such 'multiverse' theories, which Rees seems to have taken seriously in his earlier (2001) book, *Our Cosmic Habitat*, have any bearing on the future of our own? Considering that, none of these theories, unlike the kind of reciprocating universes once advocated by Hoyle, propose the recycling of the energy-matter or even necessarily repeats the laws or characteristics of nature with which we are familiar, such other 'universes' would appear to be totally irrelevant to our particular world. Yet the appearance of Rees' more recent book in 2003 (which he originally wished to title 'Our Final Century', but was overruled by his American publisher) would seem to indicate that there just might be some connection. But what exactly is it? Perhaps that question, and any possible answer to it must wait until we have considered our own more immediate fate.

2.3. *The Dying Sun*
Similar to the 'heat death' predicted for our Universe, but in a much more rapid and spectacular manner, the Sun, from whose protoplanetary disc planet Earth most likely took its origin, and which remains its principal source of physical energy, is itself, like most other stars of its size within the main sequence of stellar evolution, roughly halfway through its life-span of approximately 10 billion years. This means that the Earth itself will become increasingly uninhabitable as the Sun evolves towards its 'red giant' phase, culminating in an expansion that will engulf all the inner planets and possibly the Earth as well, before the Sun, nearly as suddenly, begins to shrink to the state of becoming a 'white dwarf ' (with the loss of about half its matter and energy) and then eventually a cold 'black dwarf' — in other words, a dead cinder in space (Adouze *et al.* [eds.] 1988: 25). So while the Universe (at least our universe) as a whole will die from lack of heat, the ultimate fate of our planet could be quite the opposite. Meanwhile, recent studies of the variations in the Earth's magnetic field, and what seems to be a puzzling decrease in its overall

strength, believed to be due to the cooling of its core, suggest the possible stripping away of the Earth's atmosphere by solar radiation. Much the same may have happened to Mars long ago, due to the fact that its smaller size (approximately half the diameter of Earth and with only about one tenth of its mass) allowed the core of Mars to cool much more quickly.

2.4. *The End of Our Universe*

The implications from all of this for the whole future of evolution on our planet are enormous. In a lecture on 'Life and the Planets' that Teilhard gave in 1945 at the French Embassy in Bejing, he quoted the British Astronomer Royal, Sir James Jeans, who had asked (and answered):

> What does life amount to? We have tumbled, as through in error, into a universe which by all the evidence was not intended for us. We cling to a fragment of a grain of sand until such a time as the chill of death shall return us to primal matter. We strut for a tiny moment on a tiny stage, well knowing that all our aspirations are doomed to ultimate failure and that everything we have achieved will perish with our race, leaving the Universe as though we had never existed... The Universe is indifferent and even hostile to every kind of life. (Teilhard de Chardin 1964: 104)

Not that Teilhard himself (like Jeans) did not protest such an interpretation of life, but his use of the quotation served to underline the inevitability of the then prevailing (and now seemingly reconfirmed) 'heat death' view of the eventual fate of our Universe. It is also the view that forms the cosmological backdrop to Teilhard's view of evolution. It is a view that Teilhard spelled out time and time again in many of his essays, but perhaps can be seen in its broadest perspectives in his most well-known work, *Le phénomène humain/The Phenomenon of Man* (1959). In it, Teilhard generally defined evolution in terms of increasingly organized complexity leading in the direction of increased consciousness (and spontaneity) in the face of or contrary to the overall tendency of matter or energy to expend itself in the increase of *Entropy*.

This term (coined by the physicist R.J.E. Clausius in the early nineteenth century) is expressed in the Second Law of Thermodynamics, and holds that in a closed system, disorder inevitably increases, thus decreasing the amount of energy available for 'useful work'. In other words, the First Law of Thermodynamics (that of the 'Conservation of Energy') paradoxically, at least on the cosmic scale, appears to be contradicted by the Second Law of Thermodynamics. The key to the paradox, of course, lies in our interpretation of what we mean by a 'closed' system. While we may not think of our Universe as 'closed' (at least in terms of space, that is, if it is continually expanding), still, in terms of the lack of input of any new energy since the Big Bang, the same situation, according to the latest findings and predictions, appears to apply as well to the Universe as a whole. So too, according to Teilhard:

> The more the energy quantum of the world comes into play, the more it is consumed. Within the scope of our experience, the material concrete universe seems to be unable to continue its way indefinitely in a closed circle, but traces out irreversibly a curve of obviously limited development. And thus it is that this Universe differentiates itself from purely abstract magnitudes and places itself among the realities which are born, which grow, and which die. (Teilhard de Chardin 1959: 51)

> Moreover, the same wearing away that is gradually consuming the cosmos in its totality is at work within terms of the synthesis, and the higher the terms the quicker this action takes place. Little by little, the *improbable* combinations that they represent become broken down again into more simple components, which fall back and are disaggregated in the shapelessness of *probable* distributions. (1959: 52)

All this, he then went on to compare to 'A rocket rising in the wake of time's arrow, that only bursts to be extinguished; and eddy rising on the bosom of a descending current—such then must be our picture of the world' (1959: 52). Such a picture would seem to echo not only that of the astronomer Jeans, but, in addition, is duplicated by the philosopher Bertrand Russell.

> That Man is the product of causes which had no prevision of the end they were achieving; that his origin, his growth, his hopes and fears, his loves and his beliefs, are but the outcome of accidental collocations of atoms; that no fire, no heroism, no intensity of thought and feeling, can preserve an individual life beyond the grave; that all the labours of the ages, all the devotion, all the inspiration, all the noonday brightness of human genius, are destined to extinction in the vast death of the solar system, and the whole temple of Man's achievement must be buried beneath the debris of a universe in ruins—all these things, if not quite beyond dispute, are yet so nearly certain, that no philosophy which rejects them can hope to stand. (Bertrand Russell, *A Free Man's Worship*, cited in Adler and Van Doren 1977: 985)[1]

If this is the case, and human evolution, as well as the biological evolution that has given it rise, while they can be seen as anti-entropic eddies or even as islands of creativity in an expanding yet dying Universe, are themselves ultimately and equally doomed, what then

---

1. The full text of Bertrand Russell, *A Free Man's Worship*, can be found in Russell (1903).

should be our response? Must not a cosmic sense of pessimism prevail? Yet despite this, Teilhard seems never to have given in to the kind of pessimism evidenced by Jeans or Russell. Why not?

3. *The Grand Options and Their Ecological Implications*

While Teilhard can never be said to have been unaware of the possibility of an ecological crisis in the offing, his earliest reference to it seems to have been, if any thing, cheerily optimistic. Thus in his long 1937 essay on 'Human Energy', he at most made a passing reference to the growing need for additional sources of physical energy asking: 'After coal, water, oil, what next?' and then answered that 'We can place our trust in physics' (Teilhard de Chardin 1969: 132) — hardly a reassuring answer for us today.

But to understand this optimism and his insistence upon it, we need to turn to a somewhat shorter essay, one which I consider of much greater importance because of what seems to be its sweeping generalizations, but which provides, I think, a much better context within which to situate Teilhard's more immediate concerns. That essay, 'Le Grand Option', first written in 1939 at the brink of the Second World War, did not appear in print until 1945 after his return to Paris and after the liberation, in a publication significantly titled *Cahiers du Monde Nouveau*. It is this essay, in particular, that gives us a better grasp or view of existential choices before us.

The option or choice that Teilhard puts before us is actually *three-fold*: optimism vs. pessimism; withdrawal vs. engagement; and finally, individualism vs. solidarity. Although these choices are couched in terms of humanity's response to the social pressures of a planet that is rapidly approaching its limits as far as its human carrying capacity — what Teilhard called the 'planetization' of humanity — the environmental aspects of this phenomenon are inescapable. Accordingly, rather than concentrate, as Teilhard did, on the structuring of human society and its political and economic structures in particular, although these too are not without their ecological impacts, what is suggested here is that we apply these same choices in a way that speaks more directly to our environmental concerns.

However, to better situate these three fundamental choices within the environmental context, we should first examine a fairly short article on 'The Directions and Conditions of the Future', written in 1948 (Teilhard de Chardin 1964: 227-37), in which Teilhard recognized that not only were there certain tendencies at work (social unification, technology, and 'rationalisation' — this latter being an urge to not only know more but master more), but also certain *conditions* that must be observed if these tendencies are to achieve their aims.

The first of these conditions has to do with 'Survival' or the health of the planet itself. While his emphasis was, as always, on the 'Conditions of Synthesis', by which he meant fostering the psychic atmosphere by which and in which people can learn to live cooperatively in greater numbers and where he (always the optimist) believed that science might provide substitutes for our diminishing stock of non-renewable resources, he was less sanguine about its chances in feeding a burgeoning population. Indeed, when it came to the 'Conditions of Health', Teilhard was not at all sure that we could ignore the problematic subject of eugenics. In other words, he was concerned about *quality* of the species in the face of the specter of runaway population growth. He had already touched upon these subjects (particularly that of eugenics and population control) especially in his long 1937 essay 'Human Energy' (Teilhard de Chardin 1969: 132-33) and mentioned them yet again in a short 1949 essay on 'The Sense of Species in Man' (Teilhard de Chardin 1970: 199-203). A year later, in his essay on 'The Evolution of Responsibility in the World', Teilhard spoke of what he described as 'a dangerous and distressing situation, inasmuch as it presents us with a whole world of vital problems: food supplies, health, the easing of the nervous strain suffered by a vast number of human beings brought into such close proximity...' All this is the result of what Teilhard called 'planetary compression' or the effect of the world's rising population, but which he also saw as 'an impressive dynamic power which can produce, together with a great deal of suffering and many mistakes, an intense spiritual energy' and which includes, besides a sense of 'solidarity', and 'a sort of generalized ultra-responsibility' (Teilhard de Chardin 1970: 212). But what would such a sense of solidarity mean for us in terms of our ecological responsibilities?

Although Teihard's language went far beyond that of more recent thinkers on this subject, still, we can find some of it echoed by Eric Chaisson, even though he seems to go out of his way to disclaim any anthropocentric claims and forswears any agenda of 'progress'. Like Teilhard, Chaisson nevertheless aims 'to frame a heritage — a cosmic heritage — a grand scheme of understanding in events of the past, a sweeping intellectual map embraced by humans of the present, a virtual blueprint for survival along the arrow of time...' admitting that 'The objective, boldly stated, is nothing less than a holistic cosmology in which life not only has a place in the Universe, but perhaps a significant role to play as well' (Chaisson 2001: 5). Thus Chaisson, like Teilhard, definitely sees humankind bearing the weight of responsibility for the future, at least for our small part of the Universe, holding that 'Humankind is now largely in charge of life on Earth; controlling most events, making key decisions, doing the selecting' (Chaisson 2001: 207) and that 'only with an awareness and appreciation of the bigger picture can we survive long enough to experience the Life Era, thereby playing a significant role in our own cosmic-evolutionary worldview' (Chaisson 2001: 208).

With these responsibilities in mind, let us now move on to the more general options or attitudes that Teilhard outlined.

3.1. *First Option: Pessimism vs. Optimism*

The most pessimistic book in the Bible, *Qoheleth* or Ecclesiastes, with its cyclical view of time (rather unique among all biblical literature) and its melancholy refrain of there being 'nothing new under the sun', nevertheless seems to assume our Sun will always be around to warm our life, no matter how short and how uncertain our own end. But as we have seen, science tells us that even the Sun is of limited duration. The first option that faces us then, is what attitude to take in the face of an inherently limited future, not just for humans as individuals, but as a race, along with all forms of life on planet Earth.

When we think of pessimism in its rawest form, we are apt to think, as did Teilhard, of the kind of Sartrian existentialism posed by Albert Camus in his typifying suicide as the ultimate question. Is life tolerable or worth the effort in a doomed universe? Ecologically speaking, the pessimistic picture drawn by Jeans and Russell would prevail. Faced with such a picture, Teilhard asked (and noted): 'Is the Universe utterly pointless, or are we to accept that it has a meaning, a future, a purpose?' (Teilhard de Chardin 1964: 42) and then added:

> On this fundamental question Mankind is already virtually divided into the two camps of those who deny that there is any significance or value in the state of Being and therefore no Progress; and those, on the other hand, who believe in the possibility and rewards of a higher stage of consciousness.
>
> For the first only one attitude is possible: a refusal to go further, desertion which is equivalent to turning back. For these no further problem arises, since they are lodged in incoherence and disintregation. We may leave them there. (Teilhard de Chardin 1964: 42-43)

These apparently harsh and dismissive words may distress many environmentalists, especially those who see environmentalism as dedicated to preserving what appears to be (and certainly is) a delicate balance, a balance that has been severely disrupted by the overwhelming presence of the human species. Teilhard's equation of 'meaning' with progress, in particular, many may also find disturbing—as if the worth of anything in nature is strictly a question of human value judgment.

However, we must also ask this question: apart from any human judgment on the matter (if such an objective statement be possible at all) must we not also conclude with the philosopher Whitehead (and one-time collaborator between 1910 and 1913 with Russell in their *Principia Mathematica* [Whitehead and Russell 1962]) that *conservationism*, understood as a kind of 'preservationism' is impossible?

> The foundation of all understanding…is that no static maintenance of perfection is possible. This axiom is rooted in the nature of things. Advance or Decadence are the only choices offered to mankind. The pure conservative is fighting against the essence of the universe. (Whitehead 1933: XIX, 2)

In other words, if we may make what may seem to be an equally harsh observation, playing this time on Whitehead's, not Teilhard's words, conservationism understood as pure preservationism is itself contrary to nature. So if we are being forced to make a choice in the face of the inevitable, optimism would counsel us, it would seem at the very least, to make the best of whatever change is inevitable.

But what sort of optimism? Should it be a kind of devil-may-care parody of *Qoheleth's* counter-refrain: 'There is no happiness for man but to eat and drink and be content with his work' (Eccl. 2.23, compare also with Eccl. 5.17; 8.15; 9.7)? How does this compare to the Epicurean slogan of 'Eat, drink and be merry, for tomorrow we (all and everything) will die' or its contemporary counterparts, as seen, for example, in many persons' (and even some nations') reaction to global warming? Or should it be an optimism which believes that humans, as responsible shapers of the future course of evolution, should be engaged in a collective effort to stabilize as much as possible what may seem to be an inevitable change in climate? Or at the very least, must we not cease to exacerbate it by irresponsible consumption of fossil fuels?

Again, Teilhard does not seem to have been impressed by any sense of crisis or impending doom. Indeed, for him the fear was that humanity would run out of *psychic* or *spiritual* energy long before it exhausted the sources of physical energy. In December 1948, Teilhard stated the issue thus:

> The problem—the spectre, I might say—of the earth's reserves of energy and food is widely, and rightly, canvassed. There is just one thing, however, which is forgotten: it is a point which I have been emphasizing for

> years. Mark my word: though man stands on great stacks of wheat, on oceans of oil, he will cease to develop his unity, and he will perish, if he does not watch over and foster in the first place the source of psychic energy which maintains in him the passion for action and knowledge — which means for growing greater and evolving — from which comes unity of mind. ('Psychological Conditions for the Unification of Man' [Teilhard de Chardin 1970: 172])

Action, knowledge, unity: these are Teilhard's overriding concerns. Without these qualities, optimism counts little.

3.2. *Second Option: Withdrawal vs. Engagement*

By 'withdrawal' Teilhard seems to have had in mind various 'oriental' philosophies and other forms of contemplative life that believes that the way to higher consciousness is to be found by following those 'who see our true progress only in terms of a break, as speedy as possible, with the world...' Contrasted with these are those who see 'some ultimate value in the tangible evolution of things' and for whom '(the true optimists), the tasks and difficulties of the present day by no means signify that we have come to an impasse in our evolution' (Teilhard de Chardin 1964: 44).

Hence, in a very short essay, titled 'The Sense of Species in Man', which followed by only a few months the one addressing the 'Psychological Conditions' necessary for humanity's unification, Teilhard insisted:

> that modern man...must reject as an illusion that he can reach the peak of his own fundamental being in isolation, egotistically, 'individualistically'... There is no way out, therefore, open towards our individual drive towards survival and super-life, other than to resolutely plunge back into the general current from which we thought, for a moment, to escape. (Teilhard de Chardin 1970: 201-202)

Again, translated into ecological or environmental stances or strategies, it seems to me that again we may find parallels. For example, if nature is truly always in a state of flux, is it enough for humanity simply to sit back and 'wash its hands', so to speak, as if we have no active role to play in the future course of nature? The kind of metaphysical dualism that has so severely separated the concept of 'spirit' from that of 'matter' (and against which Teilhard fought in practically all his thinking and writing) I believe does have its ecological counterpart — even if it is more in psychological rather than philosophical terms.

For example, when environmentalists would prefer to always 'let nature take its course', does not that very phraseology give evidence of a mind-set that sees humanity itself as somehow apart from or divorced from nature? Granted that the human species does show certain characteristics that do set it apart from, and sometimes even at odds with, the rest of nature. But does this mean, metaphysically, that we exist *apart* from nature? Instead, what I am suggesting (and which I think was implicit in Teilhard's thinking) is that the origin of what has been so much short-sighted and ecologically devastating human activity has been the kind of metaphysical dualism (often accompanied by a simplistic ethical dualism) that has separated humanity from it's material matrix.

Instead, if humans are to be ecologically responsible, we must see ourselves as a part of the natural world and as an extension of the evolutionary process. If, as Teilhard said, 'God *does not make*: He *makes things make themselves*' (Teilhard de Chardin 1971: 28), then we must realize that this co-creative activity can only be accomplished in concert with the natural world through which we have received and on which we depend for our existence.

3.3. *Third Option: Plurality or Unity (for One or for Many)?*
This, I believe, brings us to the most sensitive issue that has to be faced by environmentalists. Evolution, as we have known it, has resulted in a great plurality of life forms, a great variety of species, which to some degree are mutually interdependent. Nonetheless, the great evolutionary 'leap forward' that has taken place with the advent of the human species has been accomplished not so much by the physical emergence of the human type but rather by the social-psychological breakthrough occasioned by the advent of reflective thought. This, in turn, has allowed human evolution to progress not so much along simply the Darwinian pattern (selective transmission of randomly acquired characteristics) but even along the otherwise discredited Lamarckian pattern of the inheritance, at least through cultural transmission, of deliberately acquired traits. But this latter, it seems, is only accomplished within a *society*. Animals know, and certainly can, to some limited extent, pass on that knowledge to their offspring. But it is only humans, in 'knowing that they know', who can evolve the cultural institutions necessary for the exponential increase of that knowledge.

It is in this latter phenomenon that a decisive role is taken by Teilhard's concept of 'planetization', that is, the convergence of humanity, and with it, the convergence and resulting interaction of reflective thought upon the curved surface of the Earth. For as long as the first human groups, existing in a hunter-gatherer stage of development, were obliged to continually spread themselves thinly across the face of the planet in order to find sustenance, civilization, as we think of it, could barely gain a foothold. It is only when people were able to, or were even forced by dint of their circumstances (declining game populations, etc.) to domesticate animals, or even more importantly, plants, that the kind of settled life that eventually gave rise to the kind of division of labor and specialization that goes with it, that the great civilizations of the past could be established. And it is primarily because the planet earth is the shape it is, that these civilizations are now being forced, whether they care to or not, despite the vast oceans that separate the continents, to interact with each other. It is thus that the 'noosphere' (the thinking layer analogous to the biosphere) as Teilhard termed it, is gradually being thickened, as it were, over the surface of the planet. But as the lessons of the past century should have taught us by now, in the face of this phenomenon, that either we learn to work together for the benefit of all peoples, or else we shall surely end up destroying humankind itself.

It is not only, as the poet John Dunne put it, that 'No man is an island'; neither can any one civilization successfully isolate itself. This realization is, of course, also in part behind the logic (if not always the motivation) of the drive towards 'globalization', even if, unfortunately, the current economic practices being employed are still wedded to what some have called 'flat earth' economics – the idea that there are always more resources (and people) to be exploited or 'developed' in the service of an ever-expanding economy. On the contrary, true 'globalization' can only be carried out with images of the earth-to-moon travel pictures of 'spaceship earth' firmly fixed in our mind. If any optimism is possible, it has to be an optimism that has to be engaged for the good of all. In the end, then, it would seem that an environmental ethic, at least from a Teilhardian point of view, has to be one in which like Bentham's utilitarian ethic, seeks the greatest amount of happiness for the greatest number of people – at least for the time being. But, we must ask, to what end?

4. *The Final Question*

After facing the first and second options (pessimism vs. optimism and withdrawal vs. engagement) we asked ourselves if this all be for the sake of a plurality of individuals (and with it a heightened sense of individualism) or whether it shall be in the service of a higher unity that incorporates, as it were, the many. If it is for the latter, what then is the source of the dynamism that makes such unity possible? Teilhard had already spoken at length on numerous occasions (much more than the few cited above) about absolute need for our sense of solidarity with and rootedness in the earth that is a matrix of our very existence. But to what end? Does evolution itself have a goal? This, it seems to me, is the *ultimate* question.

In 1951, in a short note for *Semaine des Intellectuels catholique*, with a long title 'Can Biology, Taken to its Extreme Limit, Enable Us to Emerge into the Transcendent?', Teilhard wrote:

> Although we often forget this, what we call evolution develops only in virtue of a certain internal preference for survival (or if you prefer to put it so, for self-survival) which in man takes a markedly psychic appearance, in the form of a *zest for life*. Ultimately, it is that and that alone which underlies and supports the whole complex of bio-physical energies whose operation, acting experimentally, conditions anthropogenesis. (Teilhard de Chardin 1968: 212)

While this 'zest for life' may sound suspiciously like Bergson's *élan vital* and the 'vitalism' associated with it, a paragraph or so later Teilhard spoke in terms more reminiscent of Julian Huxley's description of humanity as 'evolution conscious of itself'.

> That can mean only one thing: that by becoming reflective the evolutionary process *can continue only if it sees that it is irreversible, in other words, transcendent*: since the complete irreversibility of a physical magnitude, in as much as it implies escape from conditions productive of disintegration which are proper to time and space, is simply the biological expression of transcendence. (1968: 213 [emphasis by Teilhard])

Thus, in 1953, in an essay titled 'The Activation of Human Energy' Teilhard spent two pages — more than he ever had before — totaling up the physical and environmental threats to our continued existence as a species, only to reassert his earlier conviction that 'Physical resources will not fail us' (Teilhard de Chardin 1970: 389). But again, he questions as to whether or not courage or psychic resources will run short. The basis for this question is Teilhard's belief that humans are the only creatures whose response 'is not confined to the perception of an immediate end, but comes from a confrontation with the whole of the future' (1970: 391). In other words, the question of an open vs. closed future, or as Teilhard puts it, 'An open world? or closed world? A world that ultimately opens out into some fuller-life? or a world that in the end falls back, with its full weight?' (1970: 391).

This I believe is the final question and the one which brings us back to the first — the choice between pessimism on the one hand or optimism on the other. Is there, in fact, a fundamental reason for all this optimism? Or is it, in the end, so much 'whistling in the dark'?

The reason that this final question can not be avoided is, according to Teilhard, that:

> ...from the moment when man recognizes that he is in a state of evolution, he can no longer progress (...) unless he develops in himself a deep-rooted, passionate zest for his own evolution: and there is the further reason that it is precisely this dynamic zest that could be vitiated beyond repair and annihilated by the prospect, however far ahead it may lie, of a definitive and total death. (Teilhard de Chardin 1970: 391)

True, as Teilhard admits, along with the growing sense of human solidarity and a sense of the future, it is possible, at least for a while, to stave off the doubts about the ultimate worth of human endeavor. This would certainly include, I would add, the efforts to ensure the viability of the earth as a home for humans for many, many generations to come. This sense of solidarity between the humans of today and those of the future is, as Teilhard was convinced, 'the belief – at least in theory – of the most intellectual, and the most idealistic... contemporary neo-humanists' (Teilhard de Chardin 1970: 399).

But is it a belief that can stand up to serious scientific investigation? Teilhard believed not. Instead what he saw was 'perhaps two psychological species of man: of which one can enthusiastically pursue what is no more than "temporary", while the other cannot commit himself (like Thucydides long ago) to anything that will not be "for ever"' (Teilhard de Chardin 1970: 402).

Here, of course, we are back to the primary cosmological question. Are we in a 'closed' (at least in the sense of time) universe or an 'open' one? As Teilhard saw it, unless evolution takes us over and beyond a further threshold or evolutionary break-through, that of the emergence of the *spirit,* the universe whether infinitely expanding or collapsing upon itself, the result is the same.

> Today, ninety-nine percent of men, perhaps, still fancy that they can breathe freely this side of an unbreakable death-barrier – provided it is thought of to be sufficiently far away. Tomorrow (...) mankind would be possessed by a sort of panic claustrophobia simply at the idea that it might find itself hermetically sealed inside a closed universe. (Teilhard de Chardin 1970: 403)

That observation was written only about three months before Teilhard's death some 50 years ago. Today, this same sense, even when expanded, or shrunk (depending on how you look at it) to our cosmic neighborhood, raises serious questions, even for the most dedicated of environmentalists. If our two nearest neighbors in space turn out to have once had life, but can not sustain it, even in its most elementary forms, what would this say to us, even apart from whatever we do (or fail to do) that might exacerbate the looming crisis on our own planet?

If, on the other hand, there is likely to have been a similar pattern of evolution — perhaps in countless other variations — on countless other planets circling myriads of other sun-like stars in this vast Universe (or even in other 'universes') can we reasonably believe, as did Teilhard, that the Creator has invested any special significance or value in the evolution of the human race that would save us from our own self-destruction? According to Claude Cuenot, Teilhard's first official biographer, in an informal debate with the Dominican scholar, D. Dubarle, when he arrived back in Paris in 1946, Teilhard affirmed his faith in God not allowing the Earth to be destroyed by a stray comet (Cuenot 1965: 258). But will we succeed instead in destroying ourselves? It is questions like these (and not just a publisher's eye for sensationalism) that perhaps explain the note of urgency in Rees' book (2003), or even Chaisson's pleas for an increased sense of human responsibility for the future of Cosmic Evolution. And it is questions like these that make Teilhard's views of a half-century past more relevant than ever today.

5. *Conclusion*

My own reaction to this dilemma, I must confess, remains mixed. In terms of a strictly physical view of the universe, I sense in myself a kind of foreboding, a sort of pessimism regarding the future that echoes the ancient question: '*to what good?*' Of what lasting value are all our efforts worth? Even if the Universe is infinitely expanding (or even if it might be infinitely duplicating itself) what difference can this make to me (or to any of us) if our own little corner of the Universe, planet Earth, is itself doomed? If I am thinking only of myself and my own immediate world, my efforts to protect the environment often seem rather pointless, except in terms of my own self-gratification, or at most, in terms of the well-being of those whom I hold dear. Or, as an alternative, I could give a tragic, Zen-like value to what is passing, a poignant sense of infinitude to what is impermanent or what is eminently perishable — like the cherry blossom that flourishes a few short days and dies. But is that enough? Is it enough to sustain a lasting concern for this world of ours?

Years ago, when I was engaged in study at the *Fondation Teilhard de Chardin* in Paris, I had the opportunity to meet and talk with a Jesuit who had personally known Teilhard quite well. One question was very much on my mind: was Teilhard really as optimistic as his writings made him out to be? Having studied psychology at some length I suspected that much of Teilhard's celebrated optimism really disguised a profound pessimism. I was assured that (despite stories of his occasional bouts with anxiety and depression in his later years) that this was surely not the case. But I am still not completely convinced. So often his stated optimism seems to be too good, too buoyant, to be true. Even Teilhard, in his final testament, *Le Christique,* finished a month before his death, asked himself this triple question: 'Is there, in fact, a Universal Christ, is there a Divine Milieu? Or am I, after all, simply the dupe of a mirage in my own mind?' (Teilhard de Chardin 1978: 100).

Teilhard's answer to this harrowing self-questioning was to reaffirm what he believed was the *coherence, power,* and even (as he dared put it) the *superiority* of his vision, the reason being that it alone, in his estimation, combined the love of the Universe totally with the love of God – this because he envisioned the whole universe as *converging* upon Christ. This, of course, is the part of Teilhard's grand *pleromic* view of evolution, a vision of God, through Christ, becoming 'all in all', but which few, even among believers, can follow, much less fully grasp. Yet, it is, to my mind, the heart of Teilhard's whole vision, and for those who can grasp it (even occasional pessimists like me), it is the guarantee that the cultivation and preservation of this world, with its fragile environment, will not have been in vain.

References

Adler, Mortimer J., and Charles Van Doren
    1977   *The Great Treasury of Western Thought* (London/New York: R.R. Bowker).
Adouze, Jean, Guy Israël and Jean-Claude Falque (eds.)
    1988   *The Cambridge Atlas of Astronomy* (Cambridge: Cambridge University Press).
Alspach, K.
    2004   'Guth, Linde win Gruber Cosmology Prize', *Science and Theology News* 4(9) (May): 1, 3.
Chaisson, Eric
    2001   *Cosmic Evolution: The Rise of Complexity in Nature* (Cambridge, MA: Harvard University Press).
Cuenot, Claude
    1965   *Teilhard de Chardin: A Biography* (New York: Helicon).

O'Meara, Thomas
    1999   'Christian Theology and Extraterrestrial Intelligent Life', *Theo-
                logical Studies* 60.1: 3-30.
Rees, Martin
    2001   *Our Cosmic Habitat* (Princeton, NJ: Princeton University Press).
    2003   *Our Final Hour: A Scientist's Warning: How Terror, Error, and Environ-
                mental Disaster Threaten Humankind's Future – in This Century and
                Beyond* (New York: Basic Books).
Russell, Bertrand
    1903   *Mysticism and Logic* (London: George Allen & Unwin [2nd edn
                1917]).
Teilhard de Chardin, Pierre
    1959   *The Phenomenon of Man* (New York: Harper & Row)
    1964   *The Future of Man* (New York: Harper & Row).
    1968   *Science and Christ* (New York: Harper & Row)
    1969   *Human Energy* (New York: Harcourt Brace Jovanovich).
    1970   *The Activation of Energy* (New York: Harcourt Brace Jovanovich).
    1971   *Christianity & Evolution* (New York: Harcourt Brace Jovanovich).
    1978   *The Heart of Matter* (New York: Harcourt Brace Jovanovich).
Whitehead, Alfred North
    1933   *Adventures in Ideas* (New York: Free Press, 1972).
Whitehead, Alfred North, and B. Russell
    1962   *Principia Mathematica* (Cambridge: Cambridge University Press [1st
                edn 1910–13]).
Wilson, E.O.
    1992   *The Diversity of Life* (London: Penguin).

9

Teilhard de Chardin's Engagement with the Relationship between Science and Theology in Light of Discussions about Environmental Ethics*

Ludovico Galleni and Francesco Scalfari

Introduction

A new model of the interaction between Science and Religion, based upon the works of Pierre Teilhard de Chardin and his scientific research programme, has been recently presented (Galleni and Groessens Van Dyck 2001: 5-104; and forthcoming). A short summary of these papers is given in the first part of this contribution and then its consequences for environmental ethics and the Christian attitude towards the biosphere are discussed. Finally, there is a section exploring the future implications of Teilhard de Chardin's proposal.

The reason for the interest in Teilhard de Chardin's work is that he defined new relationships towards the Earth and the terrestrial realities within Christian theology, and for science, he provided the basis of the present day scientific understanding of the biosphere and its biological complexity. Recently a number of papers have been published which have rediscovered the importance of Teilhard de Chardin's theories and their relevance to environmental ethics (see Kureethadam 2003: 61-100). This paper is an initial attempt to propose a global synthesis of his view in the light of theoretical discussions of nature conservation.

*   The authors express their sincere thanks to Paola Grattarola for her English revision, to Lisa Goddard for further revisions to the English translation, and to Chris Corbally for helpful comments on the final text.

The Making of Teilhard's Scientific Research Programme

Teilhard de Chardin was a trained palaeontologist, geologist and palaeo-anthropologist who worked mainly in the first half of the twentieth century. He was well aware that the universe continued to change with time and that this evolution involved all aspects of the earth – matter, life, animals and humankind. Teilhard, however, was also a priest who lived out his religious vocation in the Jesuit order. In his diary, Teilhard compares his vocation to that of Cardinal Newman as both sought to bring to the Church what is good in the modern world (Teilhard de Chardin 1975: 90-91). For Teilhard, the novelty to be incorporated in ecclesiastical thinking was the evolutionary approach to life that he considered held deep ontological meaning for Creation Theology (Teilhard de Chardin 1975: 264). It is with credit to the theory of evolution that we presently regard the history of humankind, a history of alliance, of redemption and salvation, as being related to the entire universe. Evolution is no longer seen as an atheistic attack on Christian theology but as the natural landscape where the history of salvation is situated. Yet the impact of evolutionary theory on theology exceeded that of the Copernican system, and its interpretation required new models for the interaction of science and theology. Teilhard de Chardin was the first to put forward such models within which he proposed that evolution was a moving towards increasing complexity which culminated in the cerebralisation seen in humankind.

Despite the suggestions of some scientists, evolution cannot just be the space for contingency, existing without any purpose or preferential direction. Evolution has to be a moving towards – of matter toward complexity and life, of life toward cerebralisation and of cerebralisation toward the noosphere (a term defined by Teilhard de Chardin, together with Vladimir Vernadskij and Édouard Le Roy).

The biblical value of moving towards, of humankind's movement *towards* alliance and redemption, is then recovered within the more general movement of evolution *towards* humankind. It is of interest that the first evolutionary theory proposed by Lamarck was directly linked to the philosophical enlightenment value of progress, a moving toward, which became the metaphysical framework of this evolutionary theory (Ruse 1996).

In Teilhard de Chardin's synthesis, the moving toward was necessary for theology because of its eschatological perspective and became the basis for his experimental research programme. Teilhard decided to study the evolution of animals looking for parallelisms and canalizations as the main outcome among these parallelisms seemed to be an increased brain size. This research programme asked for a different approach from geologists and palaeontologists. During the First World War Teilhard de Chardin corresponded by letter with Jean Boussac who was then Professor of Geology at the 'Institut Catholique de Paris'. They both argued that reductionism was insufficient and that a different approach to Geology, a holistic perspective, was necessary. This would require a different attitude toward science and a global interaction of science with all the other ways of knowing. It is curious and fascinating that it was the Professor of Geology who suggested to Teilhard, the priest, that he read the pages of the mystic Angela di Foligno.[1]

After the First World War, Teilhard de Chardin returned to the *Institut de Paléontologie Humaine* in Paris to work with Marcellin Boule. His experimental research was dedicated to the description of a group of fossil mammals of French fauna and their patterns of evolution. It is here that we first see the hints of his scientific research programme. He believed that the necessity of the emergence of humankind would leave traces that could be recovered by palaeontological investigations. There would be a moving towards increased brain size and complexity in many different animal phyla. The main parallelism that he looked for was the common evolution of separated branches toward cerebralisation.

After his doctoral thesis, he put forward the evidence for this phenomenon in a paper on the evolution of a small group of primates, the Tarsidae (Teilhard de Chardin 1971: 221-46.). This paper is one of his first scientific publications as a trained palaeontologist and here he introduces his view of a general movement of animal evolution toward cerebralisation. In Paris, after the First World War, he started his teaching duties in the '*Institut catholique de Paris*' where he received the chair of Geology. During this period, he was offered the possibility of working in the Chinese subcontinent where he had the opportunity to confront, as a scientist, an undiscovered continent, as a philosopher and theologian, alternative cultures, and finally, as a priest and mystic, the wide spaces of the Chinese landscape.

This scientific opportunity to study continental evolution provided a way to develop what was a novelty for geologists, namely a global

1.   Among the letters in Teilhard and Bussac, 1986, the one dated 27 March 1916, on pp. 46-52, is of particular relevance. Teilhard de Chardin (1975) also refers to Angela di Foligno in his journal on the 5 October 1916.

approach. Continental evolution was the only way to study the evo-lution of the whole biosphere — on a reduced scale but without distor-tions. At the time, population biology was studied on much smaller scales and so some of the characteristics of the evolutionary process were lost. These could only be discovered by an innovative approach to continental evolution. Teilhard described the opportunities that these continental studies opened to science in one of his papers pub-lished during this period. It was possible to investigate the basic mechanisms of evolution that remain when the disturbances and dis-tortions of population evolution are dispersed in large environments (Teilhard de Chardin 1971: 866-67).

The development of the idea of continental evolution, and of the global approach, is worthy of interest. It was during one of his many expeditions in the first years of his stay in China that Teilhard encountered the mystical experience of totality in the Ordos desert. It was this that crystallized in Teilhard's mind the necessity of a new approach to evolutionary biology, a global vision of evolution, which he was later to incorporate in his scientific work. This desert experi-ence also led to his writing of the Mass on the World, one of the main mystical texts of the twentieth century.

After a geological congress in Peking, Teilhard wrote to his friend and colleague Christophe Gaudefroy about the necessity of this new geology (Teilhard de Chardin 1988: 34-36).[2] In another letter sent to an unidentified friend who was also a scientist, he wrote of the aspects which are lost with the reductionist methods but which can be described using a global vision of evolution. For every change in scale also brings a qualitative change as the whole is not simply the sum of its parts. He also suggested that the idea of biology as the science of the infinitely complex was slowly emerging (Teilhard de Chardin 1967: 238-58).

Given all the elements of Teilhard's scientific research programme, it seems appropriate to consider him as one of the founders of the present-day science of complexity. The notion that the whole has characteristics that are not present in its single components, and the importance of evolution being investigated within a global perspec-tive, were central to his research. This approach enables the peculiar characteristics of evolution, canalization and parallelisms, which had been missed by reductionists methods, to be identified. In this way it is possible to present evolution as a moving toward.

2.   The letter is dated 14 January 1924: Christophe Gaudefroy was a priest and also a professor of mineralogy in the Catholic Institute of Paris.

At this point, it may be of interest to look at the debate that Teilhard later had with his colleague, the palaeontologist George G. Simpson, who had included palaeontology in the modern synthesis (Galleni 1992: 153-66) considered in light of the epistemological theory of Lakatos (1978). Simpson's research programme was organized around the role of chance as the metaphysical key to understanding the meaning of evolution and a preconceived refusal to adopt any particular position on the place of humankind in the economy of nature. Teilhard de Chardin's research programme, by contrast, put forward as its central tenet the idea of evolution as a moving towards the emergence of the thinking creature, a creature who is the only one in creation capable of accepting the proposal of an alliance from the God of Abraham. An evolutionary model based on the idea of a moving toward complexity and cerebralisation is clearly a very different metaphysical approach from the causal model of Simpson that is founded on chance. Moreover, it was Teilhard's approach that provided the positive heuristic tool capable of identifying examples of canalization and parallelisms in the fossil records.

The final evidence supporting Teilhard's theory and demonstrating its scientific integrity came from further fossil observations. For though the programme had been organized in the early nineteen-twenties, it still lacked experimental confirmation. This was to come from his work on the *Siphnaeidae*, or mole rats, which he discovered in a peculiar formation within reddish clays during his travels of Spring 1929. Teilhard de Chardin was able to follow the evolution of the mole rats over a very long time (twenty million years) and on a large scale (that of the Chinese subcontinent) enabling him to describe both canalizations and parallelisms. The original group had divided into three different branches, each of which had evolved independently but had developed, in a parallel way, the same characteristics. In each line there was an increase in size, an inception of continuous growth of the molars and a fusion of the cervical vertebrae (Galleni 1992: 153-66).

Finally, to develop his programme further Teilhard de Chardin proposed, toward the end of his Chinese period, that a new science, namely geobiology, be established which would be devoted to the study of continental evolution (Galleni 1995: 25-45). Continental evolution was the only way to study biospheric evolution on a reduced scale but without distortions; it also allowed the identification of parallelisms and canalizations. This was the first attempt to apply evolutionary tools to analyze complexity. Teilhard de Chardin had proposed Geobiology, this new science of the evolving biosphere based on the convergent efforts of all the sciences, in order to analyse the structure and the internal functioning of the biosphere, and in addition, to investigate the structural and functional place occupied by the biosphere in the system of other planetary envelopes. The final results pointed to the discovery of a more general process, the process of constituting ever more complex material units, from atoms to super molecules, from super molecules to cells, from free cells to metazoan and to social groups. The biosphere is intended to depict a whole complex object evolving (Galleni 1995: 25-45).

Teilhard de Chardin was one of the first scientists to pose the problem of complexity in the study of biological evolution and also to propose a research programme to apply the analysis of complexity to the study of the evolution of the biosphere. These novelties were the result of the interaction between science and theology. Yet, there remained another arena of interaction in which Teilhard de Chardin was to become involved. As a theologian, he proposed a new approach to the way Christians need to act in the world, one that is relevant to environmental ethics.

The Perspective of a Science of the Biosphere

A natural development of Teilhard de Chardin's approach takes place when the perspective of stability further enriches the science of the biosphere. Curiously enough, for this we have to come back to Italy at the end of the nineteenth century. An Italian geologist Antonio Stoppani was one of the first scientists who considered the biosphere as a whole entity. Stoppani was not only the most eminent Italian geologist of the second-half of the nineteenth century and the founder of the Museum of Natural History of Milan, but he was also a Roman Catholic priest and, from a philosophical point of view, a follower of Antonio Rosmini. Stoppani was heavily involved in the renewal movements of the Roman Catholic Church but he refused to accept the theory of the evolution of life. He was not able to find a way to reconcile the Bible with the common descent of humankind and apes from non-human ancestors. He was, however, a capable geologist and was very well aware that the history of the Earth was a history of continual change. His dilemma was how the data derived from geology could be connected to the idea of the fixity of living beings — his solution was a theory of stability. The results of geological investigations suggested that side by side with the continuing changes on the surface of the Earth, there was a stability of some parameters such as the salinity of the sea and the composition of the atmosphere. Living things considered as a whole entity actively maintained this stability — the biosphere. Thus, he provided an explanation for both the changes over time, typical of geology, and an overall stability which supported the absence of the evolution of life (Stoppani 1882).

The main conclusions to be drawn from this interaction of science and theology are that: in accord with Stoppani, the biosphere is an entity with the task of maintaining the stability of the parameters which are critical for the survival of life; and from Teilhard de Chardin, that it is also a whole evolving as a complex system. The contemporary development of these points can be seen in James Lovelock's Gaia hypothesis, which, by applying the concept of a system to the whole biosphere, gives the concept of stability an experimental foundation. For Lovelock, the biosphere and the stability of its parameters, as described by Stoppani, is maintained by the mechanisms of negative feedback which connect both living and non-living matter (Lovelock 1988). A new evolutionary theory is proposed whereby not only is life adapted to the environment but the environment is also continuously adapted to life.

The stability proposed by Stoppani and the evolutionary ideas of Teilhard de Chardin are thereby shown to be connected. Living and non-living parts of the biospheric system are interacting with each other in order to permit the biosphere itself to survive. Evolution thus has an adaptive value: it is the way in which the biosphere is reacting to external changes in order to maintain stability and survive (Galleni 1996: 17-32). This is a completely new perspective with a strongly ethical content — stability of the biosphere is now the main task of life.

Here, we arrive back at Teilhard and his model of scientific and theological relationships. The global theory of evolution that he suggested for theological reasons, namely the search for some level of necessity for the emergence of humankind, regarded the biosphere as a whole entity, a system. And as in every system, its task was maintaining the stability of those parameters that allowed its survival. In the case of the biosphere, it is the survival of life and the evolution of the biosphere itself.

This development in the theory of the biosphere has a strong ethical content as it has implications for the way humankind needs to act. Yet, we also need a global entity for the sphere of consciousness and for this we must again return to Teilhard de Chardin and to his concept of the noosphere, the definition of which has been taken from one of his last scientific papers, published posthumously in 1955

(Teilhard de Chardin 1971: 4580-89). Following Suess's definition of the biosphere, 'that frail but superactive film of highly complex, self-reproducing matter spread around the world' (Teilhard de Chardin 1971: 4580), Teilhard provides a definition of the noosphere as 'the psychically reflexive human surface, for which, together with Professor Édouard Le Roy and Professor Vernadsky, we suggested in the 1920's the name "noosphere"(…)' (Teilhard de Chardin 1971: 4581). The idea of totality is here recovered and is related to humans and their peculiar reflexive and 'self-conscious' type of consciousness.

At the birth of the noosphere, the rising and diffusion of the thinking creature brought a different kind of evolution where cultural characteristics were transmitted more quickly than genetic inheritance. After the first period, when humankind evolved mainly in Africa, there was a rapid spreading over the surface of the Earth during the Upper Palaeolithic period. These migrations were not for ecological or adaptive reasons but seem to be related to the need for knowledge or, at least, to the curiosity of a thinking creature. The result of this human movement was a new and peculiar form of evolution, characterized not by the acquiring of different genes, but by the establishment of distinct cultures. 'For the many fragments of mankind that have become isolated or have gained their independence in the course of time, just so many tentative technomental [*sic*] systems of the world as a whole—that is, just so many *cultures*[3]— have gradually come into existence. This is one of the major lessons taught by universal human history, from the earliest known stages until the present time' (Teilhard de Chardin 1971: 4584). This development of cultures underlines the deep biological unity of the human species. Despite this peculiar aspect of human evolution, its general characteristics, such as the rise of local populations, remain very similar to that of other animal species.

In this way, cultural evolution is for the noosphere what speciation is for the biosphere—it is the means by which diversity is being established:

> Fundamentally, according to my point of view, culturation is nothing but a 'hominized' form of speciation. Or, to express the same thing differently, cultural units are for the noosphere the mere equivalent and the true successors of zoological species in the biosphere. True successors, we insist. And how much better fitted than their predecessors to satisfy the new requisites of an advanced type of evolution! (Teilhard de Chardin 1971: 4585).

3. In italics in the text.

This is clearly the parallelism traced out by Teilhard between bio-spheric and noospheric diversification. This parallelism will be useful for the development of the present paper.

Yet, different cultures encounter one another as a result both through the physical constraints of a limited Earth surface and through the discovery of new ways of communicating:

> On the one hand, the various human cultural units spread all over the world at a given time never cease (...) to react mutually on one another at the depth of their individual growth. Whatever may be the degree of their mutual divergence, they still form, when taken together, an unbroken sheet of organized consciousness. And, moreover, on the other end, they prove able (provided they happen to be sufficiently active and sufficiently compressed on one another) to penetrate, to metamorphose, and to absorb one another into something fundamentally new. This is the well-known process of acculturation — a process possibly bound to culminate some day in a complete '*mono-culturation*'[4] of the human world, but a process, in any case, without which no formation of any continuous human shell would ever have been physically possible on the surface of the earth (Teilhard de Chardin 1971: 4586).

The risk of mono-cultural future for the noosphere has thus been identified — but is this a realistic possibility? In Teilhard de Chardin's view, this outcome would be realized, not with the diffusion of the dominant culture and the destruction of the others, but through absorption. He believed that even in a global project, diversity must be preserved. Here we find another link between the biosphere and the noosphere that is worth developing.

One of the main points of the evolutionary theory of the biosphere is the importance of biodiversity. Another key feature is stability which, in Lovelock's hypothesis, is maintained by this biodiversity. Thus, global stability is linked to local diversity. Intuitively, if there are feedback links that maintain this stability then when diversity is high, the links will be many and the level of stability enhanced.

A parallel must be traced with the noosphere — diversity provides a richness for stability. The noosphere represents cultural diversity worthy of conservation. Yet, we need to ask what are the cultural parameters that correspond to the physical parameters that, at the level of the biosphere, allow the survival of life? Surely, they are those reported in the Declaration of Human Rights of the UN Charter. This is the universal and general reference that has to be accepted by every culture. Only when these rights are fully recognized will we have diversities that are able to promote and maintain stability.

---

4.   In italics in the text.

Although difficult, this is the only way to preserve cultural diversity and its advantages for the survival of the noosphere.[5]

Of course, in Teilhard's interpretation, this present day situation of the noosphere is a result of three different forces present in the evolutionary process. Firstly, there is the general moving toward of life toward cerebralisation, shown by his investigations on canalization and parallelisms in evolution, and then the passing over of a threshold towards self reflection, which in Teilhard de Chardin's words, is 'consciousness raised to its second power; for humanity, *to know that it knows*'[6] (Teilhard de Chardin 1971: 4586). When this threshold is reached, we have a culture and new models of evolution arise. This is the execution of the main path of the universe, the natural result of the general moving towards complexity and consciousness. It is what Teilhard de Chardin calls the law of complexity consciousness.

Finally this general movement, characterized by an increasing consciousness through complexity, will not stop and will reach another threshold related to noospheric evolution. The new threshold can only be explained by returning again to the relationship between science and theology in Teilhard de Chardin's thought. This threshold, though not comprehensively treated in this paper, where only an extrapolation of the scientific data is reported, acquires its strength within a theological perspective. In fact, the threshold will be poorly proven if defined solely from a scientific perspective, but if it is related to the theological idea of the parousia of Christ, the noospheric threshold acquires a fullness of value as it is the perspective of the final moving towards the Omega point and of the Cosmic Christ (see for a theological analysis of the Cosmic Christ: Hale 1973).

---

5.   In one of Teilhard's last writings collected in 'The Future of Man', he posed clearly the problem of the stability of the noosphere. He wrote: 'According to the second answer on the other hand (the "personalist solution") a centre about which everything will be grouped, a keystone of the vault at the summit of the human edifice, is precisely what we must look for and postulate with all our strength, in order that nothing may crumble. For the supporter of this second theory, if a real power of love does not indeed arise at the earth of evolution, stronger than all individual egotisms and passions, how can the noosphere even be stabilised?' (Teilhard de Chardin 1973: 292). All of this book is of interest as it presents what might be called Teilhard's political perspective. In our paper we develop the parallelism between the biosphere and the noosphere and we are able to find ethical parameters such as human rights that correspond to the actual physical parameters. These are a capital result of the 'real power of love' as expressed by Teilhard de Chardin.

6.   In italics in the text.

With this in mind, we can go back to our analysis of the ecological implications of Teilhard's thoughts. The perspective of the Cosmic Christ as the final consequence of the moving towards of evolution is strictly related to environmental ethics. All of humankind on this very earth must follow this path. The eschatological perspective is no longer only the salvation of individuals into the Heavens, but is concerned with the whole of humankind, or better stated, the noosphere, reaching the Omega point.

The Earth thus acquires a new theological value that relates directly to the problem of the future. The Earth must be constructed in such a way as to allow the noosphere to be ready for the second coming of Christ. The terrestrial realities acquire new values. They are no longer the instruments for conquering paradise but are now necessary for the accomplishment of humankind's path on their common Earth. Every trace of the Platonic perspective of a heavenly world which is the depository of perfection, and which can be achieved only by the renouncement of terrestrial and corporal realities, is abandoned. The terrestrial realities are the necessary substratum where humankind accomplishes its task of moving towards the Omega point.

The Ethical Perspective: Acting to Maintain Biospheric Stability

The future construction of the Earth will require the efforts of humankind, but these will need to take into consideration the value of biospheric survival. The concept of the biosphere has demonstrated that stability is required for the survival of life. It is a dynamic stability as the main characteristic of life is that of evolution. This stability allows the biosphere to give rise, with a generative event, to the noosphere, and it is with the noosphere's moving toward that humankind converges toward the Omega point, the second coming of Christ. Due to the strict connections between the biosphere and the noosphere, the moving towards of the noosphere will be carried out only if there is a stable maintenance of the parameters that allow the survival of life on Earth.

Developing the general idea of moving toward, the Bible demonstrates not only how to get to heaven, but taken together with science, it shows why and how to build the Earth so that it can reach its final evolutionary step—the moving towards of the noosphere to the Omega point, the point characterized by the second coming of Christ. In this new synthesis proposed by Teilhard de Chardin, the ethical dimension of building the Earth is directly linked to the scientific dimension of the evolution of the biosphere.

The revaluation of terrestrial realities reaches its *climax* in the *Le milieu divin* (Teilhard de Chardin 1957). In this book, the perspective of human action is not restricted to the eschatological salvation of the individual soul in the heavenly Paradise. There is a completely new and different *milieu divin* which involves the very Earth. The action of the Christian in the world here acquires all of its mystical meaning. After reading Angela di Foligno, and following his experiences during the First World War and in the deserts of China, the mystic gives his assent to the perspective of the Earth. The subsequent interest in terrestrial realities which developed in Roman Catholic theology and was recovered by the Second Vatican Council, *Gaudium et Spes*, started from Teilhard de Chardin's theological vision. Many authors have recognized his influence on the Council (see, e.g., Arnoud 1996).

The research developed by one of the most outstanding South American theologians, Leonardo Boff should be emphasized at this point. One of his first books was about Teilhard de Chardin and his perspective of the Cosmic Christ (Boff 1971). This was written just after the Vatican Council when robust theologies concerned with terrestrial realities were developing in Latin America based on the experience of that subcontinent. The experience was one of domination that became linked to the perspective of liberation that was strongly supported, not only by the council documents, but also by the papal encyclical letters such as *Pacem in terris* and *Populorum progressio* (Gutierrez 2000: 27-38). The reasons for domination and captivity were investigated with the instruments of social sciences, and a distinctive Latin American approach to theology resulted — the so-called theology of liberation (Gutierrez 1971). This perspective was formed from the feelings of people who were experiencing oppression within society, and called for a move towards liberation as the path to building *Regnum Christi*. The theology of liberation thus recovered the social impact of Teilhard de Chardin's vision of building the Earth in *Christo Jesu* (Gutierrez 1971), something which had been absent in his own books and papers. Boff's work on Christology brought Christ's acts of liberation to the attention of theologians (Boff 1972).

A change of attitude inside the Roman Catholic Church occurred after the death of Paul VI, and a consequence of this was that theology returned to its traditional problems and its interpretation of the kingdom in eschatological terms alone. Moreover, it was thought that a model based on the liberal economy was useful, indeed perhaps necessary, for the Third World (Dri 2000: 39-48). At this point liberation theology and its interactions with the social sciences were looked at with suspicion. Nevertheless, the collapse of the collectivist economical model and the new models explaining the domination did require a change in the social analysis on which the theology of liberation was partially based. A different vision of the mechanisms that maintain the exploitation of a large part of humankind were needed and many paths have since been proposed (Hinkelammert 2000: 77-100).

Within the science and theology discourse, there was also a renewed attention to the very general problems of cosmology and the Anthropic principle. These were not directly related to the immediate context in which humankind lived. The focus was in looking back to the beginning and not toward the future. Into this situation, Boff (1993) brought a new perspective which linked the ecological problems and the care and salvation of the biosphere to liberation theology. He argued that the biosphere could not survive with the present day levels of exploitation — a point that was underlined by moderate groups such as the Group of Rome. In order to address the problem of the survival of the biosphere, a holistic approach would be required. This suggested the possibility of recovering Teilhard de Chardin's experience and relating the end of the exploitation of the biosphere to a new model of interaction of humankind toward nature, one that took into consideration the experience of the poor of the Earth (Boff 2000: 243-64). Liberation theology is now also a tool for a new environmental ethic. These feelings towards the Earth and the proposal of a new model of interaction requires the recovery of the liberation experiences of the poor as their culture is the only one which offers a correct way to confront nature and it is their liberation that allows the diffusion of this new perspective.

Many of the central aspects of this paper have now been presented: the biosphere and noosphere, stability, evolution as moving towards and the ultimate task. The ethical implications are now also well evident and, in fact, a new categorical imperative has been proposed: 'Act in a way that will maintain biospheric stability'.

To arrive at our conclusions, however, a final tool is required. So far, we have underlined the necessity of the noosphere in building the Earth and of the biosphere maintaining its stability. These two different tasks must now be linked in a common perspective. Clearly the biosphere has great importance for the noospheric survival and similarly, the noosphere has the capacity of altering the biosphere with the possible consequence of a common future marked by destruction and desolation. It is not easy to find a common ground and so present the need of all humankind to save the biosphere for future generations. Hans Jonas has proposed the possibility of an ontological foundation for environmental ethics which is of great interest and of great intellectual rigour (Jonas 1979). In many perspectives there is the risk that a utopia will not be understood and accepted.

Teilhard de Chardin presents a project towards the future, which, though seemingly inadequate on purely philosophical or scientific grounds, has great value when theology and science are positively interacting. This is the moving toward of the Earth and all humankind to the Cosmic Christ. In this case the utopia receives value because it is sustained by the alliance with God the Creator.

We have seen that in Teilhard de Chardin's project there is the necessity of a common link between the biosphere and the noosphere. But what is the nature of such a link? Here again science supports theology by providing the right perspective. In environmental ethics we have to avoid two risks. The first is that of a strong anthropocentric perspective where nature and the other living beings have no worth at all, but only receive their value as a consequence of their functional utility and benefits to humankind. The second is the refusal to assign any unique position to humankind so that it is only one animal species among many. This perspective is incorrect for theological and philosophical reasons, but also because the power of humankind to alter nature far exceeds that of every other species. In fact, we have to avoid both of these interpretations: humankind is not a cancer within Nature, nor the dominator of Nature.

Biological studies can give some theoretical perspectives on this issue; of special relevance are those insights gained from the Gaia hypothesis. This hypothesis is not only associated with conception of the biosphere as a system and the stability of parameters, but is also the theory which finds in symbiosis and symbiotic relationships one of the major characteristics of evolution. Symbiosis, after the proposal of Lynn Margulis, is now considered one of the most important and diffused mechanisms of evolution (Margulis 1991: 1-14). The colonization of such a hostile environment as the hydro-thermal submarine vents is possible thanks to a symbiotic relationship between chemiotrophic bacteria and animals (Vetter 1991: 219-45). Symbiosis is also the mechanism that allows life to pass the threshold between pro-karyotic and eukaryotic beings.

According to Margulis (1991: 1-14), symbiosis is a set of ecological interactions between organisms due to the protracted physical asso-ciations of one or more members of different species. Associations between partners must be significant to the well-being or the 'unwell-being' of one or both of the participants. Is it correct, however, to use the term symbiosis to describe the relationships between the bio-sphere and the noosphere?

The first problem with such a usage is that we are not dealing with organisms, but with broader entities that are hierarchically superior to organisms and species. The term here refers to a physical associa-tion among spheres. Although it is useful to present the concept of 'spheres' as different entities, this is in some way a simplification, as they cannot really be separated. The present partnership is, in fact, tightly integrated. However, this association is significant for the well-being or the 'unwell-being' of one or both of the participants. The noosphere cannot survive without maintaining fully its links, both physical-biological and cultural, with the biosphere. At this point, the present-day diversified biosphere cannot survive without an active work of conservation from the noosphere.

We use the term symbiosis when two living entities are sharing the same task. Of course the application of the term 'task' when referring to the biosphere and the noosphere needs some explanation. The task that characterizes all living beings is the ability to carry out actions in order to meet the needs encountered in the future both for the well-being of the individual and for the well-being of the species. The tasks of living beings are thus: the individual's survival as a consequence of metabolism, and the species' survival through reproduction. Symbiosis takes place when two or more individuals share common tasks, that is, they co-operate in order to realize the same task.

This is the problem: may we speak of a task at a level superior to the organism—a task of the biosphere and of the noosphere? The task of the noosphere can be considered as related to the general move-ment toward the Cosmic Christ. In a theological approach, or at least in the science and faith approach, and according to Teilhard de Chardin's perspective, this is an external task proposed by God to humankind and realized in alliance with humankind.

Is there also a task for the biosphere? Of course, in this case we have to think of a different kind of task, one that is different to the programme inside the individual self, and different from that of humankind related to the rational and intellectual acceptance of an eschatological perspective. This is found in a third level where the task is simply related to the establishment of feedback control systems able to maintain stability. If we accept this use of the word task, then we can proceed with our investigation about the symbiosis connecting the biosphere and the noosphere (Galleni 2003: 61-74).

Stability of the parameters that allow survival can be the common task shared by the biosphere and the noosphere. According to the Gaia hypothesis the biosphere is characterized by negative feedback relationships which maintain stability. If we accept that this characteristic can be defined as the task of the biosphere, the noosphere acquires it also.

Conclusions

The biosphere and the noosphere are related to Teilhard de Chardin's new vision of life and humankind considered as a whole. He believed that it was possible to apply the concepts of complexity and globality, both to life and to humankind.

It remains for theology to investigate further the relationship of God with the noosphere, and not to continue restricting it to the individual only. Both theological and philosophical perspectives are also needed to address how freedom, which characterizing human individuals, can also be characterizing the behaviour of the whole noosphere. This is not a secondary problem as in an era of globalization, the noosphere is acting as a whole, even if the free decisions are still taken by few.

In this work, the concept of symbiosis is related to the discoveries of the tight relationship between the noosphere and the biosphere. The consequence of this is that the noosphere's moving toward a final point of convergence, the Omega point, needs to take place inside the general stability of the biosphere. Stability of the biosphere is therefore the common task.

Contributing to this was Teilhard de Chardin's recovering of the connections between biological evolution and the evolution of humankind. The moving towards is a result of his investigations of mechanisms of evolution and it is also the moving towards of the noosphere. Side by side with the eschatological salvation of the individual in the Heavens, is an eschatological perspective of the noosphere moving towards the Omega point on this very Earth. The terrestrial realities are recovered because they are necessary to accomplish this second eschatological perspective.

It is the perspective of an unfinished creation that is emerging from the investigation on the philosophical and theological value of the theory of evolution (Haught 2003). For Teilhard de Chardin, the noosphere must accomplish this creation in the final synthesis of the Cosmic Christ.

We also underlined the global approach as the scientific research programme proposed by Teilhard de Chardin. We referred to its recent development in Lovelock's hypothesis and his proposal of the biosphere as characterized by the presence of relationships linking living and non-living components which result in the stability of the main parameters that allow life on Earth to survive. Finally, the concept of symbiosis and co-operation as aspects of the evolutionary mechanisms were shown to be at least as important as the struggle for life and competition.

These proposals suggested the possibility that a symbiosis between the biosphere and the noosphere is required in order to achieve their respective tasks. For the biosphere, this was the stability needed in order to maintain life on Earth. For the noosphere, it was the maintenance of this stability so that the environment will be a source of survival and delight for future generations (Jonas 1979).

Another task of the noosphere, according to Moltmann (1985), is to preserve a creation that will be a source of delight for the Creator in his/her seventh day rest. This task can be easily integrated with that of Teilhard de Chardin, namely, to build the Earth in *Christo Jesu* in order to accomplish the task of the general moving towards the Omega point.

The concept of stability suggests also the recovering of the concept of a limit, a notion of deep theological value. Interference of humankind in the biosphere should be strictly determined within the limits of biospheric survival. We ought not to alter biospheric stability and the mechanisms that allow stability maintenance.

This theological perspective is recovered in Moltmann's view that relationships between humankind and nature are no longer related to the domination perspective of Gen. 1.28 but to Leviticus 25, 26 (Moltmann 1997). The final referent of domination is still God who is not only the owner of nature but also the warrant of the moving towards thanks to the alliance proposed and accepted by Abraham. In this perspective the Babylonian captivity is also interpreted in an ecological manner: the Earth, which had not been respected by the Jews, is given its rest by God when his/her sinner people are removed from it (Moltmann 1997). The same could happen for the future: if the noosphere is not able to maintain biospheric stability required to follow the alliance and the moving toward the Omega point, then there could be a removal of this noosphere to have the biosphere ready for a future people, more open to an alliance with God.

We conclude that the model of interaction between science and theology based on the Teilhard de Chardin's work demonstrates perspectives relevant to the field of environmental ethics.

References

Arnoud, J.
  1996   *Darwin, Teilhard de Chardin et Cie* (Paris: Desclée de Brouwer).
Boff, Leonardo
  1971   *O Evalgelho do Cristo cosmico* (Petropolis: Vozes).
  1972   *Jesus Cristo Liberador* (Petropolis: Vozes).
  1993   *Ecologia-mundializacao e espiritualidade* (S. Paulo: Atica).
  2000   'Écologie-théologie: il n'y a pas de ciel sans terre', in Houtart (ed.) 2000: 243-64.
Dri, R.R.
  2000   'Néo-libéralisme et théologie', in Houtart (ed.) 2000: 39-48.
Galleni, Lodovico
  1992   'Relationships between Scientific Analysis and the World View of Pierre Teilhard de Chardin', *Zygon* 27: 153-66.
  1995   'How does the Teilhardian Vision of Evolution Compare with Contemporary Theories?', *Zygon* 30.1: 25-45.
  1996   'Prospettive per un approccio multidisciplinare al problema della biosfera che si evolve come un'unica entità complessa', in L. Galleni and P. Cerrai (eds.), *Da Pisa a Como e ritorno* (Pisa: SEU): 17-32.
  2003   'The Challenge of Biotechnology to Christian Anthropology: A Western (Mediterranean) Perspective', in V. Gekas (ed.), *Christian Anthropology and Biotechnological Progress* (Chania: Technical University of Crete): 61-74.
Galleni, Lodovico, and M-C. Groessens Van Dyck
  2001   'Lettres d'un paléontologue, Neuf lettres inédites de Pierre Teilhard de Chardin à Marcellin Boule', *Revue des Questions Scientifiques*: 5-104.
  Forthcoming 'Model of Interaction between Science and Theology based on the Scientific Papers of Pierre Teilhard de Chardin', in William Sweet and Richard Feist (eds.), *Knowledge, Science, and Religion: Philosophical Investigations* (in press).
Gutierrez, G.
  1971   *Théologie de la libération* (Brussels: Lumen Vitae).
  2000   'Option pour les pauvres: bilan et enjeux', in Houtart (ed.) 2000: 27-38.
Hale, R.
  1973   *Christ and the universe, Teilhard de Chardin and the Cosmos* (Chicago: Franciscan Herald Press).
Haught, J.F.
  2003   *Deeper than Darwin* (Boulder, CO: Westview Press).

178   *Pierre Teilhard de Chardin on People and Planet*

Hinkelammert, F.
    2000   'La théologie de la libération dans le contexte économique et social
            de l'Amérique latine', in Houtart (ed.) 2000: 77-100.
Houtart, F. (ed.)
    2000   *Théologies de la libération* (Centre Intercontinental, Louvain-la-
            Neuve; Paris: L'Harmattan).
Kureethadam, J.I.
    2003   ' "The Glow of the Hearth Matter"': A Possible Contribution of
            Teilhard de Chardin for Ecological Renewal', *Divyadaan: Journal of
            Philosophy and Education* 14: 61-100.
Jonas, H.
    1979   *Das Prinzip Verantwortung* (Frankfurt am Main: Insel Verlag).
Lakatos, I.
    1978   *The Methodology of Scientific Research Programmes* (ed. J. Worrall
            and G. Currie; Philosophical Papers, I; Cambridge: Cambridge
            University Press).
Lovelock, J.
    1988   *The Ages of Gaia: A Biography of our Living Earth* (London: Oxford
            University Press).
Margulis, L.
    1991   'Symbiogenesis and Symbionticism', in L. Margulis and R. Fester
            (eds.), *Symbiosis as a Source of Evolutionary Innovation* (Cambridge,
            MA: MIT Press): 1-14.
Moltmann, J.
    1985   *Gott in der Schöpfung* (Munich: Kaisser Verlag).

    1997   *Gott im Projekt der modernen Welt. Beiträge zur öffentlichen Relevanz
            der Theologie* (Gutersloh: Kaiser/Gütersloh Verlaghaus).
Ruse, Michael
    1996   *Monad to Man: the Concept of Progress in Evolutionary Biology* (Cam-
            bridge, MA: Harvard University Press).
Stoppani, Antonio
    1882   *Acqua ed Aria ossia la purezza del mare e dell'atmosfera fin dai primordi
            del mondo animato* (Milano: Hoepli).
Teilhard de Chardin, Pierre
    1957   *Le Milieu Divin* (Paris: Seuil).
    1967   'Lettres inédites à un savant de ses amis', *Christus* 54: 238-58.
    1971   *L'oeuvre scientifique* (ed. N. and K. Schmitz-Moormann; Olten:
            Walter Verlag).
    1973   *The Future of Man* (Eng. trans.; London.)
    1975   *Journal, 26 août 1915–4 janvier 1919* (Paris: Fayard).
    1988   *Lettres a l'Abbé Gaudefroy et à l'Abbé Breuil* (Monaco: Rocher).
Teilhard de Chardin, Pierre and Jean Boussac
    1986   *Lettres de guerre inédites* (Paris: O.E.I.L.).
Vetter, R.D.
    1991   'Symbiosis and the evolution of Novel Trophic Strategies: Thiotro-
            phic Organisms at Hydrothermal Vents', in L. Margulis and R.
            Fester (eds.), *Symbiosis as a Source of Evolutionary Innovation* (Cam-
            bridge, MA: MIT Press): 219-45.

10

TEILHARD AND THE ENVIRONMENT

Thomas M. King, SJ

The Two Processes of Earth

Teilhard was a Jesuit priest studying geology at the University of Paris, when he was drafted into the French army. After three weeks of training, he was sent to the front lines of the First World War. In April of 1916, while serving as a stretcher-bearer, he had often been under heavy shelling and survived action in the front lines at Soissons and Ypres; he had already received his first citation for bravery. Aware of the danger and knowing that his life might end at any moment, he decided to write a personal testament to give witness to his love for the universe and tell how it gave him a new understanding of God. He called the essay 'Cosmic Life'; it was the first of many essays that would later make him famous.

'Cosmic Life' begins, 'What follows springs from an exuberance of life and a yearning to live; it is written to express an impassioned vision of the earth..., because I love the universe, its energies, its secrets, and its hopes, and at the same time I am dedicated to God' (Teilhard de Chardin 1968a: 14). He then claims that we are linked organically and psychically with all that surrounds us with the result that we are 'essentially cosmic', but to realize this one must broaden one's self understanding and abandon 'all the illusions of narrow individualism and extend himself intellectually and emotionally to the dimensions of the universe' (Teilhard de Chardin 1968a: 16). He saw a scientific basis for such a claim, for he believed that life itself appeared and developed only as a function of the universe (Teilhard de Chardin 1968a: 23). And humans appeared only after long periods wherein life assumed many forms as did the earth itself. Through the ages the action of the universe has formed who we are—the universe (not just the earth) for comets, sunspots, and so on have modified the line of evolution that led to us. And each of us can see ourselves as a way that the universe has centered itself. But it is not simply a truth of our past, for we are still subject to the network of forces that gave us birth; they will shape us further as they carry us into the future. In this Teilhard is not denying our freedom. But our freedom is only an ability to select from among the energies of earth that constitute us. As a scientist studying the universe he judged us to be 'essentially cosmic'.

But it was not only the objectivity of science that enabled him to see we are integral to the cosmos and the cosmos integral to us; it is also a truth he experienced directly. Teilhard tells of such an experience:

> I allowed my consciousness to sweep back to the farthest limit of my body, to ascertain whether I might not extend outside myself. I stepped down into the most hidden depths of my being, lamp in hand and ears alert, to discover whether in the deepest recesses of the blackness within me, I might not see the glint of the waters of the current that flows on... With terror and intoxicating emotion, I realized that my own poor trifling existence was one with the immensity of all that is and all that is still in process of becoming. (Teilhard de Chardin 1968a: 25)

In the depths of himself he has found — the universe! Later on he will identify himself as 'the universe come to consciousness'. And finding our identification with the cosmos can be frightening:

> No brutal shock, no, nor no gentle caress can compare with the vehemence and possessive force of the contact between ourselves as individuals and the universe, when suddenly *beneath the ordinariness of our most familiar experiences*, we realize, with religious horror, that what is *emerging in us is the great cosmos*. (Teilhard de Chardin 1968a: 27)

What he had learned from science has become direct experience. He discovered that he was in the earth and of the earth, and it would remain at the basis for all he would say and determine his understanding of the environment.

Though frightened by the experience, Teilhard was left with a 'nostalgia for what is the greatest, the most durable, for the Absolute'. And he claimed anyone who has had such an experience 'needs to live with his whole heart, in union with the totality of the world' (Teilhard de Chardin 1968a: 27). Such expressions as universe as Absolute, living with one's 'whole heart in union with the totality of the world, 'I love the universe', or telling of an 'impassioned vision of the earth', did not readily fit with what many Christians had been hearing at that time. For Christians were told of an other-worldly ideal; they were often urged to turn away from the temporal things of earth and look to the eternal things of heaven. Teilhard wrote of his Christian faith with great ardor, yet he continued to speak of his love for the world/universe. On first reading his texts, many Christians, Catholics especially, identified with what he said. They had seen the world as more than a 'valley of tears' and responded readily to this new perspective. He would dedicate one of his books, 'To all those who love the world'. His writings had an immediate appeal to both churchmen and laymen. In Teilhard, it seemed that a Catholic priest was saying something they had long come to believe. He articulated what many seemed to know. The effect was comparable to what St. Francis of Assisi did for his time; Francis articulated a love of nature that spontaneously made sense to those in the thirteenth century: 'Brother sun and sister moon'. He too had a mystic's sensitivity to the things of earth: sun, moon, fire and water were all part of a great family — while Teilhard would use a different image and speak of all things forming one Body, the Body of Christ. Christianity had often claimed, 'Renounce the world and turn to God'. But both Teilhard and Francis told of a love of the things of earth, and by their words and example spoke to the world of their times. And each has been quoted by those concerned with the way we treat the earth.

Teilhard used many phrases to affirm his love for the world, and some–coming from a dedicated churchman — were surprising: 'I know myself to be irremediably less a child of heaven than a son of earth' (Teilhard de Chardin 1978: 121). He would speak of 'holy matter' and even write a 'Hymn to Matter': 'Blessed are you, universal matter… without you we should remain all our lives inert, stagnant, puerile, ignorant both of ourselves and of God' (Teilhard de Chardin 1978: 75; 1969c: 47). He would tell of approaching his work in science as a 'votary', and knew others would accuse him of worshiping nature (Teilhard de Chardin 1968a: 126), but he said what he saw and it 'felt' right to many Christians.

In his direct experience of the cosmos, Teilhard believed he found an 'Absolute' that drew him and yet remained hidden. It seemed to summon him to renounce his personal identity and discover more. He decided to surrender and allow himself to be rocked like a child in the arms of the great mother — the earth. Yet in doing so he felt uneasy, for surrender would imply all things blending together into One; by surrender one finds 'everything in the universe is equally true and valuable', that 'every fragment of force, every spark of life is equally sacred' (Teilhard de Chardin 1968a: 28). Nonetheless, with hesitation he surrendered. One could think of lines of the poet Algernon Swinburne: 'I must go down to the great sweet mother, mother and lover of men the sea, I must go down to her and no other, cling to her, sing to her, mix with her me'. That is what Teilhard would try.

Teilhard suggests this happened on several occasions: Once he was looking over a dreary expanse of desert and as far as he could see the steps of purple uplands rose towards distant horizons. He seemed to pass out of himself and into a wider identity. On another occasion he felt drawn into a great forest where life-laden shadows seemed to absorb his anxious strivings. And again, the waves of the ocean filled him with a yearning to find far from toil the place where dwell the vast forces that cradled him and where his over-tense activity might become ever more relaxed. He seemed to sink down into matter, 'the common origin of beings and the only end we could dream of, the primordial essence from which all emerges and to which all returns' (Teilhard de Chardin 1968a: 30).

He soon came upon a primordial consciousness as the light of life within him had diminished. Yet the move brought him peace, effort-less enjoyment, and Nirvana. Abandoning all social contact he felt a diminution of personality, and drifted passively towards a bliss-giving repose… then suddenly stopped! 'It was then that faith in life saved me. Life! When trouble lies heaviest upon us, whither shall we turn, if not to the ultimate criterion, the supreme verdict, of life's success and the roads that lead to it' (Teilhard de Chardin 1968a: 31). He decides to make a complete reversal and announces he had gone completely astray in relaxing the tension of his being.

In sinking into Nirvana, his individual identity diminished and seemed to merge with all that surrounded him. In contrast, Life appeared as a current moving in the opposite direction, towards increased structures and ever greater consciousness. He decided to identify with Life and concluded:

> I have contemplated nature for so long and have so loved her counte-nance, recognized unmistakably as hers, that I now have a deep convic-tion, dear to me, infinitely precious and unshakable, the humblest and yet the most fundamental in the whole structure of my convictions, that *life is never mistaken*, either about its road or its destination…it tells us towards what part of the horizon we must steer if we are to see the light dawn and grow more intense. (Teilhard de Chardin 1968a: 32)

Henceforth, his ideal would not simply be to sink passively into things. Rather, he would join the work of Life and actively continue its creative work. He would later phrase it: 'our most intelligent and safest course is to continue in the same direction and according to our new stature the movement that produced us' (Teilhard de Chardin 1969c: 109).

Teilhard found he was one with the cosmos, but the cosmos had two identities and both involved process. On the one hand nature/ earth was the all-embracing mother calling her children to return to peace in their common origin. This understanding would see every-thing in the universe as of equal value: 'every fragment of force, every spark of life is equally sacred'. On the other hand, nature/earth was the current of evolving life that was not dissolving complexities. It was building ever larger and more intricate structures.

Both currents were found within himself, one as a desire to lose himself and one as a desire to make something of himself — the latter enhanced his human identity. But these currents were within him only because they ran through the cosmos and he was 'essentially cosmic'. He would identify his first response with the cosmic process known as entropy. This is a term physicists use to tell of the universe moving towards an increasing break down of structures; every time energy is brought into play the order of the universe is diminished and eventually (after billions of years) all living things will have died and only inert matter will remain. In opposition to entropy he saw the current of evolution. Over the millennia evolution has been build-ing up ever more complex structures and in doing so acts in opposi-tion to entropy. 'Looked at in one way, nature is a drug, lulling us to sleep in the cradle of nirvana and all the ancient pantheisms; in a more real way she is a penetrating summons to slow efforts' (Teil-hard de Chardin 1965: 60). In his writings, he will endlessly contrast entropy and evolution (1964: 50, 81, 91, 188; 1969b: 22, 98; 1978: 84; 1971: 109; 1975: 114; 1968b: 95; 1969a: 290).

Nature was seen with two faces: In the move to Nirvana all things merged in a fusion without distinction: 'Every spark of life, is equally sacred'. This could suggest the attitude of some environmentalists: all the animals and trees have rights that are more or less equal. We should not interfere, for the world is sacred as it is and the less we disturb it the better. But the other current would see life giving rise to new and increasing structures, hierarchies of complexity. This cur-rent would not regard all sparks of life as equally sacred; it would see the human, the most complex and reflective form of life, as holding a much 'higher' place than lesser organisms.

For Teilhard, fundamentally Life has been building ever more complex structures through the ages. We are one of its constructions, a hierarchy of billions of cells, and we are called upon to continue the building. First we are to build our own selves and not dissolve them in Nirvana. And, since our persons/consciousness grow through association with others, we must work to increase human unity and build a common world. This will involve changes in the way we manage the earth and changes in politics and social structures. The world has transformed itself down through the millennia and modern industry is seen as a current phase of the process. This is what many concerned with the environment do not like in Teilhard. He would see us called upon to 'build the earth' – in continuity with what Life has been doing for billions of years. And this would involve continuing the process of change. Teilhard believed that evolution was leading to a united earth that would serve as the Body for which Christ would serve as the Soul, a World Soul of sorts that would become more evident with the passing of time. Human work has value in that it leads to a united world capable of receiving its divine Soul. He would argue this using the texts of St Paul.

A New Recognition of Earth

After Teilhard made his 'reversal' and turned his back to matter, he judged his move to Nirvana as a time he went 'completely astray'. But that judgement soon changed. In the summer of 1917 – after fifteen additional months of war – he wrote another essay, 'The Mystical Milieu', and this would tell of an 'alternating movement' (1965: 195), a movement between the earth and God. This would have it that one first must more or less dissolve into the All (the Nirvana he had rejected). He begins the essay by telling of being drawn outside himself and melting away in 'some individuality vaster and simpler than my own' (1968a: 118). The world has again drawn him out of himself and thereby he entered 'a homogeneous Milieu in which contrasts and differences are melted down'(1968a: 120). 'Everything formed a single limpid mass in which no division between things could be seen' (1968a: 122). This is much as the above move to Nirvana.

But now he finds 'the force that had been drawing the mystic towards the zone in which all things are fused together, now reverses direction and brings him back to an exact examination of the experiential multiple' (1968a: 136). Here he has again been drawn into matter, only now the very force that drew him down *makes the* '*reversal*' and with it he begins to rise with the current of Life. Now the move to Nirvana is not simply rejected; rather it is the first step that enables one to identify with the earth and gives one the drive needed to rise to the more complex forms of life – and eventually to

God. That is, his basic claim. We do not go to God directly, we go to God through and with the earth. He had suggested this in his first essay when he told of a 'Communion with God through Earth' (1968a: 57). But now the movement of identifying with the earth is not a mistake, for the earth gives one the energy one needs to rise to God. It is a first and necessary step in the process. So Teilhard would often tell of an increase of energy when back in contact with the earth. 'I regained a burst of life from contact with Africa's soil' (Unpublished Letter, LeMaitre, 2 March 1955). 'I continue to feel the helpful excitation of this new contact with the terrain' (Teilhard de Chardin 1984: 80). In other terms, it was his working in science, working with the things of earth, that enabled him to rise beyond the earth and perceive God.

At times Teilhard would express himself with a striking ardor: he tells of a visionary individual (himself?) who leaves the public places and returns to the firm, deep bosom of nature.

> Gazing into the depths of the immense complex of which he is part, whose roots extend far below him to be lost in the obscurity of the past, he again fortifies his spirit with the contemplation and the feeling of a universal, stubborn movement depicted in the successive layers of dead matter and the present spread of the living. Gazing upward, towards the space held in readiness for new creation, he dedicates himself body and soul, with faith reaffirmed, to a Progress which will bear with it or else sweep away all those who will not hear. His whole being seized with religious fervour he looks towards a Christ already risen, but still unimaginably great, invoking in the supreme homage of faith and adoration, '*Deo Ignoto*' ['To an unknown God' – see Acts17:23]. (Teilhard de Chardin 1964: 24-25)

Many Christian mystics have told of a move that resembled the move to Nirvana, but they would not tell of it as an involvement with the earth. They would enter a serenity and there wait for God. But of itself the process would not lead to an awareness of 'Christ already risen, but still imaginably great'. Teilhard would differ from them in seeing the move to Nirvana as an identification with the earth, and he would see the move as the first step towards knowing God. For Teilhard found a 'Spiritual Power' in Matter. Matter puts us in touch with the energies of earth and together with the earth we find ourselves looking to the 'Unknown God' who is to come.

Teilhard found the building process of Life bringing about ever larger syntheses and believed it was working ultimately to form a unified earth. This unifying earth is being assumed by God to form the Body of Christ. In speaking of the earth or the universe forming the Body of Christ, Teilhard was not apart from the Catholic tradition.

St Paul speaks often of the Body of Christ as a close association of
the Christian faithful, and the Catholic Church has added the word
'mystical' to clarify this sense of Body of Christ, 'the Mystical Body of
Christ'. But St. Paul also used phrases suggesting that the Body of
Christ can be extended beyond the Christian faithful. He would
speak of God's plan 'to unite all things in him [Christ], things in
heaven and things on earth' (Eph 1.10); and say that 'in him [Christ]
all things hold together' (Col 1.17). Some Catholic scholars have seen
such phrases suggesting Body of Christ can be extended to the universe. Teilhard would be among these and uses the term 'Cosmic
Body of Christ' to distinguish it from other meanings of Body of
Christ. Thus, there is both the mystical Christ and the cosmic Christ
(1968a: 58, 59). Both the mystic and the cosmic Christ will reach a
fullness only at the end of time. Presently the rising current of Life is
forming the great Body in which Christ will be the Soul. That is the
central message of Teilhard's theology: 'Fundamentally—since all
time and forever—but one single thing is being made in creation, the
body of Christ' (Teilhard de Chardin 1971: 74).

To achieve this unified earth Teilhard called for the development
of education, modern industry, commerce, transportation systems,
economic development, and a united world government. He would
write with favor of globalization (often calling it planetization). Industrial development and globalization are things that many concerned
with the environment oppose. But Teilhard would not see these as
opposed to Life; he regarded them as an extension of what Life was
doing through the ages: building ever larger and more complex
syntheses. The human drive for international development and industry are in continuity with the building movement of Life. We are now
forming a global synthesis to bring to a suitable conclusion the work
of Life.

Teilhard died in 1955, several years before Rachel Carson brought
out *The Silent Spring,* a work that awakened many to the disastrous
effects caused by industrial development. Today many see this work
as the clarion call that gave rise to the modern concern for the environment. Teilhard had too much love for the earth not to be in sympathy with them. But he believed we can, through additional science
and technology, manage the earth more effectively; beyond any
doubt he would oppose the industrial pollution of air and rivers as
this would rebound unfavorably on human life. But many environmentalists would not like the word 'manage', and see arrogance in
claims to manage the earth. But Teilhard would see us as of the earth

to such an extent it would be the earth managing the earth; but the earth centered around the human. Still Teilhard gives a highly dominant role to humanity in the future that many environmentalists would not like.

Some of Teilhard's personal attitudes to developing the earth can be seen in his letters. No passage states his ambiguities better than a letter he wrote while traveling by train through Vietnam in May of 1926. From the windows he could see large rubber plantations replacing the ancient forests:

> What impressed me even more than the luxuriance of the vegetable and animal life in these regions is the destructive and assimilative power of Man. Already the savages (the Mois) are fairly skilled in burning the bush. But before the Europeans with their roads and railroads the forest is literally melting. It is rubber, above all, which threatens to replace everything. Once I would have been furious and inconsolable at the sight of this devastation or conquest. Now I think I understand that we are witnessing the establishment of a new Zone of Life around the Earth, and that it would be absurd to regret the disappearance of an old envelope which *must* fall. (...) Temperamentally I am not disposed to think this way; it is through reflection and deliberation that I passionately welcome the life that is coming, without allowing myself to regret anything of the past. (Teilhard de Chardin 1969c: 27)

Though environmentalists would not like his reflective conclusion, his instinctive feeling for the earth adds some ambiguity to his future vision. Teilhard would often return to his more instinctive feelings: 'I feel a distaste for hunting, first because of a kind of Buddhist respect for the unity and the sacredness of all life' (1969c: 41). He could even suggest a day when we would no longer need to eat other living things: 'Going back to the respect for Life, we find ourselves, of course, in a natural system in which the mutual destruction of living things seems to be a condition of equilibrium and survival. But what is true of the animal world may perhaps diminish progressively with the establishment of the human sphere: a decline in useless destruction and, as Vernadsky predicts, the discovery of nourishment drawn from the inorganic' (1969c: 42). But all of this seems to center on the human: 'With reason, L. [an unidentified author] laments the incredible negligence of the Chinese, who are destroying and wasting all their forests without seeming to suspect that they are helping to feed the floods and to destroy their fields' (1969c: 39).

In several essays, Teilhard tells of leaving behind the human world with its claims and counter claims and going 'far from humanity's caravan routes', leaving 'the public place' and being strengthened by what he found apart from the cities. He tells of being drawn to deserts, for there and in the wildernesses he found a *'point d'appui'* apart from the conflicting claims of the city. In many places it is clear that Teilhard needed the wilderness and believed others needed to leave the cities to understand who they are. This can only come from realizing our roots in the earth. It is only in knowing our roots that we can get some sense of our destiny. In humanistic circles there are many opinions concerning the human. But he felt humanists were missing the point. He would tell of wanting to organize a conference on the human, but not wanting any humanists to attend. For he believed that humanists made of the human an enclosed world, a complete world; they tried to understand the human apart from our roots in the past. They could not understand the human anymore than one can understand a leaf without being aware that a leaf comes from a tree. As a leaf is part of a wider system, so are we. As above, we are 'essentially cosmic'. He would write *Le Phénomene Humain* (1969a) to tell of the human, yet he would spend more than the first half of the book telling of life on earth before humans appeared! For the human can be understood only as a continuation of all that went before it.

The human is seen as a continuation of all that went before us and cannot be understood apart from the earth that bore us. To be fully human we must get away from what is 'merely human' (Teilhard's phrase for the cultural world that ignores our roots) and return to the wilderness. He would call for scientific research into the unknown, but did not consider what would happen when unknown regions no longer existed. But in calling for us to leave the cities and find the unexplored wilderness (something he did as a 'votary'), he is telling us of the need to return to matter. This is something he did not see in writing his first essay ('Cosmic Life'), but did the following year. This return to matter/wilderness became a part of all of the essays that followed.

Conclusion

In reflecting back on his life, Teilhard wrote, 'I was certainly not more than six or seven years old when I began to feel myself drawn to Matter — or more correctly, by something which shone at the heart of Matter' (1978: 17). After many years of uncertainty and reflection, he came to believe that it was the Heart of Christ shining in Matter. He believed the Heart of Christ was becoming ever more present in the world and life was the universe responding to His presence. He would dedicate himself to continue that response. But the ambiguity he found as a child ('drawn to Matter — or more correctly, by something which shone at the heart of Matter') would remain. He had reflected on the instinctive feel that drew him to matter and decided it was the cosmic Christ summoning him to the future, a future that would involve globalization and industrial development.

References

Carson, Rachel
    1962   *The Silent Spring* (Boston: Houghton Mifflin, Riverside Press).
Teilhard de Chardin, Pierre
    1955   *Unpublished Letter to LeMaitre* (may be seen at the Georgetown University Library).
    1964   *The Future of Man* (trans. Norman Denny; New York: Harper Colophon).
    1965   *The Making of a Mind* (trans. Rene Hague; New York: Harper & Row).
    1968a   *Writings in Time of War* (trans. Rene Hague; New York: Harper & Row).
    1968b   *Science & Christ* (trans. Rene Hague; New York: Harper & Row).
    1969a   *The Phenomenon of Man* (trans. Bernard Wall; New York: Harper & Row).
    1969b   *Human Energy* (trans. J.M. Cohen; New York: Harcourt Brace Jovanovich).
    1969c   *Letters to Two Friends* (New York/Cleveland: World Publishing).
    1971   *Christianity & Evolution* (trans. Rene Hague; New York: Harcourt Brace).
    1975   *Towards the Future* (trans. Rene Hague; New York: Harcourt Brace Jovanovich).
    1978   *The Heart of Matter* (trans. Rene Hague; New York: Harcourt Brace Jovanovich).
    1984   *Lettres à Jeanne Mortier* (Paris: Seuil).

Part V

TEILHARD BETWEEN EAST AND WEST

11

NEWMAN AND TEILHARD: THE CHALLENGE OF THE EAST

Siôn Cowell

Prologue

Christianity, we are reminded, is both an eastern religion and a mystical religion (Clément 1993: 7). It is equally important to remember, adds one of Teilhard's first biographers, Claude Cuénot, that Teilhard de Chardin was drawn to eastern christianity because it had preserved intact the cosmic sense (Cuénot 1965: 251). The eastern Christian tradition, in the words of orthodox theologian Vladimir Lossky, had 'never made a sharp distinction between mysticism and theology, between personal experience of the divine mysteries and the dogma affirmed by the Church' (Lossky 1991: 8).

'The Church', says Teilhard, 'the reflectively christified portion of the world; the Church, the central axis of universal convergence and the precise point of contact between the universe and Omega Point' (Teilhard 1974a: 191-92). 'The Church', he writes elsewhere, 'is phyletically essential to the completion of the human' (Leroy: 1980: 98). 'We are so fortunate to have the authority of the Church', he tells theologian Bruno de Solages (De Solages 1967: 341).

The Greek Fathers, like the Latin Fathers, were representatives of the 'one holy catholic and apostolic Church', the still-undivided Church, and — as such — they still provide an important link between eastern and western Christians. The Greek Fathers deeply inspired Teilhard. And Teilhard invites us to return to the Fathers to prepare ourselves to advance towards the future.

This, it seems to me, is the challenge of the east, challenge of which John Paul II speaks when he uses the image of 'breathing with two lungs', challenge to which we who are 'pilgrims of the future' are invited to respond.

Introduction

The west looks towards the sea and the East looks towards the mountain.
—Paul Claudel (1868–1955)

From 1908 to 1912, during his stay at Ore Place, Hastings, Pierre Teilhard de Chardin (1881–1955) and his companions prepared, among other things, for missionary work in the Near East for which the Lyon province of the Society of Jesus was then responsible. At the beginning of the twentieth century the Jesuits of Lyon had three missions in the region: Saint Francis Xavier's College in Alexandria; Holy Family College in Cairo; Saint Joseph's University in Beirut. The countries of the Near East then contained important Christian communities amongst whom the Copts represented between ten and twenty per cent of the Egyptian population. On his return from three years' teaching in Cairo (1905–1908), Teilhard settled down to his theological studies in the course of which he was to 'meet' the great Cardinal John Henry Newman as well as the Eastern and Western Fathers but also, outside his strictly sacerdotal studies, the philosopher Henri Bergson.

The Society of Jesus, theologian Henri de Lubac rightly reminds us, is a missionary order. At the beginning of the twentieth century the Lyon province was responsible for three missions in the Near East: Alexandria, Cairo, Beirut.

At Ore Place Teilhard and his confrères were trained for missionary and pastoral work in countries then containing important Christian minorities which had somehow survived centuries of Muslim domination under the Arabs and Ottoman Turks. Teilhard — we know from his correspondence in 1920, in 1922 and again in 1929 — had long cherished the hope of being sent as a professor to Saint Joseph's University in Beirut. But this was not to be. And Teilhard was to spend the greater part of his priesthood in places around the world where his religious superiors in the Society of Jesus thought he would be least likely to cause a theological disturbance.

These years of exile were, however, to prove extremely fruitful. These years were to see Teilhard developing his vision of a cosmos in evolution towards its ultimate consummation in the Cosmic Christ, vision which demonstrates his considerable debt to the Church Fathers, especially the Greek Fathers. This is something of which Teilhard was deeply conscious.

Part One

Old principles reappear under new forms,
and the idea changes with them in order to remain the same.
                    — John Henry Cardinal Newman (1801–1890)

Egypt (1905–1908)

Brother Teilhard returned from Egypt in August 1908 after three years' teaching at the secondary college of the Holy Family in Cairo. Captivated by the wonders of prehistoric Egypt, he showed himself somewhat reserved towards the Coptic and Maronite Christians who then made up between ten and twenty per cent of the Egyptian population.

The letters which Teilhard wrote regularly to his parents rarely mention the Egyptian Christians. On one occasion, for example, he writes of a 'Coptic Orthodox bishop…a schismatic, venerable old man… ' (Teilhard 1963: 173). On another occasion, he refers to a lengthy Maronite mass which, he says, could easily have 'lasted as long as they wanted' (Teilhard 1963: 248-49, cf. also pp. 188, 191, 269, 272).

Teilhard's comments seem fairly typical of western Europeans of the time — and even today — who simply could not see 'beyond the unfamiliar exterior of Orthodox Church life, the beards, the icons and the candles' the cosmic vision of the Greek Fathers (Allchin 1997: 254).

Hastings (1908–1912)

It was at Ore Place, a few kilometres outside Hastings, that Teilhard, beginning in the second half of September 1908, was to complete his theological studies and prepare for his ordination. Over the next four years Teilhard would engage with historic personalities like the great theologian John Henry Newman and the Church Fathers but also, outside his strictly theological studies, the philosopher Henri Bergson whose *Creative Evolution*, published in 1907, first opened his eyes to the idea of evolution.

Solidly fixist until then, Teilhard now became a convinced evolutionist — a change of perspective encouraged by his reading of Newman and the Greek-speaking Eastern Fathers.

Newman and Evolution

In his *Apologia* of 1864 Newman reminds us that he had long sensed 'that the principal of development not only accounted for certain facts, but was in itself a remarkable philosophical phenomenon, giving a character to the whole course of Christian thought. It was discernible from the first years of Catholic teaching up to the present day, and gave to that teaching a unity and individuality. It served as a sort of test, which the Anglican could not stand, that modern Rome was in truth ancient Antioch, Alexandria and Constantinople, just as a mathematical curve has its own law and expression' (Newman 1959: 247).

'Newman insisted', says Jean Guitton, 'that development is nothing other than the incessant movement by which "old principles reappear under new forms, and the idea changes with them in order to remain the same"' (Newman 1989: 40).

Newman, we know, had long been attracted by the 'evolutionary perspective' (to use one of Teilhard's favourite expressions) of the Cappadocian Fathers like Basil of Cæsarea, his brother Gregory of Nyssa and their friend Gregory of Nazianzus, as well as the Alexandrian Fathers, especially Clement, Origen, this man with an 'extraordinary cosmic consciousness', and, above all, the great Athanasius (Von Balthasar 1959: 36).

We should remember here that it was his idea of development which enabled him to welcome the Darwinian notion of evolution: he declared himself ready to go 'the whole hog with Darwin' (Wildiers 1968: 181). 'I cannot imagine', he wrote elsewhere, 'why Darwinism should be considered inconsistent with Catholic doctrine' (Wildiers 1968: 180).

The nineteenth century, Newman's biographer Muriel Trevor reminds us, was 'the century of evolutionary theories which shattered men's idea of a static world, just as the astronomical theories of the sixteenth had shattered the image of a static earth... ' (Trevor 1974: 11).

Newman and the French-Speaking World
Newman was very well-known in the French-speaking world. His most important works such as his *Essay on the Development of Christian Doctrine* (1845 [updated 1989]), his *Apologia* (1864 [updated 1959]), as well as his major study on *The Arians of the Fourth Century* (1832–1833), were translated into French almost immediately after their publication in England.

Henri Bremond, who had completed his religious formation in England between 1882 and 1899, was deeply impressed by Newman. And one can easily imagine Bremond's later work on Newman's ideas already being known to the scholastics at Ore Place.

Bremond, who left the Jesuits in 1904, visited England during Teilhard's years at Ore Place. He was, for example, the only Catholic

priest present at the funeral of the former Jesuit George Tyrrell—
'poor Tyrrell', Teilhard wrote to his parents—who died in August
1909 without being reconciled to the Catholic Church (Teilhard
1965a: 303).

Bremond could have visited Ore Place but we doubt whether he
would have been warmly received by staff or scholastics who, Henri
de Lubac tells us, were only too well aware of 'the way in which
George Tyrrell and Alfred Loisy had used Newman and abused his
doctrine' (Teilhard 1974: 407).

We should remember here that despite ongoing suspicions in
conservative circles—notably in England—concerning his orthodoxy
Newman was no modernist. We could even say, with Jean Guitton,
that 'Newman's thought was directed, not towards preparing the
way for modernism, but rather towards preventing its being born'
(Guitton 1934: 174).

Newman and the Eastern Christianity of his Day
One cannot but regret that Newman, a great connoisseur of the Greek
Fathers, promoted to the cardinalate by Pope Leo XIII in 1879, had
virtually nothing to say about the Eastern Churches of his day. And
we know that his later correspondence makes no mention of 'the
great opening to the Eastern Churches' actively pursued by Leo XIII
in the last two decades of the nineteenth century. In the absence of
any reciprocity, as we know, this openness to eastern Christianity
was to give way to a hardening of attitudes with Pius X in 1903.

Newman, meanwhile, had died in 1890—long before Orthodox
thinkers open to dialogue with Catholicism like Vladimir Soloviev—
better known in the west today as the 'Russian Newman'—or the
founder of the Institute of Orthodox Theology in Paris, Sergii Bulgakov, had become known in the west.

Part Two

When we attain love, we have attained God:
our journey is ended and we have attained the island that is beyond the
world.
—Isaac the Syrian (C7)

Teilhard and Newman's Ideas
'Every time I met Teilhard de Chardin', Marcel Brion tells us, 'I was
aware of…this Oxford air which reminded one of an English scholar
who was both a Darwin and a Newman'.

Henri de Lubac is one of those who insists on Newman's importance for Teilhard. Teilhard 'met' Newman at Ore Place on his return
from Egypt. This was not, of course, their first meeting. He had
already heard of Newman during his years at Saint Louis in Jersey
(1902–1905).

'He was still very young', explains Édith de la Héronnière, 'when
he discovered the *Apologia* (1864) which represented for him one of
the key books to which he returned throughout his life. Newman, the
great English mystic, head of the powerful "Oxford Movement" for
anglican renewal, converted to Catholicism and was ordained priest
and then raised to the rank of cardinal.' And we can easily imagine
Newman's chief works as well as Paul Thureau-Dangin's *La Renaissance catholique en Angleterre au XIXᵉ siècle* (1899) occupying a privileged place in the libraries at Ore Place – and on Teilhard's reading
list. 'He read', de Lubac tells us, 'in *Études* two important articles by
Léonce de Grandmaison on *John Henry Newman considéré comme
maître* (December 1906 and January 1907)' (Teilhard 1974: 407).

'Newman's ideas', continues Édith de la Héronnière, 'the problems
he discussed on the relationship between atheism and Christianity,
on the question of doctrinal development, to which he devoted a long
and remarkable essay, cried out to be developed and expanded. His
constantly developing thought and his awareness of his progress and
his failures were a model for Teilhard. Accepting evolution at the
very heart of the Christian faith and the interpretation of the Scriptures, Newman argued that it was not enough simply to accept faith;
it was something we had to work at with our minds…' (De la
Héronnière 1999: 32).

Unfortunately, Teilhard's voluminous correspondence with his
parents tells us little of his appreciation of Newman. He does not
mention the cardinal in his *Letters from Egypt* (1905–1908). And he
mentions him only briefly in his *Letters from Hastings* (1908–1912). In a
letter of 8 October 1911, for example, he says how glad he was to
have had the opportunity of visiting places which had kept Newman's memory alive like St Mary's, Oxford (Teilhard 1965a: 262).

But it is only on reading his journal and his correspondence with
his cousin Marguerite Teillard-Chambon during the First World War
that we discover just how really important Newman had been to
Teilhard ten years earlier.

Teilhard and the Greek Fathers
Teilhard, we stress, greatly admired Newman – something encouraged by the theological atmosphere at Ore Place. And this thanks in

very large part to the academic staff, prominent amongst whom was Xavier Le Bachelet, Teilhard's professor of dogmatic theology, described by Émile Rideau as 'an excellent connoisseur of the Fathers' (Rideau 1967: 32).[1]

At Ore Place, Teilhard, an accomplished scholar in Latin and Greek since his days at Laval, would not be unfamiliar with Migne's *Patrologia*. But we doubt if he would have had much inclination to do so. He preferred spending what little free time he had exploring—almost always with his friend Félix Pelletier—the prehistoric sites of the Sussex Weald. Teilhard might well have thought that Fathers, and in particular the Greek Fathers with their belief in the fundamental unity of knowledge, would have approved of his numerous scientific excursions! The Fathers would, I think, have provided a welcome antidote to the rather pessimistic neo-Augustinian view of humanity which my Jesuit friends tell me prevailed in the religious houses in the early years of the twentieth century.

This is reflected in Teilhard's writings. In 'The Conversion of the World' (1936) he speaks of the importance of developing 'a christology proportionate to the dimensions actually attributed to the universe...in striking harmony with the most fundamental texts of Saint John and Saint Paul and with the theology of the Greek Fathers' (Teilhard 1965b: 122).

For Jules Carles and André Dupleix, 'not only did Teilhard know his dogma, but he was nourished on the thought of the Fathers, many of whom are present throughout his writings...his wholistic vision is subordinated to the spiritual conviction according to which there is a unique divine purpose revealed through Christ to the world. And we can ready understand how Teilhard's ideas combine with other great syntheses or visions of salvation and history... ' (Carles and Dupleix 1991: 136-37).

'The meditation of the Church Fathers, especially that of the Greek Fathers', adds Pierre Noir, 'nourished his conviction that Christ is the Milieu, that is, he is at the same time the presence who envelops and penetrates the cosmos in evolution, the Centre visé and the inexhaustible energy which animates the world and guides it towards its plenitude in God' (Noir 1993: 45).

For George Maloney, the vision of the Cosmic Christ in St Paul and St John was kept alive in the writings of the Fathers such as St Irenæus of Lyon, Origen, St Clement of Alexandria, St Athanasius, St Gregory of Nyssa, St Gregory of Nazianzus, St Cyril of Alexandria

---

1.   My translation. The original English translation is defective.

and, above all, St Maximus the Confessor, sacramental theologian par excellence of the Patristic Age. In this sense, Teilhard's views can properly be understood as 'a development out of the writings of St John and St Paul and the Greek Fathers' (Maloney 1991: 104, 107, 110).

Maloney believes that after Maximus in the seventh century there was 'an eclipse of the cosmic dimension in the study of christology, as theological reflection about Christ became largely a science of excessively rigorous rational concepts. The view of Christ as the life of the world, in the world, bringing life to the world, was increasingly obscured, only to be brilliantly recaptured by Teilhard... ' (Maloney 1968: 15).

'The work of the Greek Fathers of the first seven centuries of Christian existence was well done. The Church has need of thinkers of the twentieth century who can complete the teaching of the Fathers in terms that are intelligible to us today. We turn to one such modern teacher, Teilhard de Chardin, as representative of a modern school of Fathers eager to explore the cosmic dimensions of a christology formulated by the Greek Fathers, in ways, at times, so strikingly presaging Teilhardian thought, as when Maximus speaks, across twelve centuries, of "Christ...as a centre upon which all lines converge"' (Maloney 1968: 181).

Lars Thunberg believes Teilhard's speculations 'on the evolution of the world towards the Omega Point...seem to have a certain affinity to those of Maximus. This is the case not least in regard to their common positive evaluation of movement as a creative force, although Teilhard, of course, sees things in a more definitely historical and evolutionary perspective' (Thunberg 1985: 137; cf. *idem* 1995: *passim*).

The Evolutionary Universe
'What would happen', asks Teilhard, 'if one were to try, following a line already suggested by the Greek Fathers long ago, to transpose the evidence of revelation into a universe in movement? This is what is engaging the attention today of a number (an ever-increasing number) of Catholic thinkers... ' (Teilhard 1965b: 189).

'I fully appreciate the seriousness of the changes these new views introduce. I am familiar with the solemn canons of the Council of Trent on Original Sin. I am aware of infinite network of formulas and attitudes through which the idea that we are the guilty children of Adam and Eve has percolated into our christian life' (Teilhard 1971: 86).

Part Three

Almost everyone bears the guilt of humanity.
— Jean Giraudoux (1882–1944)

The Fall and Original Sin

The doctrine of original sin defined at the Council of Trent is wholly unknown to the Greek Fathers. And it is still unknown to the great majority of Orthodox theologians today.

The term 'original sin' was expressly created by St Augustine, probably in 397, during his polemic with Pelagius and Julian of Eclanum concerning the Fall. 'In the byzantine world', says John Meyendorff, 'where Augustinian thought exercised practically no influence, the significance of the sin of Adam and of its consequence for humanity was understood along quite different lines' (Meyendorff 1983: 143).

In this respect, the great byzantine theologian St Photius the Great — 'one of the greatest minds of the Middle Ages' — even condemns as heresy the belief in a 'sin of nature' found in western doctrines. And this moreover at a time when east and west were still united in 'one holy catholic and apostolic Church'!

The difference between east and west can, unless I am mistaken — and I am very much aware of the risks of simplification — be reduced in the final analysis to a difference of translation. Eastern theologians refer to the text which played a decisive role in the polemic between Augustine and the Pelagians in the Letter of St Paul to the Romans, chapter 5, verse 12. This text, they say, was incorrectly translated from Greek to Latin. The original Greek text reads: '…*because* all men have sinned (*eph ho pantes hemarton*)'. But the Latin text reads: '…*in whom* (that is, Adam) all men have sinned (*in quo omnes peccaverunt*)'.

The editors of the *Jerusalem Bible* tell us that today 'the proposition… can be interpreted as relative (as a consequence of which) or as a causal circumstantial (because, from the fact that), or even consecutive (following which)… ' The idea of some sort of collective guilt of the whole of humanity (which has long dominated or even strangled western theology) is quite foreign to Orthodox minds — as it is, I believe, to children of the Second Vatican Council (1962–1965).

Most Orthodox theologians, says Kallistos of Diokleia, 'reject the idea of "original guilt," put forward by Augustine… Men automatically inherit Adam's corruption and mortality, but not his guilt: they are only guilty in so far as by their own free choice they imitate

Adam... The Orthodox picture of fallen humanity is far less sombre than the Augustinian or Calvinist view' (Kallistos 1967: 229).

Are the differences between east and west of which Teilhard and his companions were almost certainly aware of Ore Place where the corridors were still haunted by the sombre spectre of Jansenism, differences accepted by the still-united Church of the First Millennium, sufficient to prevent the reconciliation of the Catholic and Orthodox Churches in the Third? I think not.

The Challenge
'The early Church of east and west', Bernard Dupuy tells us, 'always believed Christ entrusted his Church to the apostles and conferred a personal responsibility on the Apostle Peter... Church historians are unanimous today in thinking that all the "successors of Peter" in the Roman see were conscious of their special mission but that their way of carrying out that mission was understood differently in different parts of the Church, particularly in the east' (Dupuy 1991: 17). Such, continues Dupuy, was Newman's way of seeing things.

Newman, after his conversion in 1845, maintained the simple conviction, growing with the years, that the Roman Church was the Catholic Church and that the Catholic Church of the fourth century was identical with the Catholic Church of the nineteenth. And, we might add, of the twenty-first!

Teilhard agrees with Newman. 'The privilege claimed by the Roman Church of being the sole authentic expression of Christianity is far from being an unjustified pretension but is a response to an inevitable organic need... Christianity, by its very essence, is much more than a fixed system, formulated once and for all, of truths that must be accepted and preserved literally. For all its basis in a nucleus of "revelation", it represents, in fact, a spiritual attitude in process of continual development: development of a christic consciousness that keeps pace with and is required by the growing consciousness of humanity. Biologically, it behaves like a "phylum" [or "division"]. By biological necessity, therefore, it must have the structure of a phylum, that is, it must constitute a progressive and coherent system of collectively associated spiritual elements. Clearly, hic et nunc, nothing within Christianity but Catholicism possesses these characteristics. There are doubtless many individuals outside Catholicism who love and discern Christ and who are united to him as closely (and sometimes even more closely) than Catholics. But these individuals are not grouped together in the "cephalised" unity of a body which reacts vitally, as an organic whole, to the combined forces of Christ and humanity. These individuals are fed by the sap that flows in the trunk without sharing in its elaboration and youthful surge at the very heart of the tree. Experience proves, not only in theory, but also in fact, that it is only in Catholicism that new dogmas continue to germinate — and, more generally, new attitudes develop which, by continual synthesis of the old Credo and the views newly emerging into human consciousness, prepare around us the coming of a christian humanism. If Christianity is indeed destined, as it professes and feels, to be the religion of tomorrow, it is only though the living and organic axis of its Roman Catholicism that it can match and assimilate the great modern currents of humanitarianism. To be Catholic is the only way of being fully and completely Christian' (Teilhard 1971: 167-68).

Faithful to the vision of the Cosmic Christ of St Paul and St John, Teilhard was deeply inspired by the evolutionary perspective of the Eastern Fathers. But he was constantly aware of the need to transpose their ideas into a cosmos in movement towards its final consummation in the Cosmic Christ.

'Teilhard was conscious', concludes Henri de Lubac, 'of continuing the reflection of the Greek Fathers, especially of a St Irenæus or a St Gregory of Nyssa, to whom he makes frequent allusion… '

Divinisation

Divinisation, one of Teilhard's favourite notions, is expressed in the patristic adage familiar to the Church Fathers from the time of St Irenæus in the second century. 'God was made man so that man might become God.'

'Human beings', exclaims St Basil the Great, 'are animals called to become God'.

'God made himself flesh', explains St Athanasius of Alexandria, 'so that human beings might become Spirit'.

The Church Fathers, and especially the Greek Fathers, sought to discover down the centuries the mystical and sacramental symbolism of the johannine and petrine texts which speak of Christians as 'participants in the divine nature' (2 Pet. 1.4).

Redemption, according to the Greek Fathers, marks not only the victory of Christ over sin, death and hell, but also the potential divinisation of humanity and the whole universe. For Orthodox theology, the incarnation of the Word is predetermined from the beginning of the universe. The resurrection of Christ constitutes the inaugurated transfiguration of humanity and the universe 'embraced' by a divine Person…

In Christ, the world is secretly a 'burning bush', as St Maximus the Confessor argues, and humanity is embraced by the Eucharist in the same fire.

'Trembling', exclaims St Symeon the New Theologian, 'I communicate with fire… By myself, I am but straw but, O miracle, I sense myself embraced as Moses was once embraced by the burning bush.'

'At all costs', says Teilhard, 'rekindle the flame… I can do nothing but put myself back in the fire. Never retreat in the face of boredom, disgust, fear or doubt, but always advance. God, the divine fire, is the goal, the term' (Teilhard 1974: 86).

'The supreme secret of humanity', says Ukrainian philosopher Nicolaï Berdiaev, Teilhard's interlocutor after his return to Paris in 1946, 'is the birth of God in man. But the supreme secret of divinity is the birth of man in God.'

'Not all religious currents are on an equal footing at every moment', Teilhard tells us, 'but one of them (or at least a group of them) represents the place at which one must stand if one is to promote and experience more effectively the progress of the divinisation of the world' (Teilhard 1965b: 111).

Apophatic Theology

Apophatic theology is virtually unknown to the wider western public today. Apophatism, from the Greek word *apophasis*, negation, expresses the idea of God through negative propositions.

The term was first used *expressis verbis* by Dionysius the Pseudo-Areopagite in the early sixth century in his *Mystical Theology* although the idea which originated with Plato and others had already been taken up by the Fathers, especially St Gregory of Nyssa — object of a pioneer study by Jean Daniélou in 1944.

'Gregory of Nyssa's writings on the inaccessibility to God to the created mind, even when that is illuminated by faith, are classical' (Congar 2003: III, xviii). Apophatic theologians assert the inadequacy of human understanding in matters divine: God cannot be an object of knowledge at all. The doctrine is given classical expression in eastern christianity in the teaching of St Gregory Palamas on the unknowability of the essence of God.

We must now think of the possibilities of a new future-oriented theology which brings together an apophatic (or negative) theology, which asserts the utter transcendence of God, and a cataphatic (or positive) theology, which insists on the knowability of God through the Word Incarnate. Here we have the core of an answer to what John Paul II calls anti-Christian secularisation.

'Two Lungs'

Teilhard and his companions began their studies at Ore Place five years after the death of Leo XIII in 1903. This was a time when relations between Catholic and Orthodox were deteriorating. And any renewal of the policy of openness to the east would have to await the pontificates of John XXIII, Paul VI, and, above all, John Paul II, 'the pope from the east' who has dedicated his pontificate to bringing about 'the image of a Europe (from the Atlantic to the Urals) which breathes on two lungs, not only from a religious, but also from a cultural and political point of view' (John Paul II 2001). 'The Catholic Church', says John Paul II, 'is resolutely engaged on the road to unity with all churches' (John Paul II 2001b).

Towards a New Nicæa?

Teilhard died seven years before the Second Vatican Council (1962–1965) which he would probably have seen as leaving much 'unfinished business'. He had long looked forward to what he called a 'New Nicæa' — a new ecumenical council bringing together 'the Catholic Church and the Orthodox Church' — to define the relations, not between Christ and the Trinity, but between Christ and the cosmos. Above all, he feared the renewal within the framework of an evolutionary cosmos of 'the great struggles of arianism...'

'I am more and more convinced', he wrote to Bruno de Solages, 'the Church will only be able to resume its conquering march when (resuming the great theological effort of the first five centuries) it starts to rethink (ultra-think) the relations, no longer between Christ and the Trinity, — but between Christ and a universe that has become fantastically immense and organic (at least a thousand billion galaxies each surely containing life and thought...)' (Teilhard 1974: 450).

'This is why', he continues elsewhere, 'sooner or later, we must have a New Nicæa to define the cosmic face of the Incarnation'. And this because 'it is only within the framework of evolution that the great cosmic attributes of Christ, those which (particularly in St Paul and St John) accord him a universal and final primacy over creation, these attributes...only assume their full dimension in the setting of an evolution...that is both spiritual and convergent...' (1974: 450).

The council agenda is ready. The summons is seriously delayed.

Separation between Mysticism and Theology
Eastern Christian tradition, as we said earlier, has never accepted a clear distinction between mysticism and theology. Far from setting them against each other, as has been the case in the west since the sixteenth-century renaissance and reformation, theology and mysticism support and complement one another.

In the west an important minority current within the Catholic Church has never accepted the separation between mysticism and theology and, consequently, the progressive impoverishment of the western liturgy, impoverishment which involves an effective distancing between heaven and earth...

The byzantine liturgies celebrated by Pope John Paul II during his visit to Ukraine on 23–27 June 2001 remind us of the ambassadors of the Grand Prince of Kyiv exclaiming more than a thousand years ago, as they did after attending the liturgy in the Great Church of Constantinople: 'We knew not whether we were in heaven or on earth... we only knew that God was present among us. We shall never forget such beauty' (Vodoff 1988: 65-66).

Conclusion

> Have I said everything? Not at all!
> —Georges Duhamel (1884–1966)

Teilhard de Chardin sits firmly among those who refuse any separation between theology and mysticism. He is a convinced evolutionist — no one denies this — but his originality among mystics of east and west is to be both a mystic of the earth and a mystic of heaven or, more correctly, a cosmo-mystic — 'a mystic of the cosmos seen as a "divine milieu"' (Barjon 1971: 214).

Unfortunately — his long years of exile in China from 1926 to 1946, his heart attack in 1948, his final exile in the United States from 1951, his professional palaeontological work, his obedience to his superiors in the Society of Jesus, as well as, of course, Roman reservations, even hostility, towards all forms of ecumenism — all these elements seem to have prevented Teilhard from engaging in a fruitful dialogue with Orthodox theologians and thinkers, notably during his years in Paris from 1946 to 1951.

It is up to us Teilhardians of today and tomorrow to pick up the baton... Teilhard invites us to return to the roots of our faith — going through Newman and the Eastern Fathers — so that we can to advance together towards the reconciliation of the eastern and western churches in response to the urgent call of Pope John Paul II: 'May the memory of the time when the Church breathed with "both lungs" spur christians of East and West to walk together in unity of faith and with respect for legitimate diversity, accepting and sustaining each other as members of the one Body of Christ' (John Paul II 2001c). Amen.

Postscript

Let us pray.
Lord God of the universe,
You, who called your servant, Pierre Teilhard de Chardin, to burn like a flame,
Set our hearts on fire with your love,
Open our eyes to your glory,
Open our lives to your radiance,
Help us today to witness to your presence;
through Christ our Lord,
Light of the world and Light of the universe. Amen

References

Allchin, A.M.
   1997   *N.F.S. Grundtvig, An Introduction to his Life and Work* (London: Darton, Longman & Todd).
Barjon, Louis, SJ
   1971   *Le Combat de Pierre Teilhard de Chardin* (Laval QC: Presses Universitaires de l'Université de Laval).
Carles, Jules, SJ, and André Dupleix
   1991   *Pierre Teilhard de Chardin* (Paris: Centurion).
Clément, Olivier
   1993   *The Roots of Christian Mysticism* (London: New City).
Congar, Yves, OP
   2003   *I Believe in the Holy Spirit* (New York: Crossroad).
Cuénot, Claude
   1965   *Teilhard de Chardin* (London: Burns & Oates).
De la Héronnière, Édith
   1999   *Teilhard de Chardin* (Paris: Pygmalion).
De Solages, Bruno
   1967   *Teilhard de Chardin* (Toulouse: Privat).
Dupuy, Bernard
   1991   'Le fondement biblique de la primauté romaine', in *La Primauté romaine dans la communion des Églises* (Paris: Cerf).
Guitton, Jean
   1934   *La Philosophie de Newman* (Paris: Boivin et Cie).
John Paul II, Pope
   2001a   Meeting with members of the Episcopal Commission of the European Community (COMECE), 30 March 2001.

2001b   Speech, Athens, 4 May 2001.
2001c   Apostolic letter *Novo Millennio ineunte* to the episcopate, clergy and faithful at the end of the Great Jubilee of the year 2000, 6 January 2001, §48.

Kallistos of Diokleia, Bishop
1967   *The Orthodox Church* (London: Pelican).

Leroy, Pierre, SJ
1980   *Letters from My Friend Teilhard de Chardin* (New York: Paulist Press).

Lossky, Vladimir
1991   *The Mystical Theology of the Eastern Church* (Edinburgh: James Clarke).

Maloney, George, SJ
1968   *The Cosmic Christ from Paul to Teilhard* (New York: Sheed & Ward)
1991   *Mysticism and the New Age* (New York: Alba House).

Meyendorff, John
1983   *Byzantine Theology* (Fordham, NY: Fordham University Press).

Newman, John Henry, CO
1959   *Apologia pro vita sua* (London: Fontana [originally published 1864]).
1989   *An Essay on the Development of Christian Doctrine* (Notre Dame, IN: University of Notre Dame Press [originally published 1845]).

Noir, Pierre, SJ
1993   Préface pour *Le Milieu Divin*, Bulletin de l'Association des Amis de P. Teilhard de Chardin, 13 (Paris).

Rideau, Émile, SJ
1967   *Teilhard de Chardin* (London: Collins).

Teilhard de Chardin, Pierre, SJ
1963   *Lettres d'Égypte* (ed. Henri de Lubac; Paris: Aubier).
1965a   *Lettres d'Hastings* (ed. Henri de Lubac; Paris: Aubier).
1965b   *Science and Christ* (London: Collins).
1971   *Christianity and Evolution* (London: Collins).
1974a   *Toward the Future* (London: Collins).
1974b   *Lettres intimes de Teilhard de Chardin* (ed. Henri de Lubac; Paris: Aubier).

Trevor, Muriel
1974   *Newman's Journey* (London: Fount).

Thunberg, Lars
1985   *Man and the Cosmos* (Crestwood NY: St Vladimir's Seminary Press).
1995   *Microcosm and Mediator: The Theological Anthropology of Maximus the Confessor* (Chicago: Open Court).

Vodoff, Vladimir
1988   *Naissance de la chrétienté russe* (Paris: Fayard).

Von Balthasar, Hans-Urs
1959   *Origène, Esprit et Feu* (Paris: Cerf).

Wildiers, Norbert Max, OFMCap
1968   *An Introduction to Teilhard de Chardin* (London: Fontana).

12

SOPHIA, MARY AND THE ETERNAL FEMININE IN PIERRE TEILHARD DE CHARDIN AND SERGEI BULGAKOV[*]

Celia Deane-Drummond

Mary has commonly been associated with nature, especially in her appearance in folk religious traditions (Boss 2000). However, her association with the biblical figure of wisdom is, perhaps, less well appreciated. Rather than survey all the possible links between Mary and wisdom, I intend to focus particularly on Mary as portrayed in the writing of Pierre Teilhard de Chardin and compare his views with those of the Orthodox theologian Sergei Bulgakov. As we explore how Teilhard de Chardin interpreted the feminine in his cosmic vision of reality, it becomes clear that it is mainly to the Virgin Mary that he turns when considering the possibility of the feminine. Yet, while reference to the Virgin Mary is relatively scant in his work, the way she is portrayed shows the depth to which Teilhard himself integrated her into his understanding of spirituality. It also points to the cosmic significance of Mary in relation to nature *as such* in a way that goes beyond the simple identification of Mary, women and nature.

Mary as Mediator of the Feminine

Teilhard was orthodox in his heart-felt devotion to the Virgin Mary. In a letter written in 8 December 1918 he wrote that:

---

[*]   This article is developed from a paper originally given at a conference entitled *Nature and the Virgin Mary: Perspectives from Theology and Human Ecology* under the title 'Mary in Teilhard and Bulgakov: Wisdom and the Eternal Feminine' held at Lampeter University, 27 July 2002, organized by the Centre for Marian Studies.

> You know what…is my dearest wish: that God, through our Lady, may
> grant us so to share in her purity and to have so ardent a passion for her,
> that we may really be able to serve, in our own small way, to regenerate
> the world. We must have absolute faith in the power of this divine virtue
> to transform souls and spread itself; and we must see to it, too, that the
> greatest interest of our life is to feel that we are growing a little more
> within her, and are serving to radiate her influence. (Teilhard de Chardin
> 1965: 262)

Teilhard's experience had been worked out in more detail through
the concept of *The Eternal Feminine*, the title of a poem that he composed earlier that year between 19 and 25 March. He had considered
calling this poem 'Before a Veiled Virgin', aligning his thought with
that of Pascal (de Lubac 1971). He struggled for some months before
the poem finally took shape. The poem is dedicated to Beatrix, who is
the subject in the poem, echoing but not identical with the Beatrice of
Dante's poem, *The Divine Comedy*. Yet Teilhard does not begin his
poem with a discussion of the Virgin. Instead, he invites his readers
to consider in the first place what he calls 'the essential Feminine',
looking back to the early Old Testament writing on the figure of
Wisdom, described as that which came into being when the world
began (Ecclus 24.14). The force of this essential Feminine is not
marginal in the creation of the world, rather it is integral to the creative process and even, one could say, at the heart of it:

> In me is seen that side of beings by which they are joined as one, in me the
> fragrance that makes them hasten together and leads them, freely and
> passionately, along their road to unity.
> Through me all things have their movement and are made to work as one.
> I am the beauty running through the world, to make it associate in ordered
> groups: the ideal held up before the world to make it ascend.
> I am the essential Feminine. (Teilhard de Chardin 1968b: 192)

In other words he sees wisdom/essential Feminine as an inner principle of all being, the alluring force in the world that brings disparate
things together and beautifies them. Wisdom is described in the next
verse in the biblical text that he uses as the minister in God's taberna-
cle (Ecclus 24.15), the word Teilhard uses is *handmaid*, I suggest that
this is hinting at the association with Mary that he makes explicit
later. However, for Teilhard wisdom is not just the energy in the
created world, but also is involved in the first creative act that leads
to 'a vague and obstinate yearning to emerge from the solitude of
their nothingness' (Teilhard de Chardin 1968b: 193). Hence it takes
the form of a 'universal Feminine', reaching back to the foundations
of the universe. As Teilhard moves forward in his own version of the
Genesis account of the creation of the world, he speaks of how

particular beings were chosen to embody this Feminine principle. Once again he hints at what is to follow later, so he claims that 'patiently and in secret, was developed the archetype of bride and mother' (Teilhard de Chardin 1968b: 193). In this transformation the earlier roles of the Feminine in the guise of wisdom remains, a token of their beatitude. The Feminine begins to express what Teilhard describes as the 'magnetism of the Feminine', the teeming life that is common to humans, birds, insects and even the flowers, so that he can say of this aspect of the Feminine, 'I am the single radiance by which all this is aroused and within which it is vibrant' (Teilhard de Chardin 1968b: 194).

Next we have the gradual unveiling of the concrete figure of 'the Eternal Feminine' in Teilhard's perception. Yet this realization also brings with it a temptation, one that Teilhard seems to suggest is one of Mariolotry, Mary must remain merely a work of creation, rather than anything more than this:

> Soon, however, he is astonished by the violence of the forces unleashed in him at my approach, and trembles to realise that he cannot be united with me without inevitably becoming enslaved to the work of creation. (Teilhard de Chardin 1968b: 194)[1]

This leads, inevitably, to a temptation, to see in the Eternal Feminine something that humanity could grasp, suddenly she is in the guise of 'the Temptress' a 'lifeless idol to cling to', so that 'what you are grasping is no more than matter' (Teilhard de Chardin 1968b: 195). Yet the coming of Christ thwarted the possibility of temptation in this direction.[2] In spite of what we might have at first thought about Teilhard's dedication to Mary and the Feminine, his spirituality remains ultimately Christocentric. In the second section he declares boldly that the Feminine, like all creatures, needed the coming of Christ, 'Christ has given me freedom and salvation' (1968b: 197). This view is orthodox in as far as Catholic dogma states that Mary, though she was conceived immaculately, also needed Christ in order to be

1.   This resistance on Teilhard's part to any association of Mary with the idea of goddess is also noted by Henri de Lubac in his commentary (de Lubac 1968: 126).
2.   The translator, René Hague, indicates that the reference here is to human love and the temptations it brings (p. 196 n. 7), but in the light of the later passages in this poem, I suggest it is more likely to be a reference to the allure of Mariology. In my earlier work I followed the interpretation of René Hague that the temptation mentioned here was the lure of love, rather than anything specifically directed to Mary. I have since reconsidered this position. See Deane-Drummond 2000: 94-95.

saved.[3] It is through Christ, then, that the Feminine comes to be understood and even 'defined my true essence'. How has this affected her role? In one sense it is unchanged, so that he can say:

> In the regenerated world I am still, as I was at my birth, the summons to unity with the universe—the world's attractive power imprinted on human features. (1968b: 197)

Yet, hinting once again that this figure is the Virgin Mary, he claims that those who seek her on earth are mistaken, for 'my reality has risen aloft, drawing men to the heights: it floats between the Christian and his God' (1968b: 197). Such a reference points to Teilhard's faith in the Assumption of Mary, a doctrine that he explicitly affirmed (de Lubac 1971: 125; Teilhard de Chardin 1970: 215-16).[4] Yet it is at this point that the veil begins to slip, and the Eternal Feminine is named as Virginity, while still a mother. His struggles with his vocation to celibacy become clear in this part of the poem, while insisting that vocation is not a summons 'to exile love from his heart'. At the same time the Eternal Feminine takes on maternal characteristics, so that 'I am the maternal shadow leaning over the cradle' (1968b: 198). He also seems to have taken account of the fact that virginity itself is not, in evolutionary terms, what one might expect of humankind. Yet, for him, chastity allows the Eternal Feminine to issue forth in a final blossoming. He suggests that the flowering of the art of humanity and the vitality of nature is best expressed as the ideal Feminine. It is a beauty 'flung like an mantle over creation' (1968b: 199).

As Teilhard moves into the final section of his poem, he finally sweeps the veil aside and declares that he is speaking of Mary the Virgin. He makes the more radical suggestion that Christ would not have come unless Mary had lured God:

> Without the lure of my purity, think you, would God ever have come down, as flesh, to dwell in his creation?
> Only love has the power to move being.
> If God, then, was to be able to emerge from himself, he had first to lay a pathway of desire before his feet, he had to spread before him a sweet savour of beauty. (1968b: 199)

A similar idea is expressed in *The Divine Milieu* where he states that:

---

3. J. Pelikan comments on this in his impressive survey of Mariology in history (Pelikan 1996: 139-49).
4. Letter dated 25 August 1950. The name of the recipient is anonymous at their request, Prologue, René d'Ouince, p. 4.

When the time had come when God resolved to realise his Incarnation before our eyes, he had first of all to raise up in the world a virtue capable of drawing him as far as ourselves. He needed a mother who would engender him in the human sphere. What did he do? He created the Virgin Mary, that is he called forth on earth a purity so great that, within this transparency, he would concentrate himself to the point of appearing as a child. (Teilhard de Chardin 2004: 96-97)

In *The Eternal Feminine* we find a parallelism drawn between Mary the mother of all humankind and the Church, as bride of Christ. Yet even as Christ is proclaimed, the pervasive influence of the Feminine continues, she speaks of the 'tension that impels you towards God', the purity of a heart dedicated solely to love of God, hinting at the role she plays in creation as a whole, for once again we see 'my image playing over the surface of the divine fire', and as such, the Eternal Feminine (1968b: 201).

It is worth noting that René Hague (1968b: 202 n. 16) considers that the poem as a whole is not so much about Mary, as about universal love. I have argued against this view here for reasons given above. Teilhard is thoroughly orthodox in ascribing a key place for the Virgin Mary, and drawing parallels between Mary, who he saw as the ideal or pure woman and Christ as the perfect man. Why did he feel the compelling need to speak about Mary as the Eternal Feminine? Part of the answer seems to be that he thought the concept of the Godhead was 'dreadfully masculinized' (de Lubac 1971: 126). He also wrote the poem just before he took his vows of profession to the priesthood (de Lubac 1971: 20). However, Mary, as I suggested above, was still a creature, even though she embodied the cosmic Feminine principle. Teilhard does seem to have had some recourse to refer to God in maternal categories, though this is rather a weak strand in his thought. For example, in a letter written to Leotine Zanta on 24 January 1929 he declares:

once again, the great animating Power, to which it is so good to entrust ourselves, seems, in a motherly way — to have brought the inner and outer forces of the world into harmony around me.[5]

Further hints at this perspective appear in the work, *Cosmic Life*, so that now the earth itself becomes female:

And in this first basic vision we begin to see how the kingdom of God and cosmic love may be reconciled: the bosom of Mother Earth is in some way the bosom of God. (Teilhard de Chardin 1968a: 62)

5.   Cited in de Lubac 1971: 126 n. 79.

Yet the focus of his understanding of motherhood is drawn from his reflections on Mary, as I stated above, she is the Mother of all human-kind, she is also 'the Pearl of the Cosmos, and the link with the incar-nate personal Absolute — the Blessed Virgin Mary, Queen and Mother of all things, the true Demeter' (Teilhard de Chardin 1968a: 59). At the same time she is also Mother of God, Theotokos (God-bearer), and as such her significance is as one who ensures that Christ is truly human as well as divine. For 'The Mystical Christ, the Universal Christ of St Paul, has neither meaning nor value in our eyes except as an expression of the Christ who was born of Mary and who died on the Cross' (Teilhard de Chardin 2004: 79). Yet Mary's virginity and purity have a particular attraction for Teilhard, as he believes that it is in this that his own life of prayer can become sustained. In *The Mystical Milieu* he suggests the following:

> Nothing in the world is more intensely alive and active than purity and prayer, which hang like an unmoving light between the universe and God. Through their serene transparency flows the waves of creative power charged with natural virtue and with grace. What else but this is the Virgin Mary? (Teilhard de Chardin 1968c: 144)

Given the above analysis of the poem itself, it is perhaps surprising that Ursula King interprets his poem *The Eternal Feminine* in terms of what she sees as Teilhard's dedication to the universal Feminine as such, expressed variously in terms of 'wisdom, the handmaid of the God's creation, as mother nature or as the figure of Mary and the church' (King 1988: 72). According to her analysis, Teilhard placed Mary as just one of the figures of the feminine. She argues that the Temptress that he speaks about in his poem is that towards carnal love, rather than Mariolotry as I have suggested. However, although Teilhard had many close relationships with women, including his cousin Marguerite Teilhard-Chambon (1880–1959), Leontine Zanta (1872–1942) Ida Treat (1889–1978), Jeanne-Marie Mortier (1892–1982), Rhoda de Terra and Lucile Swan (1890–1965), the poem itself was more likely to be a meditation on the Virgin in the manner I have suggested, rather than his relationship with women forming a blue-print for his thinking about the feminine.[6] He did, in other texts, acknowledge that his relationships with women coloured his think-ing, so that he could say 'I have experienced no form of self-devel-opment without some feminine eye turned on me, some feminine influence at work' (Teilhard de Chardin 1978: 59). He then spoke of such influence as 'emotional', sensitising his understanding and

---

6. Sîon Cowell, personal communication.

increasing his capacity for love, so that 'no man at all can dispense with the Feminine, any more than he can dispense with light, or oxygen, or vitamins' (1978: 59). He then goes on to ask how such complementarity should be understood. He asks; Is there a higher, third way between marriage orientated towards reproduction and priesthood towards separation? It is more likely that he saw in the attraction between the sexes an energy that could be transformed for the good:

> The time has perhaps come when, in conformity with the inflexible laws of evolution, man and woman — on whom life has laid the charge of advancing to the highest possible degree the spiritualization of the earth — will have to abandon that way of possessing one another, which has hitherto been the only rule for living beings.[7]

He advocated the 'sublimation' of 'unfathomable spiritual powers that still lie dormant under the mutual attraction of the sexes' (Teilhard de Chardin 1978: 60). How was such sublimation to be achieved? It is clear that it is *in Mary* that Teilhard finds a way of being that includes the feminine, but is also expressive of the ideal of chastity.

Wisdom and Mary in Russian Sophiology

While he does not describe Mary in these terms, Teilhard's focus on Mary ever Virgin, his parallel between Our Lady as perfect woman and Our Lord as perfect man in his poem *The Eternal Feminine* echoes classical Mariology. His attribution of a more cosmic role to Mary, linking Mary with nature and also associating her with wisdom is also classical, dating back to the council of Ephesus in 431, where Mary was proclaimed Mother of God. For example, the Cathedral of St Sophia of Novgorod (1045) celebrated its feast day on the feast of Mary's Assumption. The later Russian sophiologists, writing at approximately the same time as Teilhard, also linked Mary with Sophia. Vladimir Solovyov (b. 1853), Sergius Bulgakov (b. 1871) and Pavel Florensky (b. 1882) are key figures in the development of sophiology. Vladmir Solovyov's work, for example, was both poetical and philosophical. His early encounter with Wisdom is in the form of a beautiful female figure. A few years before his death he wrote an autobiographical poem, describing the three mystical experiences of Sophia he had during his lifetime. His first experience is revealing:

> Suddenly my eyes could not focus,
> Without a trace the earth disappeared.

7. Teilhard de Chardin, 'The Evolution of Chastity', cited in King 1988: 76.

Passion's storm faded away,
I was surrounded with heavenly blue.
You too are radiant blue! A blossom
Of supernatural beauty in your hand.
With gracious goodness you smiled at me,
Nodding—then the heavenly image was gone.[8]

His subsequent experiences speak of visions surrounded by 'golden light and radiant blue', the radiance shining especially from her eyes, 'like a day's light at dawn's creation'. Given these images, it makes sense to describe these visions, as does Hans urs von Balthasar, as visions of Our Lady (Von Balthasar 1986: 292).

For Solovyov, Sophia is the Eternal Feminine, incarnate in the Virgin Mary. He arrives at an image of Sophia as a grand synthesis between humanity, the Virgin Mary and the Church, combining to produce an organic link between heaven and earth. For Solovyov, Christology alone could not produce a satisfying theology of creation, even in its cosmic forms. Another of Solovyov's works, *The Meaning of Love* shows some direct parallels with Teilhard's *Eternal Feminine*. Henri de Lubac suggests that this cannot have been a direct influence on Teilhard as although it was published in 1894 it was not translated into French until 1946 (de Lubac, 1971: 39). Nonetheless, the evolutionary aspects of creation, alongside Teilhard's determination to stress the life of chastity as an ideal, mark out differences from Solovyov. Both tended to focus on the Virgin Mary and the Church as the expression of the universal Feminine. Both suffered from a somewhat stereotypical representation of the idea of feminine.[9] Both were mystical, poetical and philosophical rather than theological formulations. Furthermore, it seems to me that while Solovyov made a conscious effort to seek Sophia and saw in the Virgin Mary an expression of that Wisdom; Pierre Teilhard de Chardin sought the Virgin and discovered in her the Eternal Feminine, as foreshadowed in the biblical writings on Wisdom. In other words while Teilhard's poem was primarily a mystical reflection on Mary, Solovyov's poem was primarily a dedication to Sophia. Henri de Lubac's comments are relevant here, in that for Teilhard:

> it is not an abstract principle which is personified in the Virgin—it is the Virgin, existing in her own individuality, who is universalised in the principle… If, then we speak of symbol, we shall not be saying that in this context the Virgin Mary is the fully realised symbol of the universal

8.   Extract from *A Poem* (1898) cited in Schipflinger 1998: 257.
9.   As applied to Teilhard, this statement needs to be qualified by the fact that he did have close women friends who were important in his life. See King 1998.

Feminine, but rather that this universal Feminine must be understood, in
its pure essence, as the Virgin Mary. (de Lubac 1971: 119)

Yet it seems to me that Teilhard's attention to the Virgin Mary as the
locus of Wisdom ultimately restricts Wisdom to the realm of creaturely nature, rather than divine agency. Before the veil is laid aside,
the Feminine is associated with the bursting forth of life in the
universe, a magnetic Feminine energy emerging from creaturely
being, but one that is still ultimately dependent on Christ for salvation and freedom (Teilhard de Chardin 1968b: 197). Furthermore,
while he does suggest that the Feminine as Virgin is active in calling
love into being in the incarnation, any seeking of her reality in 'the
flesh' amounts to a mirage, rather than the reality. The qualification
of the place of Mary through his emphasis on the importance of
Christ leads to a similar qualification of the place of Wisdom. However, there is little to suggest that this has any parallel impact on
human agency, for the vocation of humanity in science is affirmed in
a way that seems to lead to a lack of criticism of its aims and goals.
The magnetic Feminine becomes just the inspiration for even greater
achievements in technology, a means of power over nature. In his
discussion of the magnetism of the Feminine, for example, he suggests that humanity 'builds up power, he seeks for glory, he creates
beauty, he weds himself to science' (Teilhard de Chardin 1968b: 194).
We do, nonetheless, find a nascent ethic in his suggestion that in
trying to grasp after pleasures sin corrupts wisdom into folly. The
skill to distinguish between wisdom and folly is only possible for
Teilhard after the coming of Christ. No longer are we faced with a
mirage of Wisdom, rather she draws those who follow her into the
light of truth and freedom.

How are Mary and Wisdom connected in the writing of Sergii Bulgakov? He is interesting, as while one could criticize Solovyov for
committing what Teilhard saw as the temptation towards Mariolotry,
it is harder to level this criticism at Bulgakov. He was, however, thoroughly convinced of the importance of Mary, seeing her as the only
means through which ecumenical unity in the Church could be
achieved (Galaher 2002: 43).[10] Like Teilhard, he advocated Mary as
Mother of God, Theotokos. However, he was able to incorporate
wisdom into his understanding of both God and Mary by separating
Divine Wisdom and creaturely wisdom. Mary is associated with

10. His suggestion that the Virgin Mary should become the mystical unifier of
the universal Church scandalized the Protestant majority at the World Council of
Churches meeting in August 1927.

creaturely wisdom, and hence expresses everything that might be possible for wisdom as *creature*. Her creaturely nature ensures that she does not become a goddess or transform the Trinity into a Quarternity. For Bulgakov divine Sophia is integral to the ousia of God, expressed in all three persons of the Trinity. Hence, unlike Teilhard, he does not hesitate to describe God in the language of Sophia, and thereby give the Godhead a feminine face.

Yet Mary, as Mother of God, also has a special place in Bulgakov's theology (Bulgakov 1976). He also viewed her as 'a second Eve', who gives Christ his human flesh. More important, perhaps, he views Mary as one who can demonstrate what the Holy Spirit is like, even though the third person is not personally incarnate in the same way as the Logos is incarnate in Christ. Hence she:

> is not the personal incarnation of the Holy Spirit but becomes his personal, living receptacle, an absolutely Spirit-bearing creature, a Spirit-bearing human being…a created personality is completely surrendered in its createdness and is, as it were, dissolved in the Holy Spirit. This interpretation by the Spirit amounts to a change in kind. The Virgin is wholly deified, full of grace, 'a living temple of God'. (Bulgakov 1976: 92)

Mary seems to be elevated almost to an intermediate position between creaturely and divine existence, for while she is still a creature, and so differs from the God-man, Christ, she also 'differs as radically from the creation in its createdness, for she is raised and united to the divine life' (Bulgakov 1976: 92). Like Teilhard, he suggests that even though she is assumed into heaven she still in one sense 'will continue to belong to the world' (Bulgakov 1993: 119). Teilhard does allow for an *analogy* between the Virgin Mary and consummated humanity at the end of time (Rideau 1967: 563 n. 164). Yet, as an Orthodox theologian, Bulgakov is much more insistent compared with Teilhard that while Mary is still creaturely, the possibility of deification has taken place in her case. In this she enables the divinization of the human race, and thence to the created world as such:

> The Mother of God, since she gave her son the humanness of the second Adam, is also the mother of the race of human beings, of universal humanity, the spiritual centre of the whole creation, the heart of the world. In her creation is utterly and completely divinised, conceives, bears and fosters God (Bulgakov 1993: 119-20).

As indicated above, Bulgakov believes that Mary has already reached the perfected state, while other saints still wait for redemption. She is honoured not just for her role as Mother of Christ, but also as Ever

Virgin. Of particular significance for Bulgakov is the dedication of shrines of Sophia, the Wisdom of God, to Our Lady, their feasts coinciding with hers. In other words, such associations sprung from the liturgical life of the church and its prayer. Like Teilhard, Bulgakov's vision of Mary is one that is intimately connected not just with humanity, but also with hope for the whole of the created order:

> As the glory of God and the glory of the world, as the manifested love of God for the world and the manifested love of the world for God, in her prayer she glorifies God. Her own prayer is glorification, eternally realised love, flaming and triumphant in its perfect joy- God's own love for himself in his creation. But as the foremost representative of the world and of all creation, the Mother of God also offers a prayer which is not her own, and yet is hers as the prayer of all of creation. She gives wings to its prayer; raising it to the throne of God, she gives it power; she is the intercessor raising her hands to God as a high-priestess (orante) and overshadowing the world with her veil'. (Bulgakov 1976: 95)

This intercessory role of Mary on behalf of all creation is not dealt with to the same extent in Teilhard's portrait of Mary. While Teilhard speaks of Mary's cosmic role through his notion of the Eternal Feminine, he does not spell out what this means for creation, other than a much vaguer 'summons to unity with the universe'. Teilhard also seems more willing to identify cosmic processes with Mary, since he has not elaborated in the way that Bulgakov has the place of divine and creaturely Sophia, and the interrelationships between them. Hence, while Teilhard hints at a form of sophiology, through his association of wisdom with Mary, he is equally drawn to the notion of beauty as expressive of the radiance of the eternal Feminine. Bulgakov, in associating the completion of the work of Wisdom through the Holy Spirit with beauty, locating Mary in the place of humanity deified, indirectly includes beauty, but since this is meant in a perfected sense prefers to use the term glory. Mary and Sophia become the means through which Bulgakov is able to speak about the future expectation for humanity and the created world. In this way he encourages an integration of themes such as creation and redemption, instead of their separation. This is an important aspect of his theology, and one which is equally important in the construction of an adequate ecotheology. For where creation themes are emphasized in a way that weakens or excludes redemptive aspects, this leads to forms of idealization of creation that do not take sufficient account of the suffering of creation even in the creative process of coming into being. Teilhard de Chardin has been criticized for not putting sufficient emphasis on redemptive themes, and while he does make some hints in this direction, as indicated earlier, Bulgakov develops this idea further through his concept of shadow creaturely Sophia. It could be argued that neither author takes this aspect far enough – both express overall an optimistic vision for the future.

Rosemary Radford Ruether isolates a quote from Bulgakov which states that 'In the Virgin there are united Holy Wisdom and the Wisdom of the created world'.[11] This might, incorrectly, give the impression that Mary for Bulgakov is in some sense Divine Wisdom. At times he might seem to come close to this in his suggestion that 'Divine-humanity is to be found on earth as it is in heaven – in a double not only in a single form; not only that of the God-human, but of his Mother too'. Mary is also the 'feminine counterpart' to the humanity of Christ. Hence Christ cannot be separated from his mother, for to do so, 'is in effect an attempted violation of the mystery of the Incarnation, in its innermost shrine' (Bulgakov 1993: 123). Bulgakov roundly rejects any suggestion that Mary is Divine Wisdom by insisting that Divine Wisdom is in her only in so far as she allows the Holy Spirit to descend on her, she is its consecrated temple. It is only in this sense that she is God-bearer that she can be thought of as Divine. Rather, he emphasizes that it is as *created Wisdom* that the Virgin is venerated in Russia, for:

> She is created Wisdom, for she is creation glorified. In her is realised the purpose of creation, the complete penetration of the creature by Wisdom, the full accord of the created type with its prototype, its entire accomplishment. In her creation is completely irradiated by its prototype. In her God is already all in all. (Bulgakov 1993: 126)

Yet Mary seems to acquire this title of created wisdom by virtue of the fact that she is mother to Christ; that Christ's humanity came to him from his mother. As Christ represents both divine and creaturely Sophia, so 'it is in this sense, as sharing the human nature of the God-human, that his holy Mother is the created Sophia' (Bulgakov 1993: 127).

11. R. Radford Ruether, quotes Bulgakov's *The Wisdom of God* from a secondary source *The Virgin Mary*, by Giovanne Miegge (Lutterworth Press, 1955) (no page numbers are given). The full quotation reads: 'In the Virgin there are united Holy Wisdom and the Wisdom of the created world, the Holy Spirit and human hypostasis [the created person]. Her body is completely spiritual and transfigured. She is the justification, the end, the meaning of creation; she is, in this sense, the glory of the world. In her, God is already all in all' (Radford Ruether 1977: 45-46). My translation of Bulgakov's book does not include the first sentence.

Some Interim Conclusions

It is important to note that for Bulgakov created wisdom is not confined to Mary, but includes the whole creation, hence providing a theological link between Mary and nature. By separating created and divine wisdom, Bulgakov could afford to Sophia a place that was higher than that of Teilhard, but without losing the connection with Mary. Mary is divinized, clothed with Divine Wisdom, yet the ultimate expression of creaturely wisdom, uniting her not just to humanity, but to the whole cosmos. Yet, for Bulgakov, like Teilhard, the transformation of the world through Sophia is an expression of beauty. Teilhard, like Bulgakov, links the elevated figure of Mary with consummated humanity. Both theologians found different ways to express the purity and perfection of Mary, Teilhard through his suggestion that Mary's virtue allured God to become incarnate within her and Bulgakov through naming Mary as expressive of perfected creaturely Sophia, with the Holy Spirit infusing her personality so that it becomes 'dissolved' in the Spirit.

However, Bulgakov is able to express much more clearly than Teilhard the link between the action of Sophia, Logos and the Spirit in the unfolding of creation, and thereby hint at an ecological reading of her significance. For Bulgakov the Spirit works with creaturely Sophia at the beginning of creation before the first 'Let there be' of God's creative act. She is like the first mother who brings forth life to all that exists in the created world. The bringing forth of life in creation becomes a Trinitarian act, not just 'Mother' in place of 'Father', but a movement of Trinitarian love through Sophia. While he never uses the term the 'Eternal Feminine', his somewhat stereotypical representation of the feminine needs some modification. His theology does, however, lend itself to reappraisal of our image of God in a way that is inclusive of both masculine and feminine metaphors. As Brenda Meehan has pointed out, his insistence on Sophia as *ousia* of God is of particular significance, since, from the point of view of feminist theology, Sophia is not simply a feminine principle bolted on, as it were, to an otherwise masculine image of God (Meehan 1996: 159-60).

Teilhard's grand schema for cosmic role for the Eternal Feminine echoes that of the cosmic Christ, but his vision remains a mystical one, rather than one spelt out in dogmatic terms. While it is important for mysticism to be included in any systematic theology, it is only really in Bulgakov's theology that we find a clear attempt to bring together the philosophical, poetic, mystical and theological aspects of Wisdom. While his ideas bear some resemblance to the cosmic Christology of the earlier church fathers, such as Maximus the Confessor, he takes Sophia into the very heart of who God is, the very ousia of God.[12] Such a move is significant theologically as it means that Wisdom is at the very centre of theology, not just an attribute of God, but the core of who God is in God's-self. The relationship between wisdom and love is a very intimate one, wisdom is the 'loving of love' and as such included in the dynamic perichoretic community of the Trinity. Wisdom becomes the means through which creation and Creator are related to each other, she is at the frontier between the two, but comes to expression as creaturely wisdom in the created order. A theology of creation is inseparable from the concept of wisdom.

Such a vision of the relationship between God and creation impregnated with wisdom and beauty seems to me to be highly relevant for ecological spirituality today. If we love God, then we will search for wisdom. If we love God, then we will find God in the creaturely wisdom of creation, expressed in the person of Mary. A cosmic vision of Mary in Bulgakov points to what humanity might become, as glorified. However, such glorification is never distanced from the created world of nature in which humanity is situated-humanity is part of creation and any eschatology that points to a future of humanity detached from nature is far too limited and limiting. Perhaps, too, we need to remember the dark side of creaturely Sophia that Bulgakov mentions, also hinted at by Teilhard in his suggestion that the Feminine can come under the guise of Temptress. In this respect it is always possible for this good creation to be distorted or marred by sin. Indeed the development of the idea of the shadow in creaturely Sophia is necessary if we are to begin to appreciate the possibility that there are negative cosmic forces at work in addition to those caused directly by humanity. Sarah Boss argues that Mary is identified with the chaotic elemental aspects of creation, 'present in all physical things as their foundation' (Boss 2003: 5). This is very similar to Teilhard's vision of the Eternal Feminine, reaching down to the very elemental beginnings of cosmic life. Neither writer has acknowledged sufficiently, perhaps, the negative aspects built into the evolutionary process, the need for a theodicy of nature as well as humanity. In addition, for Boss to suggest that Mary 'is the Chaos

12. He does seem to take account of possible objections to this idea by suggesting that God as Absolute is not known, hence retaining the apophatic tradition. This will not satisfy theologians such as Lossky (1957: 78-79), who are more insistent that the energies of God are known, and never God's being or ousia.

that pervades all material things' (Boss 2003: 134) sounds incongruous, for goes against an interpretation of Wisdom as at the *boundary* of order and chaos (Deane-Drummond 2000), indeed the Genesis text speaks regularly of the Word of God holding back the forces of chaos (Murray 1992: 2-7).

A full discussion of evolutionary and ecological theodicy and what this might mean in the context of this discussion of Mary, Wisdom and the Eternal Feminine needs to be the subject for further discussion. In addition, while it is possible to associate theological concepts such as Sophia with practical wisdom or prudence, and beauty with temperance, both of which are important for environmental ethics (Deane-Drummond 2004), a recovery of an ecological reading of the importance of Mary is significant, for as ideal woman expressive of creaturely Sophia she can point to ways of treating not just other human beings, but the earth community in which humanity is grounded and situated.

While Teilhard did not spell out the ecological implications of his work, in dialogue with the Eastern Orthodox tradition of Bulgakov, an outline of such a reading can be developed. Both Teilhard's and Bulgakov's understanding of Mary were idealized, Teilhard even specifically mentions the concept of the essential Feminine, alongside all the other aspects which point to the Eternal Feminine. Bulgakov associated Mary with the transformation of creaturely Sophia so that it *resonated* with Divine Sophia, without losing its identity as creature. Both point to somewhat stereotypical images of Mary and womanhood, though both seek to elevate her place to the highest possible level within their theology. However, such images provide a counter to more contemporary versions of essentialism in ecofeminist spirituality that have oscillated uneasily between either the desire for a female goddess or the need to establish an essential link between women and nature as if it were the essence of what it is to be feminine (Deane-Drummond 2002). In Bulgakov Mary is divinized, but she is not a divine goddess, rather she is linked with nature through her expression of creaturely Sophia, infusing the whole of creation. In this her creaturely role needs to be emphasized.

Sarah Boss develops the idea of Mary as the seat of Wisdom to the limit in her suggestion that 'the new creation, Jesus himself, is wrought through Holy Wisdom in the person of Mary' (Boss 2003: 116). This implies identification between divine Wisdom and Mary, though she softens this somewhat by suggesting that Mary 'takes on the mantle of Holy Wisdom' (Boss 2003: 116). However, to go on to suggest, as she does subsequently, that ' "all nature" is *in* Mary and is saved *through* her. It is precisely for this reason that she may be called Wisdom' (Boss 2003: 117) stretches the analogy a little too far, taking us beyond the image of Wisdom as a covering for Mary, to identification itself, a move that was resisted by Bulgakov. Mary also represents humanity as it might become transformed through salvation in Christ, hence she points both to Christ as the source of salvation and the natural world as inclusive in Christ's redemptive compass. One could even argue that as creaturely Sophia incarnate and divinized, Mary represents both the connectivity and care for the earth that is possible for humanity to achieve. There is no need for Mary to *become* divine Wisdom in order for her to have a significant role in redemption; rather it is her creaturely nature that reminds humanity of its role in caring for the fragile earth in which humanity is placed. Neither Bulgakov nor Teilhard were familiar with current environmental issues. However, I suggest that Bulgakov's understanding of Mary, which links her through Sophia more specifically with creation and redemption, can point to an ecological reading of her significance. Sophia becomes the basis through which God both creates and redeems the world (Deane-Drummond 2000). Hence a Sophianic interpretation of Mary is linked with both the work of creation and the work of redemption in a way that can be self-consciously related to an ecological agenda.

References

Boss, Sarah J.
  2000 *Empress and Handmaid* (London: Cassell).
  2003 *Mary* (London: Continuum).
Bulgakov, Sergii
  1976 Extract from 'The Burning Bush: An Essay in the Dogmatic Interpretation of Some Features in the Orthodox Veneration of the Mother of God', first published in 1927, entitled 'The Burning Bush', in James Pain and Nicolas Zernov (eds.) *A Bulgakov Anthology* (trans. Natalie Duddington and James Pain; Philadelphia: Westminster Press; London: SPCK).
  1993 *Sophia: The Wisdom of God: An Outline of Sophiology* (Hudson: Lindisfarne Press, rev. edn). First edn, *The Wisdom of God: A Brief Summary of Sophiology* (trans. Rev. Patrick Thompson, Rev. O. Fielding Clarke and Miss Xenia Braikevitc; New York: Paisley Press, 1937; London: Williams & Norgate).
de Lubac, Henri
  1971 *The Eternal Feminine* (trans. René Hague; London: Collins).

Deane-Drummond, Celia
    2000   *Creation through Wisdom* (Edinburgh: T. & T. Clark).
    2002   'Creation', in S. Parsons (ed.), *Cambridge Companion to Feminist Theology* (Cambridge: Cambridge University Press).
    2004   *The Ethics of Nature* (Oxford: Basil Blackwell).
Galaher, Anastassy
    2002   'Bulgakov's Ecumenical Thought', *Sobornost* 24.1: 24-55.
King, Ursula
    1988   *Spirit of Fire: The Life and Vision of Teilhard de Chardin* (Maryknoll, NY: Orbis Books).
Lossky, Vladimir
    1957   *The Mystical Theology of the Eastern Church* (trans. The Fellowship of St Alban and St Sergius; London: J. Clarke).
Meehan, Brenda
    1996   'Wisdom/Sophia, Russian Identity and Western Feminist Theology', *Cross Currents* 46: 149-68.
Murray, Robert
    1992   *The Cosmic Covenant: Biblical Themes of Justice, Peace and the Integrity of Creation* (London: Sheed & Ward).
Pelikan, J.
    1996   *Mary Through the Centuries: Her Place in the History of Culture* (New Haven: Yale University Press).
Radford Ruether, R.
    1977   *Mary: The Feminine Face of the Church* (Philadelphia: Westminster Press).
Rideau, Emile
    1967   *Teilhard de Chardin: A Guide to His Thought* (trans. René Hague; London: Collins, 1967).
Schipflinger, T.
    1998   *Sophia-Maria: A Holistic Vision of Creation* (trans. J. Morgante; York Beech: Samuel Weiser).
Teilhard de Chardin, Pierre
    1965   *The Making of a Mind, Letters from a Soldier Priest, 1914–1919* (trans. René Hague; London: Collins).
    1968a   'Cosmic Life', in *Writings in Time of War* (trans. René Hague; New York: Harper & Row): 14-71.
    1968b   'The Eternal Feminine', in *Writings in Time of War*, translated by René Hague (New York: Harper & Row): 191-202.
    1968c   'The Mystical Millieu', in *Writings in Time of War* (trans. René Hague; New York: Harper & Row): 117-49.
    1970   *Letters to Two Friends* (trans. Helen Weaver; London: Rapp & Weaver).
    1978   *The Heart of Matter* (trans. Rene Hague; London: Collins).
    2004   *The Divine Milieu* (trans. Sîon Cowell; Brighton: Sussex University Press).
Von Balthasar, H. urs
    1986   *The Glory of the Lord: A Theological Aesthetics*, Volume III (trans. A. Louth, J. Saward, M. Simon and R. Williams; Edinburgh: Edinburgh University Press).

INDEX OF AUTHORS

Index of Subjects

Lightning Source UK Ltd.
Milton Keynes UK
05 February 2010

149590UK00001B/20/A